Overwhelming Injustice & Posttraumatic Blame Theory

Psychological Wellbeing in Frontline Services

Claire Carter

"Thanks Claire, As my son would say 'you're like the Hulk, but a really good, person sized Hulk who only uses massive powers to do good nice things"

Claire Carter

Acknowledgements

Thanks go to Dr. Brian W Seggie (Retd. Major - EdD MEd CertEd FCIPD FIfL FInstLM FRSA FCMI MCGI MIET CMgr IEng) for acting as supervisor on this research project and for being a supportive, encouraging and critical friend.

Thanks go to all those involved in the research, who contributed their case studies or offered their participation. This research and book would not have been possible without you. I am confident your responses and stories will help others faced with the same difficulties and experiences.

Contents

Claire Carter

Preface

Welcome to this research, into the experience of overwhelming injustice and posttraumatic blame in emergency first responder roles, armed forces and healthcare services.   This book has been peer reviewed by the International Journal of Law, Crime and Justice[1] and led to the research article 'Organisational Injustice in UK Frontline services and onset of Moral Injury, Post Traumatic Embitterment Disorder (PTED) and PTSD,'[2] published in the journal of the same name.

In the book, posttraumatic embitterment disorder (or PTED as it is known) and moral injury, (which may be referred to as MI) are explored. To understand PTED and MI, these two constructs were compared with other psychiatric diagnoses, for any potential correlation. These included Post-Traumatic Stress Disorder (PTSD), Complex PTSD (CPTSD), Burnout, Adjustment Disorder, Moral Distress and Querulousness. The main features of PTED and MI, such as feelings of betrayal, difficulty with forgiveness, embittered attitude, experience of loss, blame and desire for revenge are discussed.

The way values, morals and beliefs in a just world interact with psychological and emotional regulation, are of great importance throughout the research, as a breach of these individual or social norms can lead to PTED and MI.

---

[1] (Porter, 2021)

[2] (Carter, Organisational Injustice in UK Frontline Services and Onset of Moral Injury, Post Traumatic Embitterment Disorder (PTED) and PTSD, 2021)

The research explores predisposing factors to PTED and MI, as well as possible measures of prevention. These include, emotional intelligence, organisational safeguards and working practices, treatment and therapy, including sport and recreational therapy and posttraumatic growth.

Case studies are used, to demonstrate real life examples, of perceived moral injury or injustice and the impact these experiences can have on individuals, and others through vicariousness.

The methods used for this research are explained, including ethical considerations and research questionnaires. Analysis of the results and the potential synthesis between the constructs of PTED and MI are discussed. The hypothesis of posttraumatic blame as a theory is introduced for the first time. The book ends with conclusions, suggestions for further research and some final comments from the author. This is an independent research project.

The book will begin with an introduction, not dissimilar to an abstract, which will give you an overview of the research findings.

Introduction

Feelings of anger, resentment, self-blame, sadness, victimization, self-pity, bitterness, injustice, hurt and loss of trust in others are common to all. These emotions are part of being human. One might suggest these emotions are in-built, just as their pleasant counterparts are. Satisfaction, achievement, safety and security undoubtedly feel better. However, it is perhaps necessary to strive for a balance between the experience of comfortable and uncomfortable emotions (rather than an imbalance). The suggestion that upsetting emotions may be beneficial is perhaps controversial. If life experience was largely one of contentment, safety, satisfaction and happiness; people may be less likely to develop, expand their knowledge and skills, solve real-world problems and learn personal coping strategies for difficult times. Some degree of psychological distress is perhaps vital to growth.

Feelings of injustice can bring about a call to action, to right a wrong and safeguard others from a similar experience or danger. Anger can be a powerful energy source which motivates one to resolve an issue. Feelings of contentment and comfort may have the opposite effect; not wishing to unsettle the equilibrium and status quo. Perhaps anger, tempered by a degree of cognitive and emotional regulation can give this energy source positive, assertive and passionate direction. Unregulated anger will most likely lead to unhelpful consequences. The ability to 'switch off' or regulate highly charged or upsetting emotions is important. People can find this regulation difficult and experience persistent cognitive and emotional symptoms that may result in psychiatric disorder.

Breaches in moral codes, rules, ethics, common decency, law or policy are potential threats to individuals and societies. Perhaps agitating thoughts and feelings have a positive function in tackling these breaches, for the good of the individual and the herd (as part of being a social species, reliant on each other for protection).

This research will explore why some frontline professionals are perhaps more susceptible to enduring thoughts and feelings of a distressing nature, and get 'stuck' in this state of being. A degree of adjustment and adaptation occurs as a consequence of working and specializing in frontline services. Individuals are exposed to a higher severity and frequency of traumatic experience, immoral behaviour, heinous acts, human rapacity and tragedy than the general population. Therefore, Moral Injury (MI) and Post Traumatic Embitterment Disorder (PTED) may be more prevalent in frontline services, as well as PTSD, CPTSD, Anxiety and Depression. Cognitive and emotional regulation may become dysregulated and maladaptive due to the intensity and/or frequency of exposure. This research hypothesizes, that betrayal, injustice and moral injury in high risk professions may significantly increase the manifestation of embitterment reactions leading to disability, and inhibit recovery from psychiatric disorders. The researcher seeks to understand the cause, symptomatology, cognitive processes, treatment and prevention of MI and PTED in frontline professionals. Furthermore, PTED and MI are explored as two separate constructs which may be fundamentally the same. Questions are asked (and answered) as to whether both constructs are needed, how they may benefit frontline services and whether they can be discriminated from each other. This research draws together common themes in MI, PTED, (C)PTSD and empirical evidence to posit a new theory of the psychopathology of blame within the context of traumatic experience – Posttraumatic Blame.

Analysis of results conclude that the construct of PTSD and CPTSD now accommodate symptoms of PTED and Moral Injury (such as *"Persistent, distorted cognitions about the cause or consequences of the traumatic event(s) that lead the individual to blame himself/herself or others", "persistent and exaggerated negative beliefs or expectations about oneself, others or the world,"[3]* guilt, shame, negative self-concept and emotional dysregulation). There is significant overlap between the construct of PTED and Moral Injury, which suggests they are fundamentally the same, even if presented somewhat differently. Chronic embitterment is pathological, of clinical significance and often a symptom of PTSD which is inextricably linked to the trauma. Chronic embitterment can maintain PTSD symptoms. Therefore, chronic embitterment or posttraumatic blame are medical issues, which may require treatment and before PTSD treatment can be effective.

In the next section, I will explain the Thesis, why this project was undertaken, the early evidence which supported the idea of exploring PTED and MI in frontline services, the core questions the research seeks to answer and how the research will achieve this.

---

[3] (APA, Exhibit 1.3-4DSM-5 Diagnostic Criteria for PTSD, 2020)

Claire Carter

Hypothesis

The primary aim of this research is to provide people and groups with information and support, by identifying the experience of PTED and Moral Injury in frontline services. The research aims to explore a potential convergent validity between Moral Injury and PTED; and whether it would be beneficial to have one or both conditions classified for the purpose of diagnosis and treatment. The secondary aim is to identify if they are comorbid with PTSD and therefore requiring specific treatment to assist with PTSD recovery. Dean et al. (2019) states, "using different terminology reframes the problem and the solutions."[4] The research seeks to ascertain if PTED and Moral Injury are fundamentally the same, though presented as two different constructs.

Background

The researcher worked as an advocate and support worker in domestic abuse services for c. ten years and with police officers affected by psychological injury for five years. She has personal experience as a partner living alongside complex PTSD and embitterment symptoms.

Symptoms of embitterment, moral injury and PTSD seem to be a common experience for many officers, veterans, their partners and survivors of abuse; including revenge fantasy, feelings of humiliation and shame, anger, perceived injustice and betrayal. Some individuals appear unable to 'move-on' from feeling victimized and wronged which in turn may inhibit their post traumatic growth and PTSD recovery. The researcher observed that many officers seeking medical retirement for

---

[4] (Dean, Talbot, & Dean, 2019)

PTSD also exhibit symptoms of embitterment (as detailed in their psychiatric reports and expressed during contact). Linden (2007) report on 'the psychopathology of posttraumatic embitterment disorders' (PTED), found participants met criteria for other disorders and a high prevalence of Post-Traumatic Stress. 'Characteristic were feelings of injustice (100%), embitterment (97.7%), and rage (91.7%).

The researcher noticed a common experience of embitterment among police officers and survivors of abuse which can be enduring, with symptoms severe enough to become debilitating. Embitterment appears to be separate to PTSD, Anxiety or Depression; though these may be comorbid conditions. It could be that embitterment reduces resilience to trauma and lead to other psychological conditions. Many of those supported, stated they are unable to forgive the perceived transgressions against them. They seem unable to move forwards from the event. Officers report that their embitterment was caused by malpractice or the immoral and unethical actions of others, which conflict with their idea of right and wrong. The transgression may be intentional or inadvertent (such as incompetence, unintended negligence or carelessness). The transgression may have been actual or perceived. A transgression may occur that goes against a law, rule, or code of conduct.

Embitterment may lead to immutable loss of trust in individuals, groups, organisations or societies. The experience may create disaffection, disillusionment and underperformance. Embitterment in police officers appears to differentiate from other conditions by a marked preoccupation with the pursuit of justice, holding those responsible to account, seeking vindication and rumination on revenge.

PTSD involves significant threat to life in a physical context; embitterment could potentially involve a threat to one's basic human needs. Both are a challenge to one's survival. This may include shattering the person's intrinsic values and beliefs. The individual may be unable to assimilate the experience and adapt. Embitterment could potentially ensue as a result of threat to personal security (such as loss of shelter, finances, relationships, socialisation, self-image, reputation and achievement) or liberty (such as loss of freedom due to criminal court proceedings or other investigations).

Questions posed by this research

For the purposes of this research, the researcher will be asking (1) Do Moral Injury (MI) and PTED share the same symptomatology?, (2) Do MI and PTED share the same type of triggering event or causation? (3) Are MI and PTED comorbid with PTSD and do they share the same triggering event? (4) Do MI and PTED have specific recommended treatment options and are they the same? (5) Do we need these two separate classifications? (6) Is it beneficial to treat PTED or MI for more effective PTSD recovery? (7) Should MI be considered a disorder?

Relevant theory:

Linden (2007), identified diagnostic criteria which discriminates PTED from other disorders. 90% did not see a way to hold the perpetrator to account. His research into 'The psychopathology of posttraumatic embitterment disorders' found participants met criteria for other disorders and with a high prevalence of Post-Traumatic Stress. Feelings of injustice (100%), embitterment (97.7%), and rage (91.7%) were characteristic.[5] In his second study, 73% were triggered by critical events that were work related. Linden (2009) research (The Post-Traumatic Embitterment Disorder Self-Rating Scale - PTED Scale) suggests a prevalence of clinically relevant embitterment in the general population of about 2.5%.[6] Health and Safety Executive research with the Police Research Unit (2001) titled, 'Managing post incident reactions in the police service', identified an increased risk in the development of PTSD where police officers were dissatisfied with organisational issues. 'When a critical incident is placed within the context of other dissatisfactions within the workplace, this more demanding aspect of police work can be

---

[5] (Linden, Baumann, Rotter, & Schippan, 2007)
[6] (Linden, Baumann, Lieberei, & Rotter, 2009)

overwhelming...anger and frustration at the organisation can produce significant and long-lasting emotional distress.[7] Dunn and Sensky (2018) report on 'Psychological processes in chronic embitterment: The potential contribution of rumination,' concluded that rumination impairs problem-solving. The research states, *'The association of affective rumination with embitterment may contribute to the explanation for why embitterment becomes chronic and is often difficult to alleviate.'*[8] Linden (2018), on the 'Spectrum of Embitterment Manifestations, states that *'Embitterment is seen in reaction to injustice, vilification, or humiliation...it is known to everybody, but it can also occur in the context of mental disorders and even become an illness in itself... If embitterment grows in intensity and duration, then it can become pathological.....it is associated with severe suffering for the person as well as the family, colleagues, or even the public.'*[9]

Investigative methodology:

This fundamental research project will collect quantitative and qualitative data in the form of online questionnaires, case studies, interviews and literary review of other research. Questionnaires will be completed by Military personnel (serving and veteran), Police Officers and Healthcare professionals (serving and retired). Case studies may be provided by email correspondence or telephone, face to face or video link interviews. Interviews will be recorded on a Dictaphone and transcribed. All data collected will provide information on keywords, prevalence in frontline services, symptoms, causes, triggering events, comorbid conditions and treatment, as well as a potential indication as to whether there is convergent validity between the constructs of PTED and Moral Injury. The data will be critically analysed.

Keywords: Betrayal, Injustice, Moral Injury, Embitterment, Blame, PTSD

---

[7] (Mitchell, Stevenson, & Poole, 2001)
[8] (Dunn & Sensky, 2018)
[9] (Linden & Rotter, 2018)

Research outcomes: Findings will be published for general consumption as well as for specific affected groups. Copies of the research will be given to prominent individuals, organisations and institutions who may find it useful and for further dissemination. Suggestions for further beneficial research in this area will be made.

Dissemination plans: Relevant government bodies, organisations, charities, educational institutions and other agencies.

Word Count: Word count, excluding 'About the Author,' is 69,384. Total word count is 71,095.

Before we begin to explore PTED and MI in frontline services, we need to consider the external influences on society, the organisations, job roles and individuals at the point of completing the research. The following section is on social, economic and environmental context.

Claire Carter

Social, economic and environmental context

Coronavirus 2020

The timing of this research project coincided with the outbreak of the pandemic Covid-19. Unprecedented measures are being introduced across the world, in a bid to slow the spread, save millions of lives and protect healthcare services which are under incredible strain. Covid-19 (or Coronavirus) is a severe acute respiratory syndrome which originated in Wuhan, China in December 2019. A worldwide pandemic followed. The UK became infected in January 2020. The pilot research questionnaire (Embitterment, and injury post-trauma, in Frontline Services) was launched online on 18th March 2020. The second research questionnaire aimed at Frontline personnel (serving and retired) in first responder roles, armed forces and healthcare, was launched online on 2nd April 2020. By the 3 April, there were 38,168 confirmed cases of COVID-19 in the UK. 3,605 people had died as a result. Field hospitals are being set up in converted conference and sports centres across the UK in a bid to meet the demand for medical treatment. NHS staff and other healthcare providers, such as GPs and Care Homes are reporting a serious lack of resources (such as ventilators for patients) and personal protective equipment (such as gloves and masks). Newly qualified medics are being fast-tracked to join the effort and retired healthcare professionals are being asked to return to service. Many healthcare professionals have been unable to work due to self-isolation. Some have contracted Covid-19 and sadly died.

The threat to public health and the health service is so significant that the government has introduced statutory instruments and laws in an attempt to delay further spread. This includes new powers to keep individuals in isolation (The Health Protection (Coronavirus) Regulations 2020 – 10th February 2020)[10] and to limit or suspend public gatherings and detain people suspected to be infected (Coronavirus Act 2020 – 25th March 2020).[11] The Coronavirus Act 2020 has resulted in closures of schools, universities and non-essential shopping outlets. Sporting events are cancelled, as well as any other planned social events or gatherings. The housing market has been affected, as people are asked to delay moving home and property viewings are suspended. People's tenancies are at risk, as well as private home owners who may struggle to keep up with mortgage repayments. Funerals are to be attended by immediate family only, who are not in the 'high risk categories' (such as those with underlying health conditions and those over 70 years of age) or those in isolation due to infection. Social distancing must be observed during the funeral, which means people will be unable to comfort each other at such a distressing time. The government has agreed to these arrangements; understanding that being denied the ability to grieve through the process of a funeral, could have a significant impact on health and wellbeing.[12] "Lockdowns around the world bring rise in domestic violence"[13] as people are isolated at home with abusive partners and tensions increase.[14]

Social distancing is in force in all situations. Queues to enter supermarkets snake through the car parks and shoppers are to maintain space between each other. Travel restrictions are in place. People are advised not to travel unless it is essential or they are 'key workers' vital to keeping the country running. Police are stopping citizens to check

---

[10] (Wikipedia, Health Protection (Coronavirus) Regulations 2020, 2020)
[11] (Wikipedia, Coronavirus Act 2020, 2020)
[12] (NAFD, 2020)
[13] (Guardian, 2020)
[14] (Grierson, 2020)

their reason for travelling. They have the power to send people back home and issue fines. The government has asked people to remain at home unless 1) They are key workers, 2) They need to buy essential food or medicine, 3) to get daily exercise in isolation or with members of their household (such as a walk or run), 4) or to care for a vulnerable person. People are to stay a minimum of 6ft/2 metres away from each other at all times and are asked not to meet with family or friends. People are encouraged to work from home if they can.[15] The situation with Covid-19 has resulted in many job losses and more are expected, as the economy is impacted. Human rights and liberty may be affected as a consequence of the pandemic and measures implemented to delay the spread. The situation has become more uncertain, as cases of young people with no known underlying medical conditions have died from Covid-19. People are sadly dying alone (at home or in hospital). 13 year old Ismail Mohamed Abdulwahab, reportedly died alone without friends or family around him at Kings College Hospital, London.[16]

The Coronavirus pandemic is affecting all areas of life for citizens and frontline workers. Graham Medley (infectious diseases expert) suggests the potential harm resulting from the lockdown restrictions may outweigh the harm to our elderly population; that perhaps the Government should consider "......accepting the heightened risk to the elderly rather than harming younger generations with rising unemployment, domestic violence and mental illness."[17] It is impacting on social, ethical, moral, spiritual, environmental, biological, psychological, economic and financial, familial and relational, educational, occupational and existential domains across the UK and the world. Our 'way of life' is being altered (albeit temporarily) by, what may be considered, a naturally occurring event, predominately directed at our most vulnerable and ill population.

---

[15] (Government, 2020)
[16] (ITV, 2020)
[17] (Stubley, 2020)

At the time of completing this survey in July 2020, the number of deaths from Covid-19 in the UK is c.40,000.

Reduced public services

Over the last decade, austerity measures and cuts to spending by the Government affected public services (such as welfare, NHS, prisons and Policing).[18] This impacted on resources, including workforce numbers and the mental health of overburdened professionals. The military workforce reduced in size each year. The Government has had difficulty attracting and recruiting people.[19] There could be various reasons for this. For example, perhaps a potential decline in patriotism and community in younger generations. There have been criticisms over the Iraq war and whether Britain should have been involved. This led to the Chilcot inquiry. The report findings stated the war was unnecessary as the case for war was deficient. There were allegations that *"Tony Blair had lied or deliberately misled Parliament and the public."*[20] The war in Afghanistan and Iraq had a significant effect on those who served (including physical and psychological injury). Research carried out by Kings College London states, *"Among ex-serving personnel who deployed in a combat role to Iraq or Afghanistan, 17% reported symptoms suggesting probable PTSD compared to 6% of those deployed in a support role such as medical, logistics, signals and aircrew."* [21] There may have been a sense of Government betrayal and loss of trust resulting from the IHAT public inquiry into allegations of atrocities during the Iraq war. Soldiers were vilified, based on false witness accounts and a corrupt process in many cases.[22] There have been prosecutions of soldiers who served in Northern Ireland, such as 'Soldier F' in 2019, 47 years after the alleged incidents. This is compared with the Governments pardon for

---

[18] (Travis, 2017)
[19] (BBC, 2019)
[20] (Wikipedia, Iraq Inquiry, 2020)
[21] (KCL, 2018)
[22] (Bowcott, 2017) (Parliament, 2017)

perpetrators of terrorist acts during the same period. These events caused an outcry among the services community and beyond[23] and may have made people question the values, morals, ethics and motives of those with power and authority.

In 2019, the police service hit crisis point in the UK with unprecedented cases of PTSD among the workforce. According to research carried out by Cambridge University, an average of 1 in 5 Officers experienced some degree of post-traumatic stress.[24] Merseyside Police reported a mental health epidemic, with the equivalent of 38 years officer sickness absence taken in a 12 month period (2018).[25] The service was asked to do 'more with less' and single crewing became the norm. This was a move which increased risk of harm and violence to officers. The Police Federation stated "*Cuts to police budgets have led to a reduction in police officers and more single crewing of patrols…..The number of assaults on police officers that have been recorded has increased concurrently with an increase in the use of single crewing of patrol.*"[26] Police officers and members of the armed forces are 'servants of the crown' and are not afforded the same employment rights or individual rights as other citizens. They often sacrifice their relationships, family life, mental and physical health and safety in this role. Cuts to policing which jeopardize the health and safety of officers may be perceived as undervaluing their sacrifices and worth.

Neglect, austerity and long term cuts to the NHS are being highlighted by the Coronavirus pandemic. Sean O'Grady, writer for the Independent (2020) stated "*The NHS is getting us through this crisis. Once it's over, the people will remember exactly who tried to destroy it…we know now how much we rely on our under-appreciated, neglected public services, the welfare state and key workers…..I have to add a note of bitterness….There is a powerful*

---

[23] (Corbishley, 2019)
[24] (Giordano, 2019)
[25] (McMenemy, 2018)
[26] (PFEW, 2018)

sense of injustice around these shocking events."[27] Nesrine Malik (2020) for the Guardian writes "In this crisis, the Tory cuts can no longer be hidden by empty gestures.....Coronavirus has mercilessly exposed the damage years of austerity and shrinking of the state have wreaked." The comment "Whatever you need, that's what you're going to get!....had the air of a friend who had habitually ignored you, then one day unexpectedly needed you."[28] Between 2011 and 2017, 300 nurses died from suicide in England and Wales, according to Office of National Statistics figures. The Nursing Times stated this was "amid claims their cries for help were "repeatedly" ignored."[29]

Frontline, operational services have been greatly affected by financial cuts, increased workload, reduced workforce, difficulty with recruitment and the Coronavirus pandemic. These factors may have a significant impact on the experience of PTED, MI and PTSD in staff and organisations. In Chapter 1, an overview of PTED and MI are discussed.

---

[27] (O'Grady, 2020)
[28] (Malik, 2020)
[29] (Mitchell G. , 2019)

CHAPTER 1

PTED – Post Traumatic Embitterment Disorder & Moral Injury (MI)

The researchers' interest in Posttraumatic Embitterment Disorder was first peaked when supporting a police officer, who presented with difficulties she had not encountered before. Although he told her he was affected by PTSD and Depression; she noticed other patterns of emotional and cognitive dysregulation, which seemed to overshadow any observable symptoms of PTSD. His depressive episodes appeared to be a consequence of, or symbiotic with persistent rumination on injustice and a potentially futile desire to see a pillar of change to institutional betrayal, abuse and corruption. Although the officer sought and engaged with support; the researchers' efforts were ineffective; beyond being a 'listening ear' and bearing witness to his disclosures. He received support from family members and acknowledged that his mindset had a detrimental vicarious impact on his close family, which he regrets. He sought justice through various agencies, including Employment Tribunal.

He used his savings to support himself financially, as he was unable to work. He watched this money dwindle, to the point where the outcome was homelessness. Any ideas and goals discussed during support sessions, did not manifest actions towards achieving his hopes or desires. He seemed to 'go round in circles.' The complaints processes he engaged with, were both protracted and stressful; generating a significant amount of documentation. Organising his thoughts, a linear narrative of events, personal statements to assist with court/appeal and collating his paperwork, were overwhelming and unmanageable tasks for him. His conversation was often incoherent, in terms of structure and the researcher had the impression that much of the experiences, which were disclosed (repeatedly), were a smokescreen for 'the real issues' underlying his current cognitions and which predated his police service. For example, ideas about self and the world which were formed during childhood and early adult experiences.

Focusing on a future, which did not involve 'the cause' of holding the police service accountable and exposing their behaviour, was apparently inconceivable. For the most part, he had no interest in any enjoyable activities and displayed anhedonia. Not only did he persistently ruminate on past events; his conversation would usually turn to these ruminations too. Validation and empathy were offered during support meetings. Suggestions for alternative, positive ways to raise awareness of his concerns, which were forward focused, achievable and for which he would have control, were discussed. However, he felt unable to execute any steps or plans to bring these ideas to fruition, even with support. He stated, he felt he needed someone else to take control of every practical task which needed to be done; feeling helpless to do so himself. The volume of perceived injustices, immoral acts and insults were so significant for him, that he was cognitively overwhelmed. This tended to result in depressive episodes, where he would mentally 'shut down' with the burnout of rumination. He joined the police service, believing the organisation was moral and made a difference to the lives of victims. His beliefs about the police as an institution were undone by his experiences. During conversation, he disclosed perceptions formed during childhood about his sense of worth compared to his siblings and the lasting impact of a partners' infidelity.

The researcher describes his natural personality as idealistic, intelligent, articulate, humourous, philosophical, caring, loyal, friendly, approachable and sociable. He has high moral standards and expectations of himself and others. He has rigid perceptions. He adopts dark humour, banter and sarcasm. He is well travelled and has worldly experience. He has stated he feels anger, irritability and has little patience with others. As is often the case with psychological injury, he masks and supresses much of the negative emotions he experiences, even if they feel thinly veiled.

When presented with opportunities for personal development or change, he most often felt unable to act on this. The researcher noted the significant potential for this individual to achieve, to be successful and make a difference in the world. Furthermore, the sense of sadness that such potential is obstructed by his self-destructive outcomes, for which he is aware and feels unable to overcome at this time.

Brief therapeutic intervention (Cognitive Behavioural Therapy - CBT), was ineffective. He had suicidal thoughts, difficulty with sleep, difficulty with personal hygiene and household chores, anxiety, memory loss, withdrawal and isolation, feelings of hatred, inability to form or maintain relationships, self-sabotage, negative self-concept, feelings of shame regarding the person he had become, avoidance, inability to move-on from the perceptions of injustice, insult and wrongdoing. He has difficulty trusting others and always expects to be betrayed. This has resulted in paranoia. He expressed feelings of helplessness and the need to delegate all control for his day to day functioning over to someone else. He has little or no future orientation or forward focused plans. He tries to find hope for the future through unrealistic, eccentric and potentially unachievable goals and aspirations; as if purposely setting himself up to fail from the start.

Despite successful conclusion of court action and medical appeal process; he stated he still did not feel a sense of justice. He felt the protracted processes had made his mental health deteriorate even further and that the system was set up to break him. He stated, he feels betrayed. Furthermore, he stated he did not have the same access to justice because his mental state meant he was unable to provide a coherent account for a court hearing. Subsequently, he felt forced to settle out of court. Therefore, he was denied a possible feeling of justice, through publicly exposing the issues by way of a hearing.

Although he was aware of his avoidance, spiralling financial decline, imminent loss of security and significant stress as a result of economic poverty; he was unable to change his behaviour.

He experiences extreme revenge fantasy, which involves the humiliation, subjugation and torture of the perpetrator(s). He does not perceive offenders who behave immorally, as injurious. He does however, identify those who abuse power and authority in roles of moral standing, as perpetrators of injustice. This suggests the moral injury is less about the immoral act itself and more about who the transgressor is and their role in society. It is the shattering of preconceived beliefs and expectations of the roles people play in society that can cause moral injury and embitterment. He acknowledges that some of the experiences were not intended to cause him harm personally; rather the motivation for the transgressors' behaviour was to safeguard the organisation or other employees by way of cover-up. However, the consequence was his psychological injury.

An apology, for this individual is insufficient. He wants to witness the repentance of the transgressors. In other words, he wants demonstrable commitment to actions that prove a change for the better and sincere remorse. He wants reform and social justice, rather than personal justice.

MI and PTED can occur when there is a transgression that violates one's intrinsic values, beliefs and expectations about the world, others and self. An event or incident occurs which is perceived by the injured party as morally wrong.[30]

This can be disorientating, as one's expectations of right and wrong, their deeply held beliefs and world view are challenged or shattered. Bollmann et al. *(2015) state, "People have a fundamental need to believe that the world is a just place where individuals get what they deserve and deserve what they get."[31]*

---

[30] (Linden & Maercker, 2011) (Maguen & Litz, 2020)
[31] (Bollmann, Krings, Maggiori, & Rossier, 2015)

MI and PTED are not yet formally recognised, though there is research to suggest these conditions exist and are of clinical significance.[32] Linden et al. (2007), indicated a high prevalence of posttraumatic stress associated with PTED.[33] Features of embitterment and moral injury in a traumatized individual can increase the risk of long term psychological injury and inhibit recovery.[34] Symptoms may stem from abuse of power and authority over the individual. This could include poor leadership decisions in high risk situations, loss of trust in leadership, loss of trust in those with power over the individual, witnessing immoral behaviour and an overwhelming sense of injustice or betrayal.[35]

Additionally, there can be self-blame if one feels helpless to cope with what has happened or they failed to prevent it.[36] MI can also occur when one is the perpetrator of harm and in breach of their own values and morals.[37]

"Trauma robs the victim of a sense of power and control; the guiding principle of recovery is to restore power and control to the survivor" (Herman, 1997:159).

PTED – Post-Traumatic Embitterment Disorder

PTED can include feelings of betrayal, humiliation, rage, helplessness, injustice and desire for revenge, low mood, resignation, resentment, arousal when reminded of the event (which may result in avoidance) and normal affect when one is distracted from it. People can overcome these thoughts and feelings over time. If one is unable to process and assimilate events and emotions, the symptoms can become chronic and debilitating.

---

[32] (Linden & Maercker, 2011) (Linden, Baumann, Lieberei, & Rotter, 2009) (Maguen & Litz, 2020)
[33] (Linden, Baumann, Rotter, & Schippan, 2007)
[34] (Linden & Maercker, 2011) (Shay J. , 2003)
[35] (Maguen & Litz, 2020) (Herman, 1997)
[36] (Linden & Maercker, 2011) (Koenig, Youssef, Ames, & Oliver, 2017)
[37] (Koenig, Ames, & Bussing, 2019)

Anger, hostility, revenge phenomena and suppression of emotions are features.[38] Revenge fantasy can be a coping strategy and it can be experienced as pleasurable.[39] Major depression is commonly co-morbid with PTED. People with embitterment are less likely to seek help and there can be a greater risk of suicide. [40]

Linden and Maercker, (2011) suggests a "*premorbid personality of Posttraumatic Embitterment Disorder (PTED) as* "*achievement oriented, devoted persons with strict convictions and beliefs, that show great self-sacrifice and commitment in their job or social role*" (p.85). Traits of cynicism, mistrust and viewing others negatively are also risk factors for developing PTED.[41] They state one must be aware of the negative event and identify the incident as the cause of their embitterment.[42] Embitterment may develop from both a weak belief in a just world and an experience of injustice. The 'just world hypothesis' is an expectation that people will get what they deserve. This expectation is perhaps more significant to individuals exposed to risks that are out of their control, such as fate.[43] It may be that these traits and considerations feature heavily in frontline services and personnel.

PTED is associated with traumatized groups within the general population who 1) have experienced common yet negative life events, 2) have a prone personality to embitterment (where there is no known trigger event) or 3) PTED is comorbid with other conditions.[44] It has been associated with (and not limited to) the workplace, relationships, society, political conflict and illness. Linden et al. (2007), identified nearly

---

[38] (Linden & Maercker, 2011)
[39] (Linden & Maercker, 2011) (Graef, 1990) (Herman, 1997)
[40] (Linden & Maercker, 2011)
[41] (Linden & Maercker, 2011)
[42] (Linden, Baumann, Rotter, & Schippan, 2007)
[43] (Linden & Maercker, 2011)
[44] (Linden & Rotter, 2018)

73% were work related triggers.[45] Relationship embitterment is still under-researched.[46]

"PTED is a subclass of adjustment disorder... [and]..is triggered by exceptional, though normal negative life events such as unemployment or divorce that are typically experienced as unjust and unfair, but that are not life threatening or anxiety provoking" (Linden & Maercker, 2011:30). However, Linden et al. (2007), identified a high prevalence of post-traumatic stress. The average duration of the severe symptoms being 31.7 months,[47] which is suggestive of a disability.

PTED is being researched with the potential to be clinically recognised and included in manuals such as the Diagnostic and Statistical Manual of Mental Disorders (DSM). This is a manual referred to by psychiatry services to identify a person's condition and formulate a diagnosis. This may have positive benefits for individuals experiencing long term, debilitating symptoms. It could also impact on employment and tribunals. It has been recognised that cases of persistent embitterment in employees results in early retirement and litigation.[48]

Linden and Rotter (2018), identify four manifestations of embitterment (a) embitterment-prone personality where no specific negative life event(s) are reported, (b) complex embitterment resulting from multiple negative life events, (c) embitterment in reaction to a single traumatic event and (d) secondary embitterment comorbid with other mental disorders.[49]

Rumination on the transgression and an all-consuming pursuit of justice can maintain PTSD symptoms and inhibit recovery.[50] Sensky et al. (2015),

---

[45] (Linden, Baumann, Rotter, & Schippan, 2007)
[46] (Linden & Maercker, 2011)
[47] (Linden, Baumann, Rotter, & Schippan, 2007)
[48] (Linden & Maercker, 2011)
[49] (Linden & Rotter, 2018)
[50] (Linden & Maercker, 2011)

states there are many similarities between the symptoms of PTSD and PTED, including hyperarousal, hypervigilance, flashbacks and distress caused by reminders to the incident.[51]

"embitterment....can be at the core of severe mental illness" – Linden & Maercker, 2011:2)

One significant factor which may trigger embitterment is loss. This loss may relate to meeting one's basic human needs for security and safety. For example, relationships, employment, financial security, home, identity, self-esteem and physical integrity. When someone feels under attack in this way, their survival feels threatened. One's 'belief in a just world' and therefore belief in fairness, security and stability may be challenged or shattered. The incident may not be life threatening in the sense of physical death, though perhaps life threatening in the sense of emotional, physical and psychological needs for survival.

Linden et al. (2011), identifies bitterness as resulting from an injustice or neglect that one views as a threat and leads to loss of resources, significant others, goals (meaning and purpose), trust or bodily functions.[52] Linden et al. (2007), on the psychopathology of PTED, sets out the diagnostic criteria for the disorder. He appears to suggest some reactions to the negative and unjust event are a choice, or at least reliant on the individuals cognitive style and personality. For example the individual is *"uncertain whether they want wounds to heal."* They experience *"repeated intrusive memories of the critical event. To some extent they even think that it is important not to forget." "Drive is reduced and blocked. [They] experience themselves not so much as drive inhibited but rather as drive unwilling"* and *"Emotional modulation is not impaired and patients can show normal affect when they are distracted."*[53] Linden and Maercker (2011),

---

[51] (Sensky, Salimu, Ballard, & Pereira, 2015)
[52] (Linden & Maercker, 2011)
[53] (Linden, Baumann, Rotter, & Schippan, 2007)

state embitterment is both 'painful and rewarding' and has an 'addictive' quality. Individuals can become hostile when an opportunity for change is available, and resent it. Embittered persons are less likely to seek help. Perhaps this is why *"individuals who are prone to embitterment are also at elevated risk for suicide"* (Linden & Maercker, 2011:245). Secondary gain may be a factor affecting one's reluctance to move on from the event. For example, the perceived right to repeatedly punish the transgressor or perpetrator,[54] an energy source to fight injustice through litigation, *"the attention or influence that one gets from having been offended, or the "power" that one may feel"* (Freedman & Enright, 2017).[55]

Embitterment may be reinforced through rumination on events; it can also be reinforced by embittered others. People may seek those with perspectives congruent to their own; knowing that their view is unlikely to be challenged (which could be a painful state) and therefore, not confronted with options for change. Involvement with groups and forums which allow or actively 'stir up' bitterness reactions, may enable people to stay in an embittered state of mind. Groups, forums and support networks should validate, empathise with and acknowledge someone's experience. Then they should assist with problem-solving and helping one to regain control over their lives, emotions and circumstances. Herman (1997), suggests personal trauma can be transformed into social action and through this action find meaning, i.e. helping others and protecting others from trauma or harm.[56] Where it is appropriate to take action and challenge wrong-doing, individuals can be supported to do so - this may help with feelings of powerlessness and restoring a sense of justice. Herman (1997), suggests that to find meaning and purpose in taking action with others and 'for the greater good' or 'justice,' can protect against post-traumatic symptoms. She states, *"The solidarity of a group provides the strongest protection against terror and despair, and the strongest*

---

[54] (Linden & Maercker, 2011)
[55] (Freedman & Enright, 2017)
[56] (Herman, 1997)

antidote to trauma. Trauma isolates; the group re-creates a sense of belonging (p.214)."[57]

Moral Injury (MI)

Moral Injury (MI) is a term usually associated with the military and high risk situations where a moral transgression occurs. Bryan et al. (2015), highlights that MI, can only be present if one is aware that the experience goes against their own personal morals.[58] This may suggest that what is deemed immoral by one individual, may not be perceived the same by another.

Psychiatrist Dr Jonathan Shay first coined the term Moral Injury when working with Vietnam Veterans. He stated grief and horror can be overcome when 'what's right' has not been violated,[59] perhaps suggesting that trauma can be overcome when values, beliefs and morals are protected.

The definition of moral injury has altered since Shay. It is *"perpetrating, failing to prevent, bearing witness to, or learning about acts that transgress deeply held moral beliefs and expectations"* and resulted in *"lasting psychological, biological, spiritual, behavioral, and social impact."*[60] There have been eighteen different concepts of MI since Shay.[61] Which suggests difficulty in clearly identifying the psychopathology of MI, the causes and symptoms. Perhaps Moral Injury is a subjective experience and idea, which cannot be formalized as a construct of psychological injury.

Carey and Hodgson (2018) state, MI is a *"four dimensional bio-psycho-social-spiritual infliction with a variety of interwoven symptoms."* They propose MI

---

[57] (Herman, 1997)
[58] (Bryan, Anestis, Bryan, & Anestis, 2015)
[59] (Shay J. , 2003)
[60] (Barnes, Hurley, & Taber, 2019)
[61] (Carey & Hodgson, 2018)

should be classified as a syndrome, which will enable appropriate screening and treatment. Other researchers "*suggest a non-syndromal approach to classifying Moral Injury.*" MI can exacerbate several psychiatric disorders and result in a significant impairment of life functioning.[62]

Barnes et al. (2019), highlights that moral injury depends upon one's perception of the event and how it affects their belief system and worldview. It is noted that Moral Injury can impact on civilians and occupations other than the military, such as first responders and healthcare professionals.[63] Dean et al. (2019) state, "*Every time we are forced to make a decision that contravenes our patients' best interests, we feel a sting of moral injustice.*"[64] MI is no longer exclusive to the experience of combat. Like PTED; features of MI include feelings of guilt, shame, anger, loss of trust and lack of forgiveness,[65] betrayal, loss of meaning,[66] depression, reexperiencing, and social problems.[67] Nickerson (2018) states, Currier et al., identified greater symptoms of PTSD and depression where Moral Injury was present.[68]

Nash et al. (2013), created the Moral Injury Events Scale (MIES) to measure events that may lead to PTSD which did not specifically involve threats to life or safety and which violated morals, beliefs and values.[69]

Molendijk (2018), criticizes conceptualizations of MI as "*one dimensional*" in the sense that they are "*mechanistic and individualistic.*" He states, moral conflict with beliefs about the accepted '*values and norms*' in a social context may be factors to consider.[70] Barnes et al. (2019), state the morally injured individual has a significant impact on biological,

---

[62] (Carey & Hodgson, 2018)
[63] (Barnes, Hurley, & Taber, 2019)
[64] (Dean, Talbot, & Dean, 2019)
[65] (Barnes, Hurley, & Taber, 2019)
[66] (Koenig, 2018)
[67] (Jinkerson, 2016)
[68] (Nickerson, 2018)
[69] (Nash, 2013)
[70] (Molendijk, Kramer, & Verweij, 2018)

psychological, societal and spiritual areas of life.[71] This may suggest a view, that the individual is responsible, rather than these external factors impacting on the person. This correlates with the current MI model, where one is the perpetrator or fails to prevent the moral transgression. However, this model does not seem to accommodate circumstances where a moral incursion is directly experienced at the hands of a perpetrator (for example, someone abusing a position of power and authority).

In response to the question 'What are Morals?,' Molendijk (2018) refers to Litz et al., stating there is a moral code which can be individual or shared. For example, *"familial, cultural, societal and legal"*. There is an understanding of the rules and expected behaviour. The aim of treatment is to move the individual to a position of accepting themselves as imperfect, rather than reframe their guilt and shame as resulting from a distorted perception. For example, *"failure to realize that the actions not chosen would have probably had worse consequences than actions taken."* [72] However, Litz definition of Moral Injury as *"Perpetrating, failing to prevent, bearing witness to, or learning about acts that transgress deeply held moral beliefs and expectations"* and focus on self-blame and perpetration,[73] doesn't seem to sufficiently consider where one has been morally injured by someone else with responsibility or in a trusted position (as in Shays' concept of MI).

Currier et al. (2017) state, MI is a *"construct that addresses dysphoric moral emotions/cognitions* [i.e. guilt, self-blame] *and maladaptive behavioural attempts to manage this pain from moral violations."* They state, revenge fantasy is indicative of MI perpetrated by others; and 'acting out' is driven by feelings of shame and guilt associated with 'self-directed' MI.[74]

---

[71] (Barnes, Hurley, & Taber, 2019)
[72] (Molendijk, Kramer, & Verweij, 2018)
[73] (Molendijk, Kramer, & Verweij, 2018)
[74] (Currier, 2017)

When developing the EMIS-M model for MI, Currier et al. (2017), identified a crossover between PTSD and MI symptomatology. For example, avoidance of people, places and activities which can be a reminder of the trauma. Research identified revenge fantasy directed at others who caused the moral injury; stating, "*they appeared to stew and fantasize about exacting revenge.*" 'Shame-based acting out' results from self-blame. Currier et al., highlight the importance of incorporating religious and spiritual beliefs into the construct of MI; stating there is a "*formative role of religion in shaping moral beliefs and values.*" Furthermore, MI is only appropriate where an individual responds to moral pain with emotional and behavioural dysfunction. For example, "*dysphoric moral emotions (e.g., guilt, shame, and anger) and cognitions (e.g. self-condemnation).*" They also state, these behaviours adopted to try and avoid moral pain crosses over with other existing mental health conditions, including PTSD and Depressive Disorder.[75] A case study follows to demonstrate Moral Injury.

Case study 1: First Responder

This officer shares his story (Carter, 2014, Duty of Care - Psychological Injury in Policing): In 2003 I was first on scene to a fatal road traffic accident (RTA) involving a London bus and a five year old child. A London bus had been forced off the road and had mounted the kerb and the railing dividing the road and the pavement. The 5-year old boy had been crushed under the wheel of the bus. The child bled out in front of me and died as I held his hand underneath the bus. I struggled with the incident at the time. This was raised to my supervisors who told me to 'man up' or to 'stop being so sensitive' and 'this is the job!' Two months later I was compulsory transferred to the control room. I had several nightmares about the RTA early on which initially passed. However, I

---

[75] (Currier, 2017)

started experiencing long bouts of insomnia and stress related IBS. In 2005 I was viciously attacked by a suspect at a commercial burglary who tried to imbed a kitchen knife in my femoral artery. I had several slashes to my uniform. Attempts were made to internally discipline me as I had punched the suspect to subdue the assault. Typically, this criticism came from someone unconnected to the incident. I struggled with nightmares, flashbacks and stress/depression at the time, but my worry was redirected towards fighting the disciplinary. No concern was shown for my welfare from the event. Then began the bullying and repeat internal investigations and what I thought for so long was depression.

The term mental health was batted around regularly. I was removed from frontline duties for a suspected mental health problem. Mental health was seen as a negative and further supported the urge to have me disciplined. It was even suggested that I resigned, and when I continued to battle the disciplinary a senior officer told me he didn't want people like me in his police service. My obsessive-compulsive disorder began around this time. I didn't feel I was able to discuss my health issues surrounding the knife attack, especially when one particular supervisor felt compelled to over-scrutinize everything I did from that point on. I raised a formal grievance of bullying which was not properly investigated and covered up. Offensive messages were often written on my locker, mail and mail slot, such as 'mad Michael' or 'danger of death'.

Again in 2005 I found a murder victim in the street who had been struck across the head with an iron bar. I was performing CPR for over 30 minutes. I received a mouthful of blood/spinal fluid due to a faulty CPR mask. Spinal/brain fluid and blood were oozing from the victim and I was HEAVILY contaminated. The incident received a large media coverage. The mental health problems I was experiencing went untreated and unnoticed in the correct way, and this led to my first mental breakdown in 2005 where I apparently threw items at my bully. Bullying continued to taint my career on my return to work after two months which led to several referrals to the Occupational Health Unit.

I was awarded a punishment posting[76] to the Police Call Centre due to a second grievance I raised to the Deputy Chief Constable. Even though my allegation of bullying was heavily supported with evidence from other officers, I was told in no uncertain terms that the grievance ceased at that point whether I liked it or not.

I returned to frontline policing in 2007 having spent approximately 18 months in a non-operational role. By this time, a reputation had been created. I was deemed difficult, aggressive and to have an over enthusiastic use of force. I became a target for acting or newly qualified supervisors over the years using me as evidence of dealing with disciplinary issues. An individual in the Professional Standards Department developed an over-active pursuit of me, which momentarily stopped suddenly in 2011 when I changed my collar number.

In 2008 I was badly burnt following a severe allergic reaction to CS gas. I was removed temporarily from frontline duties due to an outrageous unfounded allegation by my supervisor that I was "obviously on steroids" because of the burn reaction. This was supported with a comment that a friend of theirs had told them I had increased my muscle mass in a short period of time. My way of dealing with my problems was to immerse myself obsessively into something, in this case weightlifting. The multiple unfounded allegations against me were often finalised without notifying me of any conclusion. In this case I was told I was under formal investigation for alleged drug use. This investigation was never concluded.

In 2008 I was beaten to virtual unconsciousness by a former professional boxer who attacked me at a domestic violence incident. I was single crewed but despite the force policy, the force control room (FCR) stated that the suspect had left therefore it was okay for me to attend alone.

---

[76] A punishment posting is a term used in the police service, when a colleague is moved to a different job or location, which is deemed unfavourable, unpleasant or inconvenient – and in response to the colleagues' behaviour or difficulties; or used as a management tool to encourage the colleague to resign from the service.

On arrival, I was met at the door by a badly beaten female who spoke no English. The drunk suspect was hiding in the premises and attacked when I entered, lifting me off the ground and pinning me to the wall by holding my body armour under the armpits. I emptied a whole can of CS spray in his face which had no effect. He then punched and strangled me repeatedly. During the struggle the virtually naked suspect defecated himself (liquid diarrhoea) and we fell to the floor and we continued to grapple. I was contaminated from head to toe with his faeces and my blood. I had open cuts and I had his faeces in my open wounds, on my face, in my hair and all up my body. I managed to get the suspect in an arm bar restraint and held him on the ground until assistance arrived. The female victim in the property was hitting me on the head and sprayed hairspray at my face. The whole time I had been calling for assistance on my radio but could hear the FCR still despatching Officers to low level incidents such as noise disturbances. I remember believing at the time that I was going to die and nobody was aware or coming to help. Two special constables arrived first on scene and immediately ran back out due to the smell. I could barely see as the room was a mist of CS gas and hairspray. I had strong skin reactions to the CS gas and was burnt again.

Whilst I struggled with the incident in silence, my colleagues found the faecal element hilarious, my supervisors tried to discipline me for swearing on the radio during the attack. No concern was shown for my welfare. I was investigated a year later by the IPCC when the same suspect died in police custody.

Following a long period of stress and depression in 2012, I was given a written warning/improvement notice at a Unsatisfactory Attendance Procedure stage 1, stating I was expected to achieve a 100% attendance record. My self-certification for sickness was withdrawn and the local superintendent told me that I was letting my team and colleagues down by being off sick. I had been recording meetings such as this on my phone covertly and I feel I was suffering with severe justified paranoia.

Concerns throughout the years of my depression, instability and change in characteristics were regularly raised, but I received no help. I had never accessed a mental health service and had only seen my GP who referred to it as depression. My experience in the police led me to believe that speaking up about problems would result in punishment. I had detailed that my depression was spiralling out of control and I asked at times for a role away from frontline policing. This was always met with an outright refusal or suggestions that I'd be posted to the other side of the county. The operational needs of the organisation came first.

My low mood was often raised by supervisors. One claimed that I was bringing the team down and that I was setting a bad example for the officer's younger in service.

In 2015, the nightmares of the four incidents started. I had been experiencing physical symptoms of stress/anxiety/hypervigilance. I emotionally broke down at a couple of incidents and found myself contemplating taking my life by trying to drive my patrol car as fast as I could into a wall, a work colleague prevented me from doing so and took me to a supervisor.

Two days prior I had detailed to my sergeant that my depression was spiralling out of control and work-related stress was too much. I was told 'you're a big tough guy, you won't go sick'. I had been on average twice a year to occupational health with no help at all and my mental health issues went unnoticed or ignored. I had been very vocal about my mental health problems for years to my supervisors. The standard response was to double crew me for a couple of weeks and to refer me to Occupational health who were seemingly untrained and over worked. I raised in my last professional development review about work related stress and my out of control depression. I was placed on an action plan to be 'more positive'.

The researcher contacted the officer at the commencement of this research project, asking if he would be willing to participate and provide information on how he thinks and feels about his experiences since retiring from the police service. The officer agreed to answer the researchers' questions via email communication only. He explained that this style of contact would prevent any 'surprises' if questioned via video link; and would allow him the time needed to reflect on the questions and answers. He drafted his answers during episodes of insomnia in the night.

Six months prior to my breakdown I had begun having panic attacks at work, chest pain, unexpected emotional outbursts, loss of time, forgetting how to do basic tasks. All of which were detailed to my supervisors during this time. Following my breakdown and attempt on my life, I was not able to return to work due to mental health difficulties and was retired in 2016.

I had been diagnosed as having Complex PTSD, severe Panic disorder, severe Anxiety, severe Depression and OCD. I developed symptoms of agoraphobia during my absence.

The researcher asked, please tell me what treatment you have had. The officer stated:

Four incidents were identified from my career as a police officer dating back as far as 2003. These included the death of a child at a Road Traffic Accident, two attempts on my life with weapons and a murder. The organisation did not provide anything despite the request from my wife, and their own force medical officer. Therefore, I was forced into a position where I had to fund my own private medical treatment (psychiatrist} due to there being a lengthy waiting list on the NHS. I have received counselling, Cognitive Behaviour Therapy and EMDR all through the NHS. None of these treatments have been effective. I have no doubt that I would have been dismissed from the organisation long before the NHS services were available if I had not sought a private psychiatric assessment and treatment. The EMDR via the NHS made elements of my PTSD worse and had to be stopped after 4 sessions. EMDR brought up additional emotions about one traumatic incident in particular, namely extreme anger and aggression. I had been prewarned by the psychologist that this was a possibility and that tackling complex PTSD with so many traumatic incidents over such a long period of time would be difficult. My condition is regularly unstable. I have been referred to the community mental health teams and secondary mental health services many times and it has been clear that they do not know what to do to help me. The two occasions that I have been discharged from the secondary mental health services have not been due to improvement but due to a change in my address putting me outside of the catchment area for that particular NHS service, and due to the coronavirus. I have been told to refer again via my GP after the pandemic, but I do not feel I will as they have not been helpful. On both occasions I have been under the secondary mental health services care, it has felt to me like a fortnightly/weekly welfare check to make sure I haven't hurt myself or others in the time between appointments with no actual therapy being given.

The researcher asked, how long ago did you leave the organisation? The officer stated he left in 2016, 4 years ago.

The researcher asked, please tell me or describe what your thoughts and feelings are towards the police service now: The officer stated, I feel very let down by the police service and harbour a lot of aggression and hatred towards the police in general. There are individuals that I fear I would not be able to control my aggression toward, if in their presence again. I have distanced myself from anything police related as it causes triggers to my PTSD, makes me extremely aggressive and causes panic attacks. I never received any assistance from the police in terms of my health when I was employed, despite regular referrals to the occupational health unit for concerns about mental health. During the Ill Health Retirement process they took every step they could to dismiss me under the unsatisfactory attendance/performance process, and even after retirement they denied all elements of the PTSD being work related which meant appeal hearings and an additional year of misery. I eventually won my injury on duty pension appeal. I had a lot of friends in the police whilst I worked there. All but one of these people abandoned me the moment I went off long term sick. Only two people tried to regain contact with me when they started experiencing work related mental health difficulties of their own, but that only adds to my own health issues. I have to avoid everything to do with the police which is very hard to do being from a police family of three generations and it taking up 18 years of my working life.

The researcher asked, please tell me or describe for me what your symptoms are and any difficulties you have with day to day activities or functioning: The officer stated, my worst symptoms are severe depression, flashbacks, triggers to my PTSD, sleep disorders and nightmares. My depression varies day to day sometimes by the hour. I have {mostly} daily nightmares of varying degrees if I manage to sleep at all. These sometimes cause me to shout/scream/struggle in my sleep. These nightmares often occur during the day where I zone out and go into what people describe to me as a trance and I have flashbacks or relive the incidents. I do have grounding techniques that help me through these. There are many triggers to my PTSD. The most significant ones are the sound of sirens, which send me into an instant panic attack. Emergency service vehicles and uniform all create panic attacks. I have a psychomotor response mostly in the left side of my body where I shake uncontrollably when under stress or in a panic state. Other triggers include children's cries/screams and buses.

I rarely drive anymore and if I do its no further than a couple of miles. I do not travel well and worry about how I would react if faced with an emergency service siren or vehicle on the road. When I panic, I see things in slow motion and my senses become warped and I do not feel I am in control of myself. I do not handle any form of stress well and I avoid people. I rarely see anyone outside of my household or immediate family. I struggle to leave the house on a daily basis. I cannot handle being in a public place or crowded space on my own. My behaviour is sometimes upsetting and concerning to others and I have a lot of hatred towards people. I am concerned what I may do if put in a stressful or confrontational situation. I have an extreme hypersensitivity/hyper vigilance response to threat and danger. It becomes unbearable at times and is a sensory overload which sends me into a state of panic. My wife often tells me I have a look on my face like I'm going to hurt someone. I've never felt I've been able to switch out of "work mode" so I constantly feel under threat. I have an extreme sensitivity to noise and I often have to wear ear plugs to cope. Some days are worse than others. My depression is extreme, It can vary hour by hour/day by day. I have regular bouts of insomnia which make my depression worse and make daily activities difficult to complete. I cannot answer why I am depressed. There is no reason but it is very debilitating, draining and makes the simplest of tasks difficult or sometimes impossible. My journey since retirement has not been much fun. I have to avoid anything Police related which is extremely difficult especially with things like tv. Whilst I do genuinely have memory loss from a lot of my police career, I do my utmost to forget the rest. I live in constant fear that they will cause further problems for me. I have come to terms with the fact that this is a lifelong condition that I will have to deal with day to day. My life has adapted to accommodate PTSD and all its baggage. I am not expected to be able to work again in a normal environment. It is not the life I wanted and certainly not one I wanted for my wife. My wife is the only reason I have survived this for so long.

The researcher reviewing this case study noted a pattern of blame directed at the officer. The organisation perceived the officer to be 'faulty' and unable to cope with the job (traumatic incidents). This may have had a significant impact on the development of negative self-concept, feelings of guilt and shame. There are several examples of Moral Injury in this case study; including the failure of those with authority to do 'what's right' and at times, in high risk situations. The persistent bullying pursuit of this officer, who was in a vulnerable state (suicidal, depressed, traumatized), appears to have contributed to the deterioration of his mental health and the loss of his career. Being attacked by a 'victim' (who the officer was trying to protect from abuse and physical assault), whilst being assaulted by the perpetrator may be another example of moral injury. Beliefs about how a 'victim' should behave may be challenged, as well as putting oneself in physical danger to safeguard an 'ungrateful victim.' Values, beliefs and morals are challenged throughout this case study; including the officer's worth, sacrifices for an unjust cause, leadership and organisational malpractice, lack of procedural justice, lack of duty of care and institutional betrayal. Expectations regarding welfare support were not met. The officer has hatred and intense anger towards the police and somewhat indiscriminate anger towards members of the public. He feels let down by the organisation and fears he may be vengeful in the presence of particular individuals who he feels are responsible. This suggests moral injury and/or embitterment alongside PTSD.

In the next section, the vicarious effect of Moral Injury and PTED on partners, will be presented through case studies.

CHAPTER 2

The vicarious effect of Injustice

This research noticed a potential vicarious effect of injustice, MI or embitterment on close relationships. Though the injustice or moral injury may not have been directed at one's partner, perhaps witnessing the effect of the incident and acting as an advocate could lead to inheriting similar symptoms and harbouring similar feelings. Two partners shared their experiences of life alongside PTSD and advocating for their husbands,' at a time when they were vulnerable and ill.

Case Study 2

The researcher asked a retired police officers' wife to explain how living alongside her husband's Complex PTSD affected her and whether she experienced any symptoms of her own as a direct result. This wife had advocated for her husband with his employer for a protracted period of time with issues around his mental ill health, threat of unsatisfactory performance procedure and ill health retirement process (IHR); including a subsequent medical appeal when IHR was refused. She was also trying to get him the medical help and treatment he needed. This case study was managed through email correspondence and not via video interview. Consent and approval was given for the publication of this case study.

The researcher asked: How has your day to day life been affected? She stated, since he developed Complex PTSD, general day to day life has completely changed. Most decisions and things we do are factored around the PTSD and whether, or not, he would be able to manage a situation or whether we have any coping strategies that might be effective in that environment. For example, we have to do a simple exercise like our food shopping at the supermarket in the middle of the week, just before the shop is due to close (8-9pm) and we travel to a town 15-20 miles away even though we live 8 miles away from a major city. This is because various locations within the City we live near are directly connected to a number of the traumatic incidents that contributed to his PTSD, worry about bumping into an old colleague who might try to engage him in conversation, a higher chance of hearing an emergency siren or seeing an emergency vehicle and the volume of people are all triggers to his panic attacks and too overwhelming for him to cope with. There have been many occasions when, despite trying to mitigate these factors, we have pulled up in the car park somewhere and he cannot get out of the car because he is so debilitated by his hyper-sensitivity to noise (he describes it like someone sticking a knife in his ear drums), hyper vigilance (constantly scanning the space for threats/danger) and suffering panic attacks from other triggers. Simple actions or decisions have to be carefully planned, weighing up the benefits and the concerns before we can do anything. Imagine having to think about the positives and negatives of going to the Cinema, collecting a pizza from the takeaway or dropping the dog off at the kennels. Most people would automatically do these things without giving it a second thought but PTSD stops you in your tracks and forces you to plan whether he can do it with you or you do it on your own.

I am also a great deal more aware of my surroundings now and acutely aware of stimuli to his PTSD. For example, if I pass a Road Traffic Collision or road closure where emergency vehicles are present, I will call him and tell him to stay away from the area. If I think there is a chance of a trigger to his PTSD in a film or TV show, I will warn him not to watch it and I avoid it too. Just recently, the Coronavirus adverts advising people to stay at home have caused no end of panic attacks for him because they use the noise of sirens and show emergency vehicles with blue lights flashing. We have adapted to this by changing the channel for 4 minutes (average commercial break time) to avoid it or streaming programmes over the Internet to avoid adverts completely. When we have visited family members with young children, I have had to discretely push the fire engine or the police car toy around the side of the sofa when they are not looking to prevent sound effect buttons being pressed and causing a panic attack as well. You find yourself constantly assessing situations for problems or danger when living with someone who has PTSD.

The researcher asked: Have you developed any symptoms? She stated, I have noticed some low level changes in my own behaviour and reactions to things that could be symptomatic of secondary trauma or learned behaviour from my husband. For example, I experienced a prolonged period of involuntary flinching when I heard an emergency siren. This would happen at home, at work and when I was out in the community, with or without him. On reflection, I think this reaction was caused by having to jump into action to protect him from another panic attack because I would automatically put my hands tightly over his ears and pull him close to shield him from the noise, or talk him through breathing exercises to recover from a panic attack. As a result, I believe I had developed my own level of hyper alertness to certain sounds that produced an involuntary reaction. I think this eased off when he started using different strategies to ride out the panic attacks rather than thinking I could stop it for him. But still, not helpful when you are in a meeting at work or having coffee with a friend! At present, I still struggle with memories of how my husband and I were treated during the Ill Health Retirement (IHR) process, particularly with regards to the Selected Medical Practitioner (SMP) and Psychiatrists who examined him at the Injury on Duty appeal hearings. These hearings felt like he and I were on trial, they were incredibly intimidating and oppressive, and served only to open pandoras box for a couple of hours before leaving me to pick up the pieces for my husband. In one particular hearing, the Psychiatrist raised his voice and spoke to me through gritted teeth, whilst threatening to remove me from the room if I spoke again, because I interjected when he was telling my husband that he used to ride motorbikes and worked in the city – things that never happened, like he was reading from a strangers file. The whole process was unbelievably punitive, void of empathy and retraumatising at a time when my husband was at his most vulnerable.

For a long time after this, I struggled with any degree of challenging situation, I felt like I'd had a gut full of grief and fighting people off for a lifetime and had no capacity to deal with anymore distress. I cried when I was on my own to let out some of the negative emotions and suppressed the memories of it as much as possible. Even now I feel shaky thinking about it. I know this point is not necessarily to do with the direct impact of his PTSD or symptoms that I have developed but it is part of the wider picture in terms of how people with PTSD are treated by other people/organisations and the impact of that on those directly around them.

The researcher noted the distress, the sense of wrongdoing and injustice experienced by this partner. As a witness to the perpetration of poor treatment, lack of empathy or fairness for someone vulnerable whom she loves; she appears to have vicariously developed symptoms. She talks of suppressing (avoiding) memories of what happened and having negative emotions. Reminders of the way her husband was treated by the organisation and medical appeal board result in physical sensations. She describes having to fight people, indicating the fight for justice for her husband.

Case Study 3

The researcher completed a video interview with the partner of a police officer with PTSD who was retired from service on medical grounds in 2016. The partner is also a police officer. The purpose of the interview and case study was explained. The officer gave verbal consent to continue. A written consent form was sent post interview with a draft copy of the case study for approval.

The researcher asked the officer for some background to her husband, his career and his mental health. She stated, he joined the Tactical firearms unit in 2000 and worked in close protection. His unit was disbanded after 6 years in the job. He dealt with some very harrowing incidents. There was a lot of pressure on him being on-call 24/7. She stated, "*we had no life.*" He never discharged his firearm during his career. His colleagues did, which resulted in the trauma of investigations. Once the team was disbanded, he went back onto section (operational frontline duties). He was given no refresher training after being out of the role for 7 years. The organisation was not supportive. There were no trainers available. The attitude was 'get on with it, it's the nature of the job.' No counselling was offered. The cracks started to grow. He had several periods off work. He and his colleagues sometimes had a hot debrief but no in depth debrief post incident. He had a breakdown in 2006. He lost 3 stone in weight and did not get out of bed for weeks. He was not eating or washing. He went on medication to help with sleep and for managing the daytime, including Diazepam. In 2015 he was diagnosed with work-related depression. PTSD was diagnosed later. He frequently had Suicidal thoughts. On one occasion he went over the woods to hang himself but did not take a rope. The NHS mental health team stated he was not poorly enough because he had not taken a rope with him to go through with ending his own life. Therefore, he could not access NHS support. Work wanted to put him on disciplinary procedure because of time off sick, despite medical reports from the psychiatrist, GP and force medical officer saying he was not well enough to work. Disciplinary action for unsatisfactory attendance stopped once the PTSD diagnosis was made. However, the organisation stated the disciplinary process would continue when he did not get ill health retirement. She stated they felt like they were always waiting for him to lose his job. The organisation would not provide him with treatment, and he could not get treatment on the NHS. He was stuck in limbo because no one would help. The police federation and the organisation stated he was too complex for counselling over the phone. Neither would fund a psychiatrist or assessment. She stated she felt the police federation was useless. She stated the federation representative was due to retire and was not interested in helping. They asked the police federation for legal advice. There was an admin error and the incorrect box was ticked on the form by one of their staff. As a result, they were introduced to a solicitor who was not appropriate for their case. When they asked for this to be remedied, they were told they had had legal advice and could not access more. He was very poorly for 18 months stuck in this void. He returned to work for brief spells. This made his health deteriorate further; particularly as he was single crewed and had approximately six different sergeants in six months. There was no consistency or support. Occupational Health were short staffed. He wanted to stay in the job.

She stated he is a very proud man. It was always his intention to get better and to stay. It was a job he loved. He did not want to leave. He wanted time to get better.

They finally got psychiatric help with the NHS mental health team. They were frustrated to learn that eight miles down the road the mental health team had a smaller case load and had space, but they were not entitled to those services because of their postcode. He continued to feel suicidal. She stated, "*I advocated for him and stated he will die if he does not get support. The mental health team in the local town gave him hundreds of counselling and CBT treatment sessions. All the clinicians suggested he needed EMDR. They would not agree to give him EMDR until his medication was reduced. However, when he reduced his medication, this made him more ill."* She stated, they were stuck in a cycle, unable to get the treatment he needed. His medication was not working so these were changed. She unexpectedly fell pregnant during this time. He was very poorly during her pregnancy. They finally got a date to see the SMP for ill health retirement assessment after a sixteen month wait. The date they were given for the appointment was the same as her due date for the arrival of their baby. They requested an alternative day. The organisation would not change it. They were told that if they did not turn up for the appointment, the organisation would recommence disciplinary procedure. She gave birth to their baby prematurely and had to take him to the SMP assessment [she became tearful as she remembered this event]. The SMP confirmed the diagnosis of PTSD and recommended his case was expedited in eight weeks. He was given a care package through the NHS, including a support worker. She stated, *"they got him from a broken man to somebody who was broken but managing to exist with some semblance of life....for the whole of my pregnancy and the first eight to ten months of our baby's life, he was not really with us. I had to remind him to eat. He could not tell you where he had been when he had taken the dog for a walk."* The organisation required him to have a second SMP appointment with an external company to gather more information. She stated, *"we had been advised by a charity and the peer support group to write down all his symptoms and how he was affected in day to day life, medication and to take this with us to the appointment. He was very tearful writing these things down. On the day of the appointment I struggled to get him upstairs or in the lift to see the SMP. It was cold. Once in the room he broke down. We did not even know her name. She did not introduce herself. The first question she asked was, please tell me about the traumatic incidents that caused your PTSD. It is laughable. He spent years building up relationships and rapport with therapists and this woman just asked him this question. The SMP did not think he was well enough to continue. She was not happy with me speaking on his* behalf. She wanted him to come back in six weeks when he was better. I said it will not help. Nothing will change in six weeks. He has already had one SMP assessment. I stood my ground. I said we had had legal advice. He had nothing further to add that he had not already given to the previous SMP. We left the list he had written. It was fortunate we had this advice and followed it, because he couldn't talk. Fortunately, the SMP accepted the document and he got ill health retirement six weeks later." He applied for an injury on duty award and this was successful. He had made notes in his pocket books following incidents at work, that no counselling was offered. He did this over many years. Consequently, he had evidence that the organisation had potentially contributed to his PTSD. His colleagues were not happy with him for logging this. She stated, "he has resentment towards 'the job' and feels pushed out. He feels bitter about being stuck on an ill health pension. He is not well enough to work. He tried to start his own business. This made him poorly. He had CBT after leaving the job. The NHS mental health team finally agreed to give him EMDR treatment while heavily medicated in September last year. EMDR was horrific to go through. The turning point came midway through treatment, that changed our lives. He is a different man. The difference is amazing.. It is sad we had to wait so long. But we are where we are. He still is not the person I knew, but this is the closest he has ever been. He is trying to live a life without trauma, but it is hard to do. He has bad days, he always will. He is still very cross that the organisation does not know how to deal with mental health. He would love to sue the organisation for making him go down the ill health retirement route; trying to get rid of him when he was poorly. They wanted to take him through disciplinary instead of providing care and treatment. In comparison, the organisation paid over the odds for someone with a broken leg to get rehabilitation. He is bitter and feels they are responsible for his PTSD and loss of the job he loved, because they did not give him support and treatment. The 'job' has taken that from him. He has lost self-esteem. Life as a house husband now can feel demeaning. Couples counselling has helped him to reframe his thoughts. He felt he had become a 'dogs' body' who does what he is told and what chores to do. The trauma has been dealt with through EMDR. I wish there was a magic pill to get rid of the injustice. That is what he *needs to do now. The trauma has been managed but he is preoccupied with the injustice and losing his job. This may be made worse because I am still in the job. I try not to talk about work when I'm home. There needs to be a sweep up after EMDR, to get rid of crap brought up after sessions. The EMDR only deals with trauma. Other issues like the injustice are not dealt with during treatment."*

The researcher asked: Have you developed any symptoms yourself living alongside your husbands' condition? She stated, "yes, I have had CBT and I have been on antidepressants because of this. I suffer with tinnitus which is stress related. I accept I have it (through my husband and work), the job has a lot to answer for. I don't want to bottle it up like my husband did and end up like him. CBT has helped me to deal with things. I learnt to live with the fact it's his condition, I haven't got to take it on. I have always been one to say, if I can't fix it then what can we do to change it? I lost a lot of friends and family. They said my husband is a lost cause and why put myself through this? I think he's poorly, it's not his choice. He stuck by me through my medical conditions. I married him in sickness and in health. Part of my husband will always be there. CBT helped me to recognise it's my husbands' PTSD and depression. I go out now and have my time. Historically, I'd go down with him, stop seeing friends and going out, becoming withdrawn. It was hard to do something for myself. CBT put a lot in place in my head. Take time for me. I would feel guilty, what if he were to do something (suicide), could I live with that? There is no doubt in my mind that one day he will do it. I've done absolutely everything I can. What will be will be is my thought process now. I would ask my parents to look after their grandson so I could do my own things. They couldn't understand why my husband could not look after him while he was at home. I haven't got help for me. Family and friends tell me to leave him. Why would I walk away when he's poorly. In March he wasn't willing to get support, he was withdrawn and said no one wants to help. He couldn't see the light at the end of the tunnel. He stopped engaging. I always said the moment you stop looking after yourself, we go. So we left for a week and he began engaging again. I have to explain to our son when his dad is having a sad day. I have had no support through work. On days when my husband was suicidal and I could not *get into work, I was called into question for my sickness absence. I had been up with him and the crisis team all night.*

Every day I wonder if it's going to be a bad day with my husband. It's hard. I'm always hypervigilant to his moods. I'm constantly on call. Work would say, "but it's not you who is poorly."

The researcher asked: do you feel let down by family and friends? She stated, *"yes, they don't understand why I'm still with him. I kept quiet for years, not because I'm ashamed but because it's easier. Now I talk about it. CBT has helped me to do that.*

The researcher asked: did you feel guilty for going out, being happy and enjoying yourself when your husband was not well? She stated, *"yes, I did then, but not now. I have learnt to change the way I think about it.*

The researcher asked: Is the attitude towards mental health in fully operational frontline departments different to other departments, such as Monday-Friday jobs. She stated, *"Yes, definitely, It's a different culture. I loved working in the Criminal Investigation Department (CID), but it's full on and you're stuck to a job. I hate it. CBT helped me understand I don't hate the job, I hate some of the people and procedures; so I try to change that and shout about injustice in the organisation and act as a champion for change at work. My job is crap in the way they handle people. It's laughable. The police couldn't organise a piss up in a brewery. I have come to understand it's not personal, it's crap management. A new chief started in 2017 and blue light champions were introduced to act as peer support for mental health at work. They do more now to assist staff. 2013 was horrific. My husband was poorly, I suffered bereavements in close succession, I had a medical scare, I found out I was pregnant and lost twins. At the time I had a high case load and files needed to be in for court. I would find out someone close to me had died in the morning and had to go back to work in the afternoon. It's laughable. I used to think, can't you live without me for a day so I can say goodbye to a friend? Now, in my new role, I take time off to take my son to the dentist. Big difference. They are stressed to the hilt in CID. I went back after maternity. I was a good detective working on organised crime. I made waves about how women are treated after maternity leave. I was penalised and punished and put back into uniform. Part of me wants to leave. Part of me wants to fight. I've been back three years since maternity leave. I have quality time with my son and work a 9-5 job. It's not what I want, or what I trained for but this role helps me to get external qualifications for when I want to walk. They've done me a favour. If I'd gone back, I'd be where my husband is now. I think every cloud has a silver lining. So, the organisation has done me a favour by moving me to a different department and role.*

The researcher stated: you talk about every cloud has a silver lining, they have done you a favour, if you can't fix it then you change something and it sounds like you look for the good in the bad. You are proactive and a problem solver. She stated *"oh, I am bitter. If I had my ten minutes with some of the bosses I've had over the years…..I'm bitter. But I do what I can so no one else has to go through it. Who employs HR (Human Resources Department)? they are next to useless. Without people with that fight in them nothing would change."*

In summary, this wife and officer demonstrates the vicarious symptomatology of living alongside and supporting a close other with psychological injury and embitterment. The experience of her husband inextricably impacts on her own life and sense of safety, security and belief in a just world. She talks about procedural injustice, poor management, feeling let down by family and friends, loss of a specialist career for her and her husband, and the role of advocating for the rights of her ill partner. It appears a proactive, problem-solving approach and utilising the bitterness she feels for fighting injustice, is her coping strategy for the many traumatic challenges she has faced. She gives meaning and purpose to her experience by fighting organisational injustice. CBT has helped her to differentiate between her husbands' difficulties and herself as an individual. This has enabled her to challenge vicarious symptoms such as withdrawal and 'going down with him.' She has been helped to reframe her perceptions, thoughts and feelings, to recognise her personal limitations and need for self-compassion and care. She feels punished by the organisation for raising the issue of personal difficulties in combination with a highly pressurized role. The organisation responded by moving her from her specialized job into one with less pressure and regular working hours.

Though perceiving this as a 'punishment posting', she has also been able to consider the situation from more than one perspective. She recognizes the benefits that have come with the change and the improvement to her quality of life. These cognitions have been identified by Linden et al. (2011), as protective against developing PTED.

The Institute for Social and Economic Research at the University of Essex - Understanding Society' longitudinal survey, found that Women are more likely to provide informal care than men and over longer periods of time. They are more likely to have a greater degree of onerous care-giving responsibilities (i.e. complex care needs). Women providing care for three years or more or intermittent care, exhibit more symptoms of psychological distress than others and starting to give informal care can have an impact on mental health. Symptoms of psychological distress experienced by men providing care remains the same whether they are long-term care-givers or provide occasional care.[77]

Further research into the vicarious effect of injustice, Moral Injury and embitterment on close others, could lead to developing greater understanding of the wider impact of MI, PTED and PTSD.

The next chapter explores the potential correlation between PTED and MI with other psychiatric diagnosis.

---

[77] (Informal care-giving and mental health, 2018)

CHAPTER 3

Potential correlation with other psychiatric diagnosis or constructs

(Complex) PTSD

There is some evidence to suggest MI or PTED may be a comorbid condition with PTSD (as already discussed). Sabic et al. (2018) state, 'embitterment' is frequently found in war veterans with PTSD.[78] Lehrner and Yehudi (2018) state, "*the additional signs and symptoms of PTED, rather than the core diagnostic criteria, appear to have the most overlap with PTSD. Many of the clinical descriptions of PTED could be observed in trauma survivors.*"[79] There is also evidence to suggest PTSD may not always be motivated by fear or anxiety. It may be driven by betrayal and this is a significant factor in both PTED and MI. PTSD has been defined as an anxiety disorder which is evoked by fear. However, recent research has found that in some cases of PTSD the driver is not fear. Deprince (2001) found that betrayal predicted PTSD 'above and beyond' fear. Furthermore, that fear did not significantly predict PTSD arousal or anxiety.[80] PTSD was classified as an anxiety disorder in DSM-IV. It has now been re-classified as a Trauma and Stressor-related disorder in DSM-5. Pai et al. (2017) state, "*PTSD entails multiple emotions (e.g., guilt, shame, anger) outside of the fear/anxiety spectrum.*"[81] Barnes et al. (2019) state, MI and PTSD are often comorbid. Some studies in military

---

[78] (Sabic, Sabic, & Batic-Mujanovic, 2018)
[79] (Lehrner & Yehuda, 2018)
[80] (Deprince A. , 2001)
[81] (Pai, Suris, & North, 2017)

personnel and veterans discovered that for a significant minority of people, the traumatic incident leading to PTSD was not fearful or threatening.[82] Criteria for PTSD in the latest version DSM-5, includes both the 'fight and flight' reactions. The manual also includes 1) Arousal - such as aggression, recklessness and self-destructive behaviour, hypervigilance and sleep disturbance 2) Avoidance – of memories and reminders which elicit distressing thoughts and feelings, 3) Re-experiencing – such as intrusive memories, flashbacks and dreams and 4) Negative cognitions and mood – which could be characterized by affect dysregulation, blame, withdrawal from others, loss of interest in activities and gaps in memory of the traumatic event.[83] Both MI and PTED include self-destructive behaviour/self-sabotage, blame, negative self-concept, emotional dysregulation and anger.[84] In PTED patients experience intrusive memories of the event.[85] In MI individuals can experience avoidance of reminders to the event.[86]

In DSM-IV manual for psychiatric diagnosis, there was a criterion that PTSD resulted from a fear-based reaction. In DSM-5 this was removed as "*intense fear, helplessness or horror…..proved to have no utility in predicting the onset of PTSD.*"[87] However, the World Health Organisation (WHO) criterion for PTSD in ICD-11 continues to include fear and horror.[88]

DSM-5 has evolved the diagnosis of PTSD to include some symptoms which correlate with MI and PTED. For example, self-blame, negative self-concept and 'feeling alienated from others.'[89] The manual also identifies, "*Persistent, distorted cognitions about the cause or consequences of the*

---

[82] (Barnes, Hurley, & Taber, 2019)
[83] (APA, DSM-5 Factsheets, Changes in PTSD Criteria, 2020)
[84] (Currier, 2017) (Linden & Maercker, 2011)
[85] (Linden, Baumann, Rotter, & Schippan, 2007)
[86] (Currier, 2017)
[87] (APA, DSM-5 Factsheets, Changes in PTSD Criteria, 2020)
[88] (WHO, 2019)
[89] (Nickerson, 2016)

traumatic event(s) that lead the individual to blame himself/herself or others."[90] Not only does this indicate feelings of guilt and shame;[91] it is perhaps reasonable to assume that difficulty with forgiveness of self or others is associated with blame too (which are all features of PTED and MI). Where there is 'blame,' one may expect a perpetrator (self or other) to be present; either by action (inflicting harm) or inaction (failure to prevent harm). Feelings of guilt and shame could stem from an inability to cope with what happened. Linden and Maercker (2011) on PTED state, there is *"Attributing blame, responsibility and intentionality"* (P.54) and *"the victim can exaggerate the intention of the harm-doer"* (P.37) which is a distorted cognition.

Criterion D2 of the DSM-5 on PTSD is *"persistent and exaggerated negative beliefs or expectations about oneself, others or the world."* [92] For example, 'no one can be trusted,' or 'I am worthless.' PTED and MI share this feature with PTSD. A breach of moral codes and values within traumatic experience can undermine one's beliefs about the world, self and others. This can result in negative self-concept, (including low self-esteem), loss of trust in others, loss of meaning and purpose and the belief and expectation that the values and morals of others or the world, are not shared with the individual. This is explored further in the section 'values, beliefs and morals.'

The full diagnostic criteria for PTSD with the presence of 'Disturbances in Self-Organisation (DSO)' may elicit a diagnosis of Complex PTSD[93] (according to the ICD-11). Complex PTSD (CPTSD) is not included in the DSM-5. The DSO are made up of three symptom clusters, 1) Affective Dysregulation (problems regulating emotions and feelings) such as over-reactions, overwhelming emotions, rumination on the event(s)

---

[90] (SAMHSA, Exhibit 1.3-4 DSM 5 Diagnostic Criteria for PTSD, 2020)
[91] (Molendijk, Kramer, & Verweij, 2018)
[92] (SAMHSA, 2020)
[93] (Nickerson, 2016)

and sleep disturbance,[94] 2) Negative Self-Concept such as "*beliefs about oneself as diminished, defeated or worthless and accompanied by feelings of shame, guilt or failure related to the traumatic event*"[95] and 3) Disturbances in relationships, such as "*difficulties in sustaining relationships and in feeling close to others*" [96] CPTSD has a significant impact on social, occupational, educational and personal areas of life.[97] As previously discussed, PTED and MI are also characterized by psychosocial factors and symptoms of DSO as outlined in the ICD-11 criteria for CPTSD. For example, feelings of shame, guilt, helplessness, resignation, self-blame, lack of trust in others and thinking about the event(s) over and over again. CPTSD is most likely occurring as a result of repeated, prolonged or interpersonal trauma, institutional abuse, childhood abuse, exposure to the coercive control of a perpetrator and people exposed to treatment for trauma.[98] A single traumatic incident is more predictive of PTSD and multiple traumas are more predictive of CPTSD.[99]

PTED differs from the construct of (C)PTSD in that PTED criteria stipulates there has been an exceptional, yet common negative life event (i.e. not a life threatening one). MI can result from the same type of traumatic events as (C)PTSD (such as sexual assault and life threatening situations) where there is an element of betrayal, injustice or moral breach.

Querulant Delusion and Querulant Litigant

A querulant person, is one who obsessively feels wronged and often complains or relentlessly seeks redress. This can often result in litigation

---

[94] (Franco, 2020)
[95] (WHO, 2019)
[96] (WHO, 2019)
[97] (WHO, 2019)
[98] (Nickerson, 2016)
[99] (Cloitre, Gavert, Brewin, Bryant, & Maercker, 2013)

and grievances. Mullen and Lester (2006) state, Querulous behaviour is on the increase as a result of a cultural shift towards a *"proliferation of complaint organizations and agencies of accountability......drawing more and more people into asserting their individual rights through the pursuit of claims and grievances."* They state, the outcome has brought *"suffering for the querulous and disruption to the organizations through which they seek their vision of justice."* Mullen and Lester state, there should be a resurgence of interest within the field of psychiatry, into the phenomenon of Querulous behaviour.[100] Querulousness within psychiatry has largely disappeared, perhaps in response to the growing social demand for justice and holding others accountable for perceived or actual breaches of one's rights. Therefore, to label litigants as querulous could undermine the credibility of their complaints. The suggestion is that there is no appetite for discouraging complainants from pursuing their claims. Lester et al. (2004) state, there is a small group of people who are unusually persistent complainants, who are a burden on the resources of agencies and organisations.[101] Linden (2020) states, the main symptoms of Querulant delusion (as identified by Kraepelin, in the early 20th century) are *"embitterment, negativism, helplessness, self-blame, unspecific somatic symptoms, phobic avoidance of persons or situations related to the event, intrusions, phantasies of revenge and aggression. Another name is 'Posttraumatic Embitterment Disorder."*[102]

Lester et al. (2004) study, identified that persistent complainants were significantly less likely to consider their complaint resolved at the point of closure of their case. They were more likely to attend complaint agencies without an appointment and more likely to demand a new 'case worker.' Financial compensation and improved services were commonly sought by all types of complainants. However, persistent complainants were more likely to seek public acknowledgment of their mistreatment

---

[100] (Mullen & Lester, 2006)
[101] (Lester, Wilson, Griffin, & Mullen, 2004)
[102] (Linden, 2020)

and an apology, as well as demands for the dismissal or prosecution of those responsible. *"More extreme forms of revenge, such as public exposure and humiliation, were demanded exclusively by the persistent complainant."* Persistent complainants were more likely to demand justice on matters of principle and *"insisted on their day in court."* They were also more likely to change the grounds of their complaint over time, compared with other type of complainant. Written complaints were often unintelligible, *"inappropriately lengthy and difficult to follow"* and various types of emphasis were used, such as underlining and highlighting specific words. Persistent complainants were overtly offensive and dramatic, made unnecessary repetitions and used direct and veiled threats. Only 10% of persistent complainants were able to express their complaints coherently and rationally. Their persistent pursuit of claims; are more likely to damage their close relationships and financial situation.

The expectation that vindication and retribution is a possible outcome of the complaint, is not in line with the remit of complaint organisations to provide conciliation, reparation and compensation. Lester et al. (2004), suggest further research to explore whether *"persistent complainants were more likely to be subjected to hostile, rejecting or blaming responses"* early on in the complaint process, which led to the chronic behaviour of some complainants.[103] Dr Lester (psychiatrist) states, *"No one is born a querulant."* He states, querulant complainants are driven by the pursuit of justice to the point of devastating their own lives. They can be demanding, persistent, uncooperative, difficult to negotiate with, will not accept other than their own demands and can be aggressive. The querulent person may have obsessional, paranoid or narcissistic personality.[104]

---

[103] (Lester, Wilson, Griffin, & Mullen, 2004)
[104] (Lester, 2020)

ICD-10 has a classification of the litigious subtype of 'persistent delusional disorder' and the DSM-III to DSM-5 includes 'delusionary disorder – persecutory type,' which are variants of querulant delusion or querulant litigant.[105]

Gerevich and Ungvari (2014) adopt Heinrich von Kleist's Novella, 'Michael Kohlhaas,' as a 19th century case study for describing the litigious querulant. *"Michael Kohlhaas, a querulant horse trader, carries out an armed uprising disproportionate to the minor injustice of the unlawful seizure of his horses. Following unsuccessful attempts at legal recourse, Kohlhaas takes up arms against the authorities, and in the course of his uncompromising pursuit of justice eventually sacrifices his own and his family's lives….Kleist portrays Kohlhaas' psychopathological development from a psychologically balanced, emotionally warm family man to one who causes utter destruction…"[106]* This characterisation fits with the statement made by Dr Lester, that no one is born querulant. What begins as misinformation resulting in two of Kohlhaas' finest horses being impounded and maltreated by the authorities - ends with the death of Kohlhaas. A fate, which may have been avoided if his early requests for a return of the unlawfully seized horses had been granted. Because the defendant had a high social status and influential relatives, Kohlhaas' legal case was rejected. In todays' terms, this would be a closing of ranks around the defendant and a failure to do 'what's right' by those with legitimate power and authority, leading to moral injury. As Kohlhaas frustration escalated over the situation and lack of resolution, so too was he driven to seek revenge and a way to force the authorities to provide justice. He organises a 'peasant uprising', which threatens the social order. He finally has his malnourished horses fattened up and returned, however, his fight for justice ends with his destruction as he is executed for the rebellion. Kohlhaas seeks justice at all costs. Prior to this incident, he is described as very reasonable, modest, a model citizen, generous, fair minded and a loving husband and

---

[105] (Gerevich & Ungvari, 2014)
[106] (Gerevich & Ungvari, 2014)

father. He becomes disaffected when legal institutions reject his claim and his belief in a just world order is shattered. He appeals and appeals through the correct institutional channels, to no avail. He loses faith in authority. Kohlhaas felt driven to right a wrong for the benefit of the wider society and so that others may not suffer the same injustice. His altered world view resulted in anhedonia and loss of interest in home, family and occupation. He was branded a 'vexatious litigant.' His role as husband and father became less worthy of his time and efforts. The noble pursuit of justice for the greater good took precedence over all else. *"He plunges into the 'hellish torment of unsatisfied revenge."* Querulousness develops over time with the repeated rejection of one's complaints.[107] Therefore, suggesting the deterioration in psychological health and escalation of difficult and protracted litigation could potentially be ameliorated or diffused in the early stages of a grievance or complaint. *"The various agencies of accountability contacted in Australia, estimated that such unusually persistent complainants only made up a fraction of one per cent of those who pursued grievances but consumed between 15 and 30% of all resources."*[108] To state one has querulent delusion or paranoia, may be stigmatising and undermine any legitimate claim of injustice.

Rather than being delusional (perceived rather than actual wrongdoing); the persistent complainant may have grounds for complaint and an 'overvalued idea' of the injustice, as well as a resolution (or punishment of the person(s) responsible), which is disproportionate to the wrongdoing.[109]

In summary, there is a potential cross-over between PTED, MI and querulant behaviour. The fact querulant litigants have been classified within legal services and complaints agencies; is an indication of the high likelihood of embittered and morally injured persons seeking legal recourse. Furthermore, there is an associated cost to organisations, in

---

[107] (Gerevich & Ungvari, 2014)
[108] (Mullen & Lester, 2006)
[109] (Skilling, Øfstegaard, Brodie, & Thomson, 2012)

terms of resources and finances for difficult and protracted complaints. Studies identify a need for organisations to respond to complaints sensitively from the outset and to manage complainant's expectations on the outcomes, to avoid triggering the development of querulousness in individuals and deterioration in psychological health.

Adjustment Disorder

PTED has been proposed as a subtype of Adjustment Disorder, which is a stressor-related condition. PTSD is categorized under the same group of trauma or stressor-related disorders. The DSM-5 (published in 2013) diagnostic criteria for Adjustment Disorder, states symptoms develop within three months of a stressful event. The emotional and behavioural response to the stressor is disproportionate to the severity of what happened; as such, the symptoms are of clinical significance. The degree of distress may cause significant impairment in important areas of life, such as work or socialisation. It is important to note that a diagnosis of Adjustment Disorder should only be made if the cause and nature of symptoms does not meet the criteria for another psychiatric disorder or the exacerbation of one which already exists. A diagnosis of Adjustment Disorder does not apply to normal bereavement. Symptoms are expected to abate and cease within six months of the stressor ending. The criteria in DSM-IV that the disorder is acute if symptoms last less than six months and chronic if symptoms last over six months, has been removed from the latest version.[110]

PTED criteria stipulates "*A single exceptional negative life event precipitates the onset of the illness.*"[111] PTED may be an appropriate diagnosis where there has been an event which is exceptional, negative and yet common; such as divorce or redundancy. The experience may be experienced as

---

[110] (SAMHSA, 2020)
[111] (Linden, Baumann, Rotter, & Schippan, 2007)

traumatic. However, not traumatic in the same context as PTSD or Complex PTSD. Criteria A for PTSD (DSM-5) requires the cause to be relating to an incident which was "*exposure to actual or threatened death, serious injury, or sexual violence.*"[112] The ICD-11 definition of Adjustment Disorder (published 2019), provides more clarity on how it is distinctive from PTSD. For example, an absence of specific or severe symptoms and typical stressors as common life events which one struggles to cope with and adapt to. The definition is as follows: "*Adjustment disorder is a maladaptive reaction to an identifiable psychosocial stressor or multiple stressors (e.g. divorce, illness or disability, socio-economic problems, conflicts at home or work).... The symptoms are not of sufficient specificity or severity to justify the diagnosis of another Mental and Behavioural Disorder and typically resolve within 6 months, unless the stressor persists for a longer duration.*" Symptoms include rumination on the stressor which produces worry and upsetting thoughts, as well as worry about the consequences. One has difficulty adapting to the stressful situation, which causes significant impairment in important areas of life, such as social, educational, occupational and personal.[113]

Burnout

Burnout has been classified in ICD-11 for the first time, as a syndrome. It relates only to the workplace. Symptoms include exhaustion, withdrawal from one's occupation and a cynical and negative perception of one's job.[114] Burnout can manifest when one is repeatedly asked by the employer to perform duties, which are in conflict with ones' own values. In addition, there is a heavy workload, little or no control over the work environment and decisions being made (particularly on quality of service provision). There is an absence of good support from colleagues and supervisors and lack of dignity and respect. One may

---

[112] (APA, 2020)
[113] (WHO, 2019)
[114] (WHO, 2019)

experience self-blame when unable to help people who are suffering.[115] *"Burnout is a process, not an event" (Farber, 1983, cited in Salston & Figley, 2003)."* Burnout may result in 'boredom' and underperformance in staff.[116] The syndrome can be particularly prevalent in occupations which are emotive, specialist, morally charged and which carry high levels of responsibility and risk. For example, healthcare professionals and first responders. Research has shown a strong correlation between burnout and PTSD, with burnout being a predictive factor for post-traumatic stress.[117]

Embitterment is prevalent in the workplace[118] and appears to share some features similar to Burnout, such as a potential conflict with one's values, the development of the condition over time, cynicism, negativism, withdrawal, loss of control, feeling helpless to cope or effect positive outcomes. This can result in negative self-concept. Sensky et al. (2015) state, *"Clinical experience suggests that, while embitterment can often be traced back to an initial trigger, a key feature of the condition is its escalation over time."*[119] The research into embitterment in NHS trust staff, found that embitterment was more likely present in individuals who perceived low 'procedural justice' and support from the organisation. Embittered staff are 'significantly more likely' to take high levels of sickness absence. Embittered persons in the workplace can impact negatively on their colleagues and on those receiving care.[120] Michailidis and Cropley (2018), research into occupational embitterment, noted the prevalence of embitterment in the workplace.[121] Szczygiel and Mikolajczak (2018), undertook research which concluded that 'Emotional Intelligence' buffers nurses against the development of Burnout. They identified *"(in*

---

[115] (Salston & Figley, 2003)
[116] (Salston & Figley, 2003)
[117] (Woojin, 2019)
[118] (Sensky, Salimu, Ballard, & Pereira, 2015)
[119] (Sensky, Salimu, Ballard, & Pereira, 2015)
[120] (Sensky, Salimu, Ballard, & Pereira, 2015)
[121] (Michailidis & Cropley, 2018)

descending order of frequency) anger, irritation, sadness, disappointment,
embitterment, and depression" as the most significant negative emotions
experienced by nurses. Those with higher traits of emotional intelligence
were less affected by the experience of Burnout.[122] Emotional intelligence
as a protective factor against the development of Burnout, is perhaps a
correlation with the 'Wisdom' model protecting against the development
of PTED (see 'Predisposing factors and Prevention'). There appears to
be a connection between embitterment and burnout. However, these
two occurring phenomenon were seen as separate to one another in the
literary review of research. This is an area of investigation which may be
of benefit.

Moral Distress

Lamiani et al. (2015), carried out a review on multiple publications
regarding the construct of Moral Distress (MD); one which relates
specifically to the healthcare profession. The concept of MD was first
identified in 1984. Lamiani describes MD as, *"The experience of acting not*
accordingly to what one believes is professionally right, because of internal or
external constraints." MD appears to present similarly to Burnout; as this
construct explores occupational dissatisfaction, leadership styles,
resources available to provide appropriate care to patients, sense of
powerlessness, lack of autonomy, peer support and collaboration.
However, Lamiani states MD is distinct from Burnout because of the
"perceived violation of one's own professional integrity and obligations and the
concurrent feeling of being constrained from taking the ethically appropriate
action."[123] He states, the subject of MD is understudied, nor did studies
explore the potential impact of MD on patient care. Individual factors,
such as character, coping strategies and personal beliefs were not fully
explored in the research. The effect of MD results in low job satisfaction,

---

[122] (Szczygiel & Mikolajczak, 2018)
[123] (Lamiani, Borghi, & Piergiorgio, 2015)

low satisfaction regarding provision of quality care, burnout and desire to resign.

The only symptom cluster highlighted in Lamiani's research on MD are anger, frustration and guilt.[124] Therefore, this research has excluded Moral Distress from further consideration of comparison to Moral Injury or Post-Traumatic Embitterment Disorder.

In the next chapter, characteristic features of PTED and Moral Injury are explored, such as feelings of betrayal, difficulty with forgiveness and embitterment.

---

[124] (Lamiani, Borghi, & Piergiorgio, 2015)

Claire Carter

CHAPTER 4

Features of PTED & Moral Injury

Betrayal

Smith and Freyd (2013) state, Institutional Betrayal is when "*common trusted and powerful institutions, [act] in ways that visit harm upon those dependent on them for safety and well-being.*" For example, harassment and insensitive investigations. Their research explored the impact institutions may have on individuals following traumatic experience. They state, institutions may be responsible for a 'second assault' when one seeks help, including medical or judicial support. A victim of trauma may be stigmatized or blamed. There may be a 'closing of ranks' within an organisation seeking to protect its reputation, which is valued over and above the welfare of the individual. Institutions can foster abuse. Research suggests that institutions may exacerbate post-traumatic reactions by contributing to existing trauma. This could include "*systemic difficulties in service provision for veterans with chronic health issues.*"[125] These are arguably common difficulties for other frontline workers with existing trauma too, as well as medical discharge or retirement process. The key factors are 'trust' and/or 'dependency' on the institution.[126] Betrayal has been found to predict dissociation and withdrawal in PTSD over and above the experience of fear, and fear does not significantly predict PTSD anxiety and arousal.[127]

---

[125] (Freyd & Smith, 2013)
[126] (Freyd & Smith, 2013)
[127] (Deprince, 2001)

Being asked to make personal sacrifices morally, physically, emotionally and psychologically for what was believed to be a just cause - only to discover later this was not the case or personal sacrifices are not valued, may lead to feelings of betrayal. One may feel unsupported and even vilified for doing their job, by the very people who asked them to do it. Betrayal of one's trust can have a long lasting effect. Feelings of betrayal feature in PTED, MI and PTSD.[128] Freyd (2019) states, people may choose to be blind to betrayal, remain unaware or forget in order to protect a relationship which they may depend on for survival. Examples could be where a child is dependent on an abusive caregiver, or where one is dependent on an institution for financial security.[129]

"The pressure of work, and the lack of support from his colleagues and supervisors, had also become too much for him. My husband feels complete and utter deep-rooted bitterness and hatred towards the people in the police force who had a duty of care towards him, but who failed him time after time, despite the fact that they knew about the PTSD" – (NICE Guidelines, 2005)

Conflicts which are political in nature can create large scale embitterment. Linden and Maercker (2011), explored embitterment and forgiveness in the context of conflict in Northern Ireland and culture-bound anger in parts of Asia as just two examples of this issue across societies.[130] In the UK, following the Iraq war, Iraqi Historic Allegations Team (IHAT) was set up to investigate allegations against soldiers. Those allegations included torture and murder. The inquiry came under criticism for bringing cases where there was no 'credible evidence to support them.' A tribunal later found a solicitor contracted by IHAT (a unit set up by government), guilty of false witness accounts about the actions of UK armed forces personnel. The solicitor stood to benefit from the claims and was subsequently struck off.[131]

---

[128] (Deprince A. , 2001) (Koenig, 2019) (Linden & Maercker, 2011)
[129] (Freyd J. , 2019)
[130] (Linden & Maercker, 2011)
[131] (Bowcott, 2017)

"Over 3,500 allegations of abuse were taken up by IHAT, many of which were not supported by credible evidence. The report found a range of failings in the conduct of the investigations into those claims alongside a MoD support package which was fragmented, inaccessible and largely unknown. The report concludes that because of this, those under investigation have suffered unacceptable stress, have had their lives put on hold and their careers damaged.....The overall impact of this has been the erosion of the bonds of trust between those who serve, and their civilian masters" (Defence sub-committee, 2017).[132]

Brian Wood had a 16 year military career. He was awarded the Military Cross on his return from the Iraq war. He was one of the soldiers involved in the IHAT inquiry and subsequently published a book called Double Crossed – A Code of Honour, A Complete Betrayal. He talks about the media coverage, some of which was proven to be false and the public nature of the inquiry putting soldiers and their families at risk. He states the government let it happen. Brian stated, *"We were sent to war to do what we'd been told by politicians, only to then come back and find ourselves fighting another battle to clear our names"* (p.195). Support was not offered to him and his family, particularly when the inquiry went public. He stated, *"The emotional impact was huge.... I'd gone from being rewarded for my actions by Her Majesty the Queen to having the government undermine what I'd achieved (p.195). It was us who paid the price for the governments' mishandling of the inquiry...it damaged families, damaged careers and fuelled PTSD....I feel hurt by the government....I lost trust and faith in the system...when I needed it most, it failed me....it is hard to have to put your life on the line and then to come back and hear things like 'well, you probably should not have been there in the first place"* (p.196).[133]

Sometimes it's not only the accused individual who can feel betrayed. It is their community. It can create wholesale distrust in authority, when people believe there has been double-standards, scapegoating, injustice,

---

[132] (Parliament, 2017)
[133] (Wood, 2020)

prioritising political aims or closing ranks. One's liberty, reputation, livelihood, psychological health and way of life can be jeopardized by people and systems in power.

Cubela et al. (2007), suggest the experience of injustice only has a negative affect when the level of adversity is too great to be assimilated into the psyche.[134] Frontline workers are often in a role with higher physical and psychological risks. They may believe their organisation will support them in exchange for the risks they take. Ones' strong belief in a 'just world' is not undermined by exposure to violence.[135] It is shattered by betrayal and injustice which can be destabilizing to one's belief in personal worth or value.

The next case study demonstrates feelings of institutional betrayal and the impact on psychological health.

Case Study 4 – First Responder

This officer offered her medical report to inform this research. These are excerpts taken from her psychiatric assessment. The report highlights 'second assault' and the negative impact the employing organisation can have, on dedicated and traumatized employees, expecting and seeking support, safety and security. It reads:

She has Chronic PTSD and moderate depression, related to traumatic experiences encountered whilst working as a police officer. This has had a significantly negative impact on her life. She experiences significant distress associated with images and details of the incident. She is experiencing negative impact on her relationships with friends, family and colleagues. Her social functioning has also been negatively impacted. She avoids going out and struggles to experience pleasure or positive

---

[134] (Dalbert & Donat, 2015)
[135] (Dalbert & Donat, 2015)

emotions. She is particularly distressed by her perceived lack of support from the Police Force. She stated, "they say if you need help, ask. I pleaded and they didn't help." "I just needed a break, and they made me plead." She feels the Police Force are not taking responsibility. She states, that she reached out for support on several occasions and it was not forthcoming.

She states, she was instructed to work at times that she did not feel able and recalls being told to "do her job" when she has reported difficulties. It is of note that negative social reactions are hypothesised to perpetuate symptoms of PTSD.

Research has shown that highly traumatised individuals suffering from PTSD require a safe and stable environment with adequate social support for their symptoms to improve. Unfortunately, what seems to have compounded her feeling of being somehow changed or damaged in some way is her perceived lack of support from her employing organisation. There seems to have been an apparent absence of any clear plan or framework of action ongoing in terms of the human resources and occupational health elements. She has clearly internalized the idea that she is somehow surplus to requirement and is not highly thought of enough to be supported through her significant difficulties. This is highly unfortunate, as in my treatment sessions with her she plainly expressed the pride she felt at being a serving police officer.

In my opinion, whilst she continues her role in the police force, she is unlikely to see significant improvement in her symptoms without psychological intervention and support from her employer. I believe that it is important that the relationship between her and the police force is repaired, which would involve the force acknowledging her distress, acknowledging what she considers to be the police force's accountability and responsibilities and supporting her recovery. Due care will be required on the part of the employer organisation to ensure that she is supported in terms of any reintegration into the police service at this stage.

In summary, the psychologist states this officer's PTSD is potentially being maintained and/or compounded by the lack of support from the organisation. Law enforcement is a vocation, not a job. It requires commitment and often sacrifice of personal interests or health and wellbeing. There was an expectation the organisation would demonstrate their appreciation for her with care and support. The officer spoke of pride in her role and believed she was valued by her employer.

This belief was undermined when the support she asked for was not provided; resulting in negative self-concept about her worth. Difficulty with forgiveness and the presentation of embittered attitude are explored in the next section.

Difficulty with forgiveness

People can often be unwilling or unable to forgive a perpetrator or transgressor who has caused them harm. An embittered person may find the idea of forgiveness wholly abhorrent. Forgiveness for the perpetrator may not be necessary in order to move on from the event.[136] Forgiveness is not to condone or forget what has happened.[137] Rather, it may be the process of trying to understand the perpetrator, what has transpired and one's own role in events - to find meaning and purpose in what has happened.

Linden et al. (2007), in the Psychopathy of PTED states the embittered person may feel *'unsure if they want the wounds to heal'* and that it *'is important not to forget.'*[138] Perhaps one feels that to forget what happened is to lose a sense of meaning and purpose derived from the experience. Tedeschi and Calhoun (2004) state, a degree of continued distress is needed for posttraumatic growth and personal development.[139]

---

[136] (Linden & Maercker, 2011)
[137] (Freedman & Enright, 2017)
[138] (Linden, Baumann, Rotter, & Schippan, 2007)
[139] (Tedeschi & Calhoun, 2004)

Ruminating could be a seemingly helpful (yet unhelpful) behaviour. For example, a reminder never to repeat the mistake of trust in others. Lehrner and Yehuda (2018) state, "*Remembering trauma may also have adaptational value in terms of ensuring that communities and individuals maintain vigilance for their safety and survival and stand in solidarity with other communities facing violence and injustice.*"[140] Worthington (2004) states, rumination on a grudge sees ones' 'physical arousal soar', such as increased heart rate and blood pressure and emotional reactions such as anxiety, sadness and anger.[141] Linden and Maercker (2011) state, rumination on the incident can maintain PTSD symptoms.

Perhaps one may perceive forgetting as equal to forgiveness. One may feel unready to forgive. If the traumatic event was witnessed and involved others, one may feel it important not to forget in honour of their memory. Guilt or shame and subsequent self-punishment (difficulty forgiving oneself), could contribute to thinking of the event over and over again, as well as reinforcing a negative self-concept. Considering difficulty with forgiveness in this way, could explain embitterment as a psychological process of cognitive and emotional dysregulation; and not a personality or attitude trait.

Embittered Attitude

During the process of this research, the question has arisen as to whether embitterment is pathological or a 'choice,' an attitude and personality trait. Understanding embitterment reactions could change the way we perceive others, their personality and their difficulties. It is important to understand the possible underlying reasons for embitterment. For example, in the piece on 'difficulty with forgiveness,' I suggest how unforgiveness may seem helpful to the individual (yet be unhelpful). Maladaptive behaviour can often be a way of meeting one's

---

[140] (Lehrner & Yehuda, 2018)
[141] (Worthington, 2004)

needs. For example, an unwillingness to forget the transgression because the event may lose its meaning and purpose, such as a fight for justice. Perhaps it seems important to keep the violation alive in memory of others, such as loved ones lost. It can also be a way of avoiding significant life changes which are daunting, such as career change or new relationships when one has been hurt before. An embittered person could be viewed as stubborn, grumpy, difficult, obstructive, cynical, pessimistic, moody, draining, hostile, attention seeking and full of self-pity. This can create an unsympathetic or unempathetic reaction in others. Telles-Correai et al. (2018) states, "*according to Szasz, one should not speak of mental "disorders" but of deviations from socially accepted norms and values.*[142] *It would not be a question of the violation of the natural order, but of the social order.*" In other words, suggesting the violation of social norms is at fault and not the individual or their biology.

Can embittered reactions be a goal-orientated and future-focused strategy (even if subconscious)? Linden and Maercker (2011) state, PTED is the opposite of future orientated. One becomes stuck, including rumination on past events and an inability to move-on from the incident. One can become self-sabotaging.[143] However, what if one's future-orientation is to maintain their status quo and avoid change as a preference; perhaps despite social pressure to accept change as a normal response to the situation? The proverbial "digging one's heels in" springs to mind. Perhaps we should ask, "what is the motivation for embitterment?" and not "what is the cause of embitterment?" What might be the secondary gain (if any) driving this cognitive state and behaviour? For example, embitterment disorder and moral injury are associated with a strong desire for justice and re-establishing a sense of personal power and control over one's life and circumstances. Posttraumatic Growth is dependent on continuing levels of distress and rumination, and embitterment is a behaviour resistant to significant life

---

[142] (Telles-Correai, 2018)
[143] (Linden & Maercker, 2011)

changes. Therefore, the nature and quality of rumination is perhaps important for determining positive or negative outcomes.

Linden and Rotter (2018) state, there are four categories of embitterment which include consequence of traumatic experience, comorbidity with other disorders or a prone personality where there has been no traumatic incident reported.[144] This would indicate that embitterment reactions can be both a personality trait and/or a medical consideration. Linden and Maercker (2011), identifies a personality predisposition characterized as cynical, pessimistic, perfectionist and neurotic and one who supresses or inhibits emotions. In addition, there is the experience of subjugation, where one is kept oppressed unjustly by those in a position of power and authority. Furthermore, he describes a premorbid personality as "*achievement oriented, devoted persons with strict convictions and beliefs, that show great self-sacrifice and commitment in their job or social role.*"[145] Injustice, moral injury and violation of deeply held values and beliefs are the cause and embitterment reactions are the consequence. Embitterment is a word, which encapsulates many symptoms. These include: blame of self or others, negative ideas about oneself (such as low self-esteem), guilt, shame, difficulty with forgiveness, loss of meaning and purpose, loss of trust, feelings of humiliation, injustice and betrayal, anger and desire for revenge.

This list could be expanded further to include resentment, hatred, disaffection, hostility, self-pity and victimization.

Linden and Maercker (2011) state, we can all experience embitterment and "*Very few will develop PTED. The trigger may be a specific kind of injustice experienced in combination with a weak belief in a just world (Dalbert 1997) and presumably other social and personal factors*" (p.38).

---

[144] (Linden & Rotter, 2018)
[145] (Linden & Maercker, 2011)

This seems to suggest embitterment can be experienced as a temporary emotional reaction and in chronic cases it can become pathological.

As previously mentioned in this research, the DSM-5 on PTSD states that there may be *"Persistent, distorted cognitions about the cause or consequences of the traumatic event(s) that lead the individual to blame himself/herself or others" (DSM-5, 2013:272).*[146] This highlights blame as a potential consequence of trauma and symptom of PTSD. Pai et al. (2017) state, *"Each symptom must be anchored to the traumatic event through a temporal and/or contextual relationship. The DSM-5 stipulates that to qualify, the symptoms must begin…or worsen…. after the traumatic event. Even though the symptoms must be linked to a traumatic event, this linking does not imply causality or etiology."*[147] Therefore, blame and subsequent embitterment may be anchored to the traumatic incident and PTSD. This is demonstrated in case study 5 (see below). This could have implications for 'institutional betrayal,' which acts as a 'second assault' linked to the original trauma and chronic embitterment towards those perceived as responsible for the traumatic incident. For example, where it is felt there has been a neglect of duty of care leading to anger, blame and pathological embitterment. Medical professionals will have to consider that the presentation of an 'attitude' and symptoms of embitterment (or moral injury) are a 'medical concern.' Furthermore, they will need to consider that these symptoms need specific treatment as they can maintain PTSD symptoms.[148] The next case study demonstrates the potential triangulation between PTSD, institutional betrayal and embitterment reactions.

---

[146] (Molendijk, Kramer, & Verweij, 2018)
[147] (Pai, Suris, & North, 2017)
[148] (Linden, Baumann, Lieberei, & Rotter, 2009) (Koenig, 2019)

Case Study 5 – First Responder and his wife

Preparation for this case study: The officer signed a consent form for participation in this research and to undertake an interview. He confirmed he had support in place during this process. He forwarded medical reports for the researcher to view. These documents included two reports prepared by Clinical psychologists. One psychologist being an expert witness for court and in the subject of PTSD, (including work with first responders and military veterans). Other documents related to a medical appeal hearing. The researcher sourced information online relating to this officer's traumatic experience, which was a significant public order incident. After initial paper review, the researcher arranged a video interview with the officer and his wife, over a secure system. Prior to beginning the interview, the researcher explained the aims of the research project and that breaks could be taken during interview if required. She advised that it may be difficult to read a copy of the case study, which would reflect their experiences and situation. The researcher suggested it may be beneficial for the officer's wife to read the case study first and communicate this to the officer, acting as a buffer to the contents. Both participants agreed this would be a good idea and that the officer's wife usually read emails on his behalf for this reason. After reviewing the finalized case study, the participants confirmed their agreement for inclusion in the research and publication.

The occupational doctor wrote of this officer in his medical report, that: Precipitating factors include perceived stress at work. The emotional worry about placing himself into a stressful environment may be leading to some subconscious resistance to the idea of returning to an environment where he'll be at risk of facing exposure to potential traumatic events again.

Perpetuating factors include perceived loss of career and ongoing civil claim against the employer. Maintaining factors: potential dispute with management, feeling let down by the force and embitterment. Protective factors include a supportive relationship. He is suffering anxiety symptoms including recurrent panic attacks, centred around his employer. The content of his dreams; are not about the incident and therefore more consistent with anxiety than PTSD. His mental state is not consistent with PTSD and he is not experiencing flashbacks as he did before. [He is displaying] dysfunctional behaviours, maladaptive thoughts, intensive anxiety symptoms and negative thoughts about the police. He understands that he is going through a crisis of grief over losing his role and identity at work. He is not appreciating the significance of his pre-existing depression on the development of his symptoms. [He has] (reactions to severe stress with associated anger [and] intrusive re-experiencing symptoms). He has negativity towards a possible improvement that might result in him being asked to return to work as a police officer. This indicates a pre-determined mindset to the outcome of treatment, supporting that there is a psychosocial issue. Successful psychological therapies often require the belief of a cure and motivation to engage with treatment. He seems very aggrieved with the force…and a sense of ongoing embitterment and distress. Being embittered, angry or having antipathy toward the police, or perceived lack of support are not a medical condition. There is a systemic issue that cannot be treated, that is the breakdown of a working relationship of trust between employer and employee. Non-medical factors are influencing his progress. He himself, has indicated that he does not believe that his health will improve until he has left the service. He has requested consideration of ill health retirement.

He currently feels he is in the final stages of 'battle' with the organisation. He has many symptoms of PTSD. He goes through phases of anger, denial, shame and grief.

Background to this case: This officers' case went to a medical appeal board to dispute the doctors' decision not to grant ill health retirement. The researcher noted the following from reviewing all the reports. It was highlighted that his anxiety symptoms stemmed from perceived stress at work and emotional worry about the risk of exposure to harm (avoidance). The occupational GP opinion, was that the officer has a predetermined mindset against treatment, as successful outcomes could result in a return to work. However, the two psychologist reports, stated he has fully engaged with all the treatment offered to him and diagnosed PTSD. Furthermore, the psychology report stated, either the officer is within the subset of people for whom treatment is ineffective or he is not yet in a safe, stable state to fully engage with treatment and this may not be achievable until the officer has left the policing environment. This is because he will most likely be re-traumatized. His psychology report stated, the DSM-5 diagnostic model and SCID diagnostic instrument were used in assessment. His legal representative appealed the decision (among other reasons), stating that "embitterment might be an issue but there is still an underlying medical condition. He would break down if he returned to the policing environment." The occupational GP stated, he felt there had been an underlying personality issue which was not likely to change with treatment. The Occupational GP stated, "there was no startle reaction or hypervigilance during assessment, and he was capable of normal activities." In contrast, the psychologist noted the officers' visible anxiety during assessment. The occupational GP asks, "if there is a significant mental health issue, how can he be capable of looking after the children." The clinical psychologist states, the officer has difficulty within the policing environment and in normal day to day life, such as with short term memory, forgetfulness, disproportionate anger, excessive use of force, irritability and incapacity in detailed administrative tasks. The occupational GP states, "the hurt and humiliation from being reminded of the incident needs to be addressed so that he can move beyond his current emotional state." He understands that he is going through a crisis of grief over losing his role and identity at work. The psychology report stated, the officer had given a "very clear impression of a man who was dedicated to his career." The appeal board noted that "various authorities consider the appellant to be disabled by PTSD."

However, the board disagreed with the diagnosis and believed him to be affected by a phobic anxiety, maintained by embitterment. The psychologist clearly stated in their report that the officer's symptoms had persisted for four years and therefore surpassed the criteria for adjustment disorder. It appears the medical appeal doctors had the opinion that embitterment is a personality issue and not a medical condition. No one linked the embitterment to the index trauma. It was a public order incident in 2015, in which the officer was hit with a projectile in the face. He was not wearing full personal protective equipment (such as a helmet). The medical report submitted to the appeal stated, he had answered urgent calls for assistance from fellow officers. However, the officer stated he attended with his colleagues in the capacity of 'riot police' and therefore, there was some forward planning before arriving on scene.

He blamed the organisation. It was for this reason that he pursued a civil claim (as mentioned in the medical report). The appeal board felt that the incident was not significant enough, as he sustained no injury and continued with work. It seems the board did not account for the perceived level of threat the officer may have felt in a large crowd, with individuals targeting officers. Over 400 people were arrested, eight police officers were injured and there was a rise in violence at the annual event. It was the highest number of arrests since 2008. There were 21 assaults on officers. Riot police were called in after officers had been hit with bottles. Some members of the public were stabbed. One officer was bitten and another stabbed.[149] However, the medical appeal board and occupational GP quoted ICD-10 criteria for PTSD, as requiring the incident to be of exceptional severity. Neither the GP or appeal board believed the incident met this criteria. Furthermore, the board stated he had several years of training with public order; implying that this would negate any traumatic effect. Both the GP and the board failed to refer to the DSM-5 criteria for PTSD (published in 2013, two years prior to the

---

[149] (Morgan & Randhawa, 2015)

incident in 2015). Criteria A requires that the person is exposed to real or threatened serious injury, directly experiencing or witnessing the event as it occurred to others and/or learning that the event occurred to a close friend which must have been violent or accidental. Finally, the traumatic incident may be experiencing repeated or extreme exposure to aversive details of the traumatic event(s). For example, the retelling of the incident at work and details of injured colleagues. Symptoms in criteria B can include the following: Intense or prolonged psychological distress at exposure to internal or external cues that symbolize or resemble an aspect of the traumatic event(s) or marked physiological reactions to internal or external cues that symbolize or resemble an aspect of the traumatic event(s). For example, the policing environment. Symptoms in criteria C relate to the avoidance of triggers and stimuli to the trauma, such as "people, places, conversations, activities and situations." Symptoms in criteria D include, "persistent and exaggerated negative beliefs or expectations about oneself, others or the world. Persistent, distorted cognitions about the cause or consequences of the traumatic event(s) that lead the individual to blame himself/herself or others and a persistent negative emotional state (such as fear, horror, anger, guilt, or shame)." Criteria E needs to be two or more of the following symptoms: Irritable behaviour and angry outbursts (with little or no provocation), reckless or self-destructive behaviour, hypervigilance, exaggerated startle response, problems with concentration or sleep disturbance." Criteria G requires that "the disturbance causes clinically significant distress or impairment in social, occupational, or other important areas of functioning." Therefore, one does not need to be impaired in all areas of functioning to qualify. The officer may be able to function in childcare and unable to function in an occupational setting, because of the associated stressors in that environment. The psychologist report noted the officer's difficulty with short term memory, forgetfulness, crowded places, disorientation to place, difficulty with administrative tasks and disproportionate anger. The occupational GP stated, "he is not appreciating the significance of his pre-existing depression on the development of his symptoms." DSM-5 does not stipulate that there can be no pre-existing conditions (i.e. depression), or state that pre-existing conditions may contribute to the onset of PTSD.[150] It appears the occupational doctor does not believe the appellant has PTSD. He stated "he has dreams which are police related but not to the index event. It raises issues as to the validity of a diagnosis of PTSD. This statement is in conflict with the psychologists' report, which stated the officer frequently has distressing dreams about the index event. DSM-IV states, "Recurrent distressing dreams of the event" is one of five potential re-experiencing symptoms. However, this version of the manual had been replaced by DSM-5 at the point of assessment and appeal. DSM-5 states "Recurrent distressing dreams in which the content and/or affect of the dream are related to the traumatic event(s)" is one of five potential intrusion symptoms (of which one or more should apply). Therefore, the content of the dreams may be 'related' to rather than 'of the' traumatic event; and if this symptom is missing, yet one other intrusion symptom is present, the officer would still meet criteria B. The occupational GP and appeal board agreed with a diagnosis of phobic anxiety. The researcher was not able to find a classification of 'phobic anxiety' in DSM-5. The closest classification in DSM-5 is Anxiety Disorder. Examples of the potential causes of Anxiety Disorder are "marked fear of anxiety about a specific object or situation (e.g. flying, heights, animals, receiving an injection, seeing blood)." One is asked to specify which type of stressor is applicable - Animal Type (e.g., spiders, insects, dogs), Natural Environment Type (e.g., heights, storms, water), Blood-Injection-Injury Type (e.g., needles, invasive medical procedures), Situational Type (e.g., aeroplanes, elevators, enclosed places), Other Type (e.g., phobic avoidance of situations that may lead to choking, vomiting, or contracting an illness; in children, avoidance of loud sounds or costumed characters). This disorder would not be an appropriate diagnosis where "The disturbance is not better explained by the symptoms of another mental disorder, including.........reminders of traumatic events (as in posttraumatic stress disorder........)."[151] ICD-10 (which was the latest ICD version at the time of assessment) had a classification of phobic anxiety disorders. The disorder is characterized by the following types of phobia: Agoraphobia, Social phobia (fear of scrutiny from others and subsequent social avoidance) and specific phobias as outlined in DSM-5 (such as fear of animals, flying and heights.). [152] The researcher did not note referencing made by either the occupational GP or medical appeal board to support and evidence their decisions and opinions. This demonstrates a failure to understand the medical criteria for PTSD and Phobic Anxiety and that perhaps, both the occupational GP and appeal board are not current on their knowledge of the conditions and diagnostic criteria.

The researcher completed a video interview with the officer and his wife. They stated: His period of sickness absence has lasted around two years. He returned for a couple of months on reduced hours, in an office role after early ill health retirement was refused. He felt this has made him worse. Police premises and crowded places (such as train stations used to get to work) are the main triggers for his symptoms. He stated, he would be ready to punch anyone who came near him in crowded spaces. He has been told he will never be able to return to frontline operational duties again because of his anger.

He stated, he has no point of law he can use to appeal against the medical appeal board decision and that he may need to apply for ill health retirement again in the future.

He feels they should do more to support adjustments in the workplace. He stated, the organisation say they have done enough, "you're not working from home, you're coming in." He has been told he is protected

---

[151] (SAMHSA, 2020)
[152] (WHO, 2016)

by the Equality Act, by the force doctor. He is now seeking a claim of disability discrimination against his employer via an Employment Tribunal. The personal injury claim he made for the traumatic incident is still ongoing after five years and is with his legal representative. He stated, his EMDR (Eye Movement Desensitization and Reprocessing) therapist suggests he is still living it and fighting it. He hasn't had closure. There are still ongoing issues. How can he be in the right place mentally to make a recovery? The psychologists think his condition is probably complex PTSD with depression thrown in as well. The psychologist states, in his opinion the embitterment was a symptom of the PTSD and a return to work would make the symptoms worse. The officer stated he feels 'embitterment' is being used to ignore the medical condition and save money on ill health retirement. It is very convenient. He has been told that if he goes off sick within the next three months, he will be subject to unsatisfactory performance procedure at work. He has had Trauma-Focused CBT and is now receiving EMDR organised by a police charity. He has trouble with sleep, angry outbursts (verbally), short temper and poor concentration. He is not keen on public transport because there may be something he needs to deal with as an officer. His wife recalled a psychotic episode when at the airport going on a family holiday. This resulted in seeking help from the mental health crisis team. He can't remember much of it.

His wife stated he lost the plot, shouting and screaming, frantically searching for a rope. He stated, "*I wanted to be somewhere else.*"

The researcher asked, "have you thought about pursuing another occupation or alternative employment?" He stated, he would love to leave and do something else. It all comes down to finances. "*I'm not in a position where I can just walk out on the job.*" His wife stated they have thought 'enough', but without something to walk in to with pay in the same area, they feel like their hands are tied. He stated, it is about 'the fight' and not wanting to let the other side win. He feels like he is a victim in it all. He blames the loss of his career, identity, ability to provide for his family, loss of camaraderie, loss of trust, PTSD and symptoms on the incompetence of the senior officer on the day of the traumatic incident. He stated, he would not be in this situation now if the senior officer had made a different decision. In relation to the incident, he stated that the supervisor already had knowledge, that people were targeting the 'police line' at the event before they went in. They could see 'missiles' being thrown from where they were. There was plenty of time to sort out personal protective equipment. The decision was made not to do so. He stated, if they had made a different decision, none of this would have happened and he would be working now. He had been involved in other riots before. This time he felt his life was threatened. He stated, he had always felt protected and safe in other situations. This time he felt vulnerable. It was different.

He also attributes problems to 'ignorance towards mental health.' He stated, "*it is unseen. You haven't got a broken arm. People think you are 'pulling a fast one' and you are a malingerer.*" He stated he is now fighting the organisation. One man against a great big corporation. He stated, "*I want some sort of semblance of victory. Where do you draw the line, when do you say enough is enough? Financially I can't do it.*" The researcher asked; "If money wasn't an issue, would you be able to walk away?" The officer replied "*No. It's a bit about finances, but it still doesn't feel right. It's the duty of care. It is their ignorance. It is like a lie. On joining you are told you are part of a family now. We will look after you.*" He stated he felt disbelieved in relation to having PTSD. The researcher asked; "if a timely apology had been made for the injury at the time or soon after, would that have changed the way you feel now and your symptoms?" The officer stated, "*initially, yes. But it goes hand in hand with aftercare and this was missing.*" His wife stated, when she met him, he was a very proud police officer and proud of what he did. He spoke highly of his colleagues. She stated he was never phased by the work he did. After that incident (in 2015) he changed completely. At this point in the interview his wife became upset and tearful. The researcher asked, "have you done any forward planning? For example, plan A is going back, Plan B is education and training to do something different. Have you thought about other options if you do leave?" The officer stated, *"yes, I've thought about training courses in various trades, I've got a degree, it depends on having the financial backing."* He stated, the issues he is dealing with now are so energy sapping. He felt everything was out of his hands and he was having to rely on other people to do their jobs, just to resolve the issues. It makes him feel like he has no control. The researcher asked, "when is it going to stop, what is your desired outcome?" He stated, *"to be out of the job completely, ideally with some financial security to then start fresh. Then I know my wife and kids are set up and okay. We don't have to worry about her having to take on another job, which she has done before. To not have to worry about, 'I've got this to do today and that to shell out for."* The researcher asked, "do you think that would be more stressful than having to go through two legal action claims, potentially a second ill health retirement process and unsatisfactory performance procedure?" He stated, *"as much as we're in it together, I don't see it as my wife's fight really. It's all on me. Because I don't feel like I'm providing enough. It's a loss of my identity. I'm dealing with the grief of no longer being in that unit, in that closeness with people you would trust with your life, cover your back when you are doing raids. Spending more time with them than you would your own family. I haven't had any contact with them whatsoever, it's been shut down since I went off, so it's been around two years, yet I have been in the unit for about ten years. Now doing an office job after being operational is mundane and demeaning."* He stated it had resulted in low self-esteem.

The researcher asked, "would you go back to the job you were doing previously if you made a full recovery and you were no longer symptomatic?" He stated, *"No. There is a loss of trust."*

The researcher asked, "do you feel the door is firmly closed on your police career now? To which the officer replied, *"yes."*

In summary, this case study demonstrates the apparent failure of the occupational medical professionals to link the embitterment reactions to the index trauma and desire to avoid the stimulus to trauma (such as the police environment and unavoidable busy areas on route to work). "Work environment factors such as dissatisfaction with organisational support predicted PTSD symptoms in police officers" (Carlier et al., 1997). The independent psychologist seemed to be of the opinion, that the embitterment reactions were part of his PTSD symptomatology (and not a separate issue). The occupational doctors have perceived the embitterment as a personality issue and not a medical one. It seems the context of the incident (which the officer perceived as traumatic) was not taken into account. For example, he felt it was life threatening. He was exposed to the incident directly and witnessed harm to others (including colleagues). The diagnostic criteria for PTSD was not fully explored. An occupational doctor (GP equivalent) gave an opinion which disagreed with two specialist consultants in Psychology. As a result, their professional diagnosis was overturned by the appeal board.

The officer presents as someone who has embitterment symptoms and moral injury. His experience fits with Dr Shay's definition of moral injury, which is a failure of those with legitimate power and authority in a high risk situation, to do what's right.[153] His embitterment reactions are comorbid with PTSD, which is often the case in moral injury. He has expressed a sense of injustice and betrayal. He implies his deeply held values and beliefs about the police service have been undermined; saying, "*It is like a lie. On joining you are told you are part of a family now. We will look after you.*" The officer mentions many common symptoms associated with moral injury and PTED such as, low self-esteem, humiliation (at having to do demeaning work now), feeling like a victim (this happened to him), feeling powerless (little or no control over his situation), loss of trust, loss of meaning and purpose, sense of grief and loss, blame and a strong desire for justice, shame and self-blame (feeling unable to provide for his family and to cope with what has happened). He is experiencing impairment in significant areas of life, such as occupational, social and

---

[153] (Shay J. , 2003)

economic. It appears his way of trying to remedy these thoughts and feelings, to right a wrong and to feel he has control over his life and situation is to pursue a litigious route until this has been exhausted. It seems he may be unable to fully explore what other opportunities there could be beyond his fight with the organisation at this time.

The experience of blame, shattered values, morals and beliefs, revenge fantasy and loss are significant characteristics or symptoms of PTED and MI, and are discussed in the following sections.

Blame

Embitterment, Moral Injury and 'blame' may be interchangeable in terms of their correlating reactions. For example, one may say blame is a symptom of embitterment or may say embitterment is a symptom of blame. Embitterment could be an overarching term to encapsulate symptoms such as anger, hatred, blame, self-blame, guilt, shame, difficulty with forgiveness, sense of injustice and betrayal (as in PTED). However, we could perhaps perceive embitterment and associated reactions, as resulting from 'blame'. Can embitterment exist if there is not first the concept of blame? Perhaps in order to feel embittered or betrayed, there must first be an injustice or wrongdoing, a humiliation suffered for which self or other(s) are responsible. Blame is attributed and subsequently becomes a driver for unforgiveness, revenge fantasy, feelings of shame and guilt, sense of injustice and bitterness. Blame of self or others is a common denominator in PTED, Moral Injury and PTSD. Therefore, where 'blame' is identified in PTSD as a significant symptom, a comorbid condition of chronic embitterment, PTED or Moral Injury could be considered. Additionally; where a traumatized patient presents as an embittered person, one may consider this an expression of the symptom 'blame of self or others,' as specified in DSM-5, PTSD diagnostic criteria. The context of the embitterment will most likely be important to determine whether it is related to the traumatic incident, or separate to the event. This is perhaps demonstrated in Case study 5, where medical professionals failed to link the embitterment reactions to the index trauma and perceived the cause to be a personality issue and general grievance with the organisation.

Shaver's (1985) model of blame identifies a process of attributing the cause, then responsibility and finally, blame.[154] Therefore, there is a negative or traumatic event, an evaluation of who is responsible for the incident that caused harm and then blame is attributed. If the evaluation of the incident produced no perpetrator or transgressor (including self), then blame does not result.[155] Perhaps moral injury or embitterment could not apply. Malle and Monroe (2014), say blame is attributed when the act was 1) intentional, 2) the outcome preventable, 3) the behaviour within the perpetrators' control, 4) the perpetrator had an obligation to prevent the incident and 5) the capacity to do so. In case study 5, the officer directed blame for his psychological injury on the supervisor (not the assailant or associated trauma). The officer in charge had an obligation to minimize risk of harm to colleagues, the capacity to provide full personal protective equipment (as well as the resource of time to facilitate this) and utilize knowledge and training to inform decisions. The outcome (the officer's injury), may not have been intentional. However, the supervisor intended to send officers into a riot situation without PPE. In other case studies throughout this research, the officers blamed the organisation for their PTSD and not the violent offenders or extremist terrorists. It appears the officers are blaming those they perceive to have a duty of care toward them and not the individuals who were responsible for the violent crimes or directly responsible for the threat to their physical safety or that of others. This pattern leads the researcher to question whether the primary cause of trauma is a distressing or fearful incident and the cause of psychological injury may be attributed to a person(s) or organisation who has capacity, intention, control and

---

[154] (Alicke, 2000)
[155] (Malle & Monroe, 2014)

obligation to prevent the traumatic experience or ameliorate its effect. Not everyone who is exposed to traumatic events will develop PTSD. Could the element of 'blame' (including self-blame), be a key factor in determining why some who experience trauma go on to develop PTSD and some do not? Blame has been identified as a symptom of PTED, MI and (C)PTSD. However, has the psychological process of attributing blame, as having a causal effect on the development of PTSD been explored? The attribution of blame should be warranted. The perception of 'wrongness' depends on one's personal schema. Therefore, there is no need for this judgement to be warranted. For example; the analogy of 'live and let live' – moral disapproval of another persons' lifestyle or sexual preferences, minus the feature of 'blame.' An acceptance that others may have different values, morals and beliefs.[156] Publicly blaming another can be damaging. To cast blame without good reason, grounds or evidence is socially unacceptable.[157]

When one argues a moral judgement without rationality or reason, this is known in psychology as 'moral dumbfounding.' For example, "What they did was very wrong. I can't tell you why, it just feels wrong."

Greene (2018) states, urgent clarification on 'blame' within DSM-5 criteria (D3) for PTSD is needed. She states, the criterion that 'blame' is distorted does not consider that 'blame' may be justified or appropriate. Furthermore, Greene states there is "*evidence that blame is associated with other PTSD symptoms, is clinically relevant........[and] may be an important intervention target in therapy.*" She is of the opinion there are notable differences between blame of self and blame of others which need to be identified and a distinction needs to be made between blame which is 'normal' and 'pathological.'[158]

---

[156] (Malle & Monroe, 2014)
[157] (Malle & Monroe, 2014)
[158] (Greene, 2018)

Values, beliefs and morals

Beliefs can be altered through debate, education, experience and open mindedness. Morals can be influenced or manipulated to fit any situation, as it can often be a matter of perspective. Values are an intrinsic part of an individual – one's blueprint. When one tries to move away from their values, it can cause psychological and emotional pain. Herman (1997) states, one way to protect against the development of PTSD is to stay true to ones' morals and values.[159]

To have strong beliefs, is to potentially be closed to all other possibilities. A closed mind can be less resilient to change, life crisis, trauma, immorality, injustice and transgressions.[160] A belief in a just world where one gets what they deserve and deserves what they get, could lead to symptoms of embitterment or moral injury when those beliefs are challenged or undermined by negative life events.[161] One may feel unable to adjust to new beliefs or continue on as before. They may *"go through distress and confusion as they try to understand why this terrible thing happened to them"* (Collier, 2016).

If one does not stay true to their values, they risk injuring themselves by tearing at the very fabric of their being. Dissociation from the truth and events, such as forgetting what happened or betrayal blindness may be necessary for protecting against psychological pain and for survival. [162]

Malle and Monroe (2014) state, *"Morality regulates individual behaviors so they come in line with community interests and sustain social relations."*

---

[159] (Herman, 1997)
[160] (Linden & Maercker, 2011)
[161] (Linden & Maercker, 2011)
[162] (Freyd J. , 2019)

'Norms and values', rules and morals, are important for individual inclusion and belonging, resource sharing among the social group, trust and protection of vulnerable people and their rights.[163]

Sometimes people are faced with no-win situations where either course of action will have harmful consequences. This can cause a painful state for the individual. One cannot do right, for doing wrong. *'Psychologists call this 'double bind' and it drives people mad'* (Graef, 1990:17). *"A moral dilemma entails a situation in which one is confronted with competing moral principles that one considers important, but which cannot simultaneously be honored; one principle has to be violated in order to respect the other. In a moral dilemma, there is thus no unequivocal "right" or "wrong" decision"* (Molendijk, 2018).[164]

When beliefs in a just world are gone

One's plan filled, organised, predictable and 'normal' life may feel like it was another lifetime. What was known and believed to be secure and safe may no longer exist in the world. One can feel like they are always one breath or heartbeat away from crossing the line to anarchy, to break through social norms and expectations and tear down the walls that keep them in. There is a thin veil holding them back, keeping their rage in check. Belief in authority may be corrupted and one may no longer tolerate being controlled. Some may lose control of their emotions and behaviour.

"people say hi, how are you? The immediate answer is not too bad thanks. Really, I just want to scream IT'S ALL F**KED! MY WHOLE BODY AND MIND ARE READY TO EXPLODE AND IT'S JUST A THIN LAYER THAT IS KEEPING ME FROM MAKING A MESS! I HATE EVERYONE INCLUDING MYSELF AND I AM SO SCARED OF MY OWN SHADOW THAT THE SMALLEST THING

---

[163] (Malle & Monroe, 2014)
[164] (Molendijk, Kramer, & Verweij, 2018)

SENDS ME WIBBLE" - an account from Duty of Care, Psychological Injury in policing[165] - Carter (2014).

One may experience embitterment, perhaps chronic and severe enough to become a disorder. Feelings may be turned in on oneself rather than outward onto others. One can feel victimized and become entrenched in this mindset. Those around the embittered person can be greatly affected by their moods, negativity and inability to move past the event. People can become consumed by the need to seek justice or become very litigious in nature. One can persist with their perceived right to punish the transgressor for the wrongdoing, over and over, in a bid to show everyone how they were treated and the pain they continue to endure.

"Embitterment often coincides with a rejection of help (e.g. the world will see what it did to me)....the aims of successful therapy....to overcome the preoccupation with the traumatic event, to give up the right to continuously punish the person who has 'wronged' the victim...." (Linden and Maercker, 2011:123). Some may seek revenge and others may ruminate on revenge, knowing they cannot act on it.

Revenge

Revenge fantasy may feature where there has been trauma, abuse, Moral Injury or embitterment disorder (PTED), including abuse of power and authority or repeated exposure to threat and harm. Revenge phenomenon often features in PTSD, MI and PTED.[166]

The perpetrator, abuser or betrayer may be the subject of vengeful thoughts, such as ruminating on when, where and how revenge will be enacted. These thoughts and feelings can be both unpleasant and pleasurable, cyclical and addictive, perhaps helpful in the short term and

---

[165] (Carter, Duty of Care - Psychological Injury in Policing, 2014)
[166] (Linden & Maercker, 2011)

potentially damaging to mental health over the longer term - including leading to other mental health conditions. Rumination on revenge can maintain PTSD and PTED symptoms. Feelings of anger and thoughts of revenge may occur to quell fear (fear of powerlessness, victimisation, threat and humiliation - which seems helpful). However, rumination and vengeful thoughts can continue to activate fear, anxiety and PTSD. Revenge fantasy and ruminating on justice can keep a person stuck in the past and inhibit recovery, bringing no relief. It can also keep one in a state of hyper-arousal. When one feels helpless to find a resolution to an event that was threatening to them or their values and beliefs; it may lead to rumination and intrusive thoughts. These recurrent, negative thoughts may lead to chronic symptoms of embitterment. Revenge fantasy may be the only way to create a scenario in which one can find relief. Therefore, revenge fantasy may be experienced as pleasurable. However, it can also have a negative affect because rumination (repetitive thinking) continues to maintain the symptoms. It is reinforcing.[167] *"If the injustice seems unlikely to be resolved in reality…people restore justice cognitively"* (Linden and Maercker, 2011:31). In revenge fantasy the victim may become the perpetrator. In this way they may regain their sense of power and control which was felt to have been taken away. Herman (1997) states, revenge fantasy may be in response to persistent and prolonged abuse, threat, betrayal or trauma, where there is a sense of not being able to escape the situation and powerlessness to stop the abuse of power and authority over the individual. Revenge fantasy may be graphic, violent and pleasurable. Thoughts or feelings of revenge may be directed towards people in general, a type of group or an individual. Thoughts may turn to the killing, torture, humiliation or subjugation of the abuser. The risk of homicide-suicide is increased if an individual can get hold of powerful weapons and turn revenge fantasy into reality.[168]

---

[167] (Linden & Maercker, 2011)
[168] (Linden & Maercker, 2011)

When PTSD is present, there can be reduced ability to cope with systems, processes and procedures which are necessary and life events like divorce and family breakdown. This can also trigger revenge fantasy against family members, work colleagues, medical professionals and so on.

Revenge fantasy may seem like a kind of antidote to feelings of powerlessness and victimisation. *"the roles of perpetrator and victim are reversed.....the victim imagines that revenge is the only way to restore her own sense of power. She may also imagine that this is the only way to force the perpetrator to acknowledge the harm...done."* (Herman, 1997: 189)

For some people it can be disturbing - They may have a *"fear of becoming a monster"* (Lansing, 2012:49). So perhaps, just as it may feel cathartic and remedial, it can also create other problems relating to one's self-image and frustration that the revenge fantasy cannot be acted upon. Coming to terms with this reality may mean a process of grieving and replacing revenge fantasy with an alternative path to justice - such as court action, peer support, raising public awareness, being heard and having one's experiences validated.[169]

One individual in 'Talking Blues' describes his reactions to violent riots. He sought psychiatric help and described a vivid dream of himself murdering people indiscriminately who had been a threat to him during this event. He recalls it being the most enjoyable dream he has ever had in his life.[170]

Revenge (or retaliation and sabotage) for injustice or humiliation can be more covert. For example, call centre workers purposefully keeping customers on hold for longer than necessary, redirecting customers to the wrong department or deliberately disconnecting a call.[171] Within hierarchical organisations where subordinates are unable to challenge

---

[169] (Carter, Duty of Care - Psychological Injury in Policing, 2014)
[170] (Graef, 1990)
[171] (Linden & Maercker, 2011)

senior officer decisions or behaviour, subversive acts of retaliation may occur. Eleven research participants responded to a questionnaire on underhanded and sneaky acts of retaliation or revenge in frontline services. Some examples given were underhanded and sneaky ways that supervisors or senior officers bullied subordinates or treated them unfavourably. For example, 1) punishment postings (being moved to a different job), moves across county making getting to work difficult 2) job applications blocked 3) being picked for unpleasant tasks 4) Sergeants setting up traps to stick officers on (disciplinary). Examples of ways in which subordinates retaliated were A) giving any officer a map – (seen as an insult to the officer) B) reporting an inspector to the anonymous national complaints number C) whilst suffering from a very nasty cold, deliberately went and used the telephone in my bosses office. I might have sneezed, oh and snorted a bit. He had 10 days off work with a cold he developed a short time later D) doing a bad job to make them look bad and bad mouthing them E) tea contamination, moving stuff around on desks. Low level stuff really. When senior officers had personal toilets, using them on nights and not flushing was popular. Almost hangable being caught on the Divisional Commanders toilet! F) fake reports of racism or sexual harassment to get back at officers G) enlisting them onto free offers that humiliated them, sex sites, free sex aids, wigs, inappropriate covert medication (e.g. laxative in tea), spitting in drinks, sending partners comments stating they were cheating.

Nearly one third of respondents stated these types of retaliation or revenge are culturally accepted or commonplace within their organisation. 72% of respondents stated sneaky, underhanded retaliation or revenge was the only way to realistically get a feeling of justice or regain a feeling of personal power as a subordinate in a hierarchical organisation. When asked why, respondents stated the organisation hates to be challenged in any way, even when it is wrong and will not let things lie. Openly challenging wrong doing is career suicide. There is no recourse through normal complaints channels. In the long term it can derail your career for the future.

It can lead to being ostracised from the team. There was no other way to fight against the culture or the bully. Middle management are incompetent. Doing it the right way causes the complainant more difficulties than the person who is wrong and it takes far too long. Nearly 87% of those respondents who took part in acts of sneaky, underhanded forms of retaliation or revenge stated this brought them satisfaction or sense of relief. Approximately one third of all respondents (36.36%) did not act out of revenge or retaliation. 81% of responses related to the police service. The remainder related to armed forces. Nearly 91% of respondents were male. Over half of respondents (54.55%) were educated to post graduate level, approximately one third (36.36%) were educated to college level and 9% educated to undergraduate level. Nearly 91% of respondents were white British. Under two thirds (63.64%) were aged 45-59. Under one third (27.27%) were aged 60 or over. 9.09% was mixed race and aged between 18 and 29.

The number of responses to this questionnaire are too small to draw any conclusions. However, the survey has highlighted a potential area for further research into types of revenge or retaliation in hierarchical organisations, as a coping mechanism against injustice or humiliation in frontline services; and a potential psychological protection against feelings of powerlessness, loss of control, moral injury or embitterment.

The experience of loss

Many types of loss are features of Moral Injury and PTED, yet the concept of grief as a feature is not made explicit. For example, loss of beliefs, meaning and purpose, trust, personal identity, family or friends, security, certainty, future orientation, self-esteem, career or vocation and significant personal investment (sacrifices). The loss which results from an injustice and violation of one's deeply held values, morals and beliefs can touch multiple areas of one's life.

Zisook and Shear (2009), describe the differences between uncomplicated (normal) grief and complicated grief (which may relate to major depression and require intervention).

As with the development of embitterment, grief is a process of trying to assimilate and accept loss. One learns to live with the experience rather than continue to live in the experience. For some, embitterment reactions, similar to complicated grief are enduring. Zisook and Shear (2009) state, "*there are grievers who do not want the grief to end, as they feel it is all that is left of the relationship with their loved one. Sometimes, people think that, by enjoying their life, they are betraying their lost loved one.*"[172] Linden and Rotter (2007) stated, embittered people are not sure they want the wounds to heal.[173] Perhaps complicated grief and chronic embitterment follow the same pathways or psychological processes; for one may have lost oneself and mourn the loss of the person they used to be. Litz et al. (2016), identify traumatic loss (in combat) as complicated grief. Zisook and Shear (2009) state, the 'griever' fluctuates between rumination and avoidance of reminders. Litz et al. (2016) state, exposure therapy is not appropriate for complicated grief (and therefore, traumatic loss), because the treatment is designed for avoidant persons and people with complicated grief tend to seek reminders and ruminate on the past. One may feel detached from significant others. Risk factors are lack of social support, multiple life stresses - resulting in saturation and reduced resilience to cope with the loss and a history of mood or anxiety disorders. Complicated grief may lead to PTSD or major depression.[174] The experience of grief goes through various stages and can include: disbelief, shock, numbness, denial that the loss or change is happening, anger and blame directed at others, feelings of bitterness or resentment, feeling vulnerable or helpless, sadness, confusion, hurt, avoiding emotions by being proactive with taking control, withdrawal from others, guilt,

---

[172] (Zisook & Shear, 2009)
[173] (Linden, Baumann, Rotter, & Schippan, 2007)
[174] (Zisook & Shear, 2009)

impacting negatively on others, acceptance that this has happened and finding ways to live with the experience and move forward.[175] Tedeschi and Calhoun (2004), on Posttraumatic Growth state, *"Many people who survive traumatic events report that many months later they can still be struck by a sense of disbelief."*

To an extent, this process may involve "grief-work," in the sense that the loss involved in the trauma is gradually accepted."[176]

Anger, bitterness, preoccupation with the loss, confusion about one's role in life, diminished sense of self, avoidance of reminders, inability to trust others since the loss, difficulty moving on with life, emotional numbness, difficulty with positive reminiscence, loss of meaning in life and difficulty or reluctance to plan for the future, are potential symptoms of prolonged grief disorder (PGD) according to ICD-11 and Persistent Complex Bereavement Disorder (PCBD) in DSM-5. Jordan and Litz (2014) state, *"The disruption associated with bereavement can trigger various disorders, including not only PGD but also major depression and posttraumatic stress disorder (PTSD). Failure to fully face the reality of the loss may prolong emotional reactivity to loss reminders, while avoidance of loss reminders, unwillingness to adopt new roles, and an aversion to seeking support from new individuals may constrict a person's behavioral repertoire and prevent him or her from discovering new sources of meaning and pleasure. Disengaged from the social sphere, the bereaved may thus keep his or her attention narrowly fixed on the past and the meaning, pleasure, and intimacy it contained before the loss."*[177] There appears to be a significant cross over between symptoms of PGD or PCBD with PTED or MI, including comorbidity with PTSD. However, PGD and PCBD can only be diagnosed where there has been a 'death of a close other.'

---

[175] (Holland, 2018)
[176] (Tedeschi & Calhoun, 2004)
[177] (Jordan & Litz, 2014)

These conditions do not accommodate loss of vocation, loss of a partner through divorce or separation or other significant loss. Maercker (2018) states, a diagnosis of Adjustment Disorder would be appropriate in these circumstances.[178]

Research into the potential for bereavement counselling to ameliorate embitterment reactions and moral injury may be beneficial.

Predisposing indicators that an individual may experience chronic embitterment or MI and possible measures of prevention, are discussed in the next chapter.

---

[178] (Maercker, 2018)

CHAPTER 5

Predisposing factors and Prevention

Survival depends on protecting against, 'a broken heart' (or social pain), as well as physical safety. Trauma in either case can result in changes in the brain. Berkfeld and Braus (2011), explain that extreme social pain may be on par with chronic physical pain in terms of brain plasticity. '*The broken heart has to recover from its psychological injury just like a broken leg would after enduring physical damage*' (cited in Linden & Maercker, 2011: 114). Embitterment can have a significant effect on people's lives, their brain function and emotions.[179]

Galatzer-Levy et al. (2013), evaluated police officers periodically from the point of training at the police academy as new recruits, and over the course of 48 months on duty. The research observed responses to potentially traumatic incidents every twelve months. Four trajectories were identified, 1) Resilience 2) Reactive-worsening 3) Chronic distress-recovering and 4) Anticipatory distress-recovered. Lower levels of negative emotion in recruits during training predicted resilience when exposed to traumatic events on the job. Higher levels of positive emotion in recruits during training also predicted resilience to traumatic exposure. The largest group were resilient (72%). The second largest group was reactive-worsening (19.7%), where levels of distress worsened over time and were maintained. This group of recruits demonstrated the lowest levels of positive emotion during training. These groups were followed by substantially smaller groups of chronic distress-recovering (4.8%) and anticipatory distress-recovering (3.5%). Therefore, resilience

---

[179] (Linden & Maercker, 2011)

and a higher level of positive emotions, offer significantly greater protection against the development of psychological injury and predispose individuals to having healthy coping strategies for recovery following distress.

These may be considerations useful to the recruitment process and for monitoring stress responses throughout frontline service.[180] The results appear to indicate a significantly higher likelihood that symptoms of trauma will be maintained in less resilient individuals whilst in service, than the likelihood of their recovery.

Blom et al. (2012) state, that "*a negative attachment history may promote embitterment. The....study identified attachment anxiety - more than attachment avoidance - as a possible vulnerability factor for the development and maintenance of embitterment.*"[181] One is more resilient when they have secure attachments and trust in caregivers; knowing that people important to the individual will be there to give support, comfort and reassurance following distress. This knowledge and secure attachment can reduce anxiety and have a calming effect. A sense of security promotes trust in others and encourages emotional regulation. Repeated rejection and unreliability creates insecurity and difficulties with close relationships (as often featured in complex PTSD). Insecure attachments can lead to one doubting their own value or worth and worries that the support they need will not be available when needed. In the absence of secure attachment, one may develop avoidant attachment or anxious attachment. An avoidant person will remain independent and be untrusting of others. Therefore, they will suppress emotions of attachment. An anxious person will be fearful of rejection and persistently seek reassurance and love in order to feel secure and valued. Sex may often be used to obtain reassurance, comfort and approval. Attachment anxiety can be exacerbated by feelings of abandonment or separation. Secure attachments can be developed in the anxious or

---

[180] (Galatzer-Levy, et al., 2013)
[181] (Blom, van Middendorp, & Greenen, 2012)

avoidant types with therapy and reliable, trustworthy relationships.[182] The findings of Blom et al. (2012), could perhaps be applied to the employer-employee, caregiver and receiver relationship in high risk occupations. The impact of trauma and distress may be reduced when colleagues feel supported by trusted others and those with a duty of care towards them; particularly where individuals have less resilience. It is not uncommon for frontline workers to feel a sense of abandonment or rejection when psychological or physical injury on duty results in their loss of vocation. Anxiety attachment can be improved upon and individuals supported to develop secure attachments in the workplace.

Linden and Maercker (2011), identify that ways individuals cope with a situation can include rumination, distraction or reassessment of the event. One can repeatedly think about problems and their negative consequences, turn their attention to other things, so as to avoid rumination or choose to think about the experience from various perspectives and reframe it's meaning. The latter can help one to assimilate what has happened and move on from the incident. Supressing emotions and ruminating on events can change usual reactions into maladaptive and pathological ones. However, the practice of reassessing the event and taking action to solve problems may be a protective factor against the development of embitterment. One is less likely to view the incident as unjust when able to assess multiple perspectives on an event, including a constructive criticism of ones' own role in the situation. Empathy and understanding toward others may contribute to resilience against embitterment; as well as traits of optimism, humour and forgiveness. Linden and Maercker (2011) refer to this as 'wisdom'. They state, people who develop embitterment may have been less open-minded early in life; seeing "*change as a threat rather than an opportunity*" (p.79). The perception that one has little or no control over their situation or environment and is helpless, may lead to embitterment.[183]

---

[182] (Heshmat, 2015)
[183] (Linden & Maercker, 2011)

Therefore, the organisation can help prevent embitterment by enabling employees to have more autonomy and control over their role and the workplace.

Rumination can be negative, or experienced in a positive form as 'reflection' or reflective practice. Rumination replays events over and over with a focus on the pain, the injustice and negative consequences. One can become stuck in the past. Whereas reflection allows for problem-solving skills that may assist with finding a resolution and moving on from the event. Dunn et al. (2018), research into chronic embitterment and the potential contribution of rumination in healthcare staff, refers to work-related rumination. Respondents were divided into two groups, 1) affective rumination and 2) 'problem-solving pondering.' Embitterment scores correlated with affective rumination and not problem-solving pondering.[184] Therefore, utilizing problem-solving skills is a protective feature against the development of embitterment. What is perhaps unclear is how rumination and embitterment can persist when one is actively trying to take control of their situation and find a resolution. For example, in seeking justice through litigation or grievance procedure. Perhaps the action, desired outcome and means by solving the problem are disproportionate to what can be achieved in reality. For example, where the desired outcome is unreasonable or where one's perception of the injustice as intentional is unfounded. DSM-5 identifies "*persistent and exaggerated negative beliefs or expectations about oneself, others or the world*" in PTSD.[185] Perhaps comorbid conditions can affect one's ability to seek a reasonable or realistic course of action.

Examples of personal wisdom as a resource or coping style are: 1) looking for the positives in a situation that allow for growth (as well as acknowledging the negative consequences) – seeing the good in the bad. 2) Looking for the opportunities created by the event, rather than fear change. 3) Reflecting on the situation to better understand how it

---

[184] (Dunn & Sensky, 2018)
[185] (SAMHSA, 2020)

happened; including an honest evaluation of one's own part in the event and the perspectives of others. 4) Finding meaning in the experience (such as it happened for this reason....this is how I can use the experience to give the incident purpose) 5) Reassessing the event and trying to learn from the experience, so as to inform one's future. 6) Be a problem solver and be proactive in positive ways – take action. 7) Learn to be open to, or comfortable with change. Have a flexible approach to life and oneself. 8) Seek to understand the views of others and be open to new and varied perspectives. 9) Accept that life is uncertain and one may not be able to control events. However, one can master the self, cope with situations and manage emotional reactions to events. 10) Exercise self-compassion and understanding.

The practice of wisdom to overcome trauma may be a protective factor against 'self-centredness' and embitterment.[186] Wisdom is a *"slightly detached perspective, an observer's perspective – an empathetic observer"* (cited in Linden and Maercker, 2011:70). *"some (few) people become wise in the course of their lives, others become embittered, and most of us become neither"* (cited in Linden and Maercker, 2011:75).

Rumination or brooding may be a factor in the development of embitterment. Positive rumination by way of reflection on the meaning, opportunities and lessons which the situation brings, can be factors in post-traumatic growth.[187] The way one perceives, assesses and deals with crisis and the world can be reinforced over time. Therefore, it may be beneficial to practice the skills of reflection, openness, accepting some uncertainty, problem solving, regulating emotional responses using logical and analytical approaches to the situation and viewing situations from multiple perspectives (including views on oneself).

Difficulty forgiving is a key factor in both PTED and MI (perhaps too in PTSD). Forgiveness is beneficial to health. However, asking an embittered

---

[186] (Linden & Maercker, 2011)
[187] (Linden & Maercker, 2011)

or wronged person to forgive may land like a lead balloon and the suggestion met with hostility. Some of the reasons one may be reluctant to forgive have been detailed in this research. For example, the perception that to forgive is to forget, or that one cannot continue to seek justice if they have forgiven the transgressor. Worthington (cited in Wier, 2017) states, that forgiveness may be seen as a weakness. "*To that I say, well, the person must not have tried it,*"[188] for learning to forgive takes practice and strength. One might think of it as 'a hard pill to swallow.' The benefits of forgiveness may far outweigh those of remaining embittered or vengeful, such as better mental and physical health and reduction in stress levels which could otherwise lead to anxiety, depression and psychiatric disorder. Forgiveness improves self-esteem[189] and in the process may reinstate a sense of personal power and control over one's emotions and life. One study found mental ill health was not predicted for people who experienced higher levels of stress over the course of their lifetime and scored high on forgiveness. The opposite was true for those who were unforgiving. "*The power of forgiveness to erase that link was surprising, Toussaint says,*" "*We thought forgiveness would knock something off the relationship [between stress and psychological distress], but we didn't expect it to zero it out*" (cited in Wier, 2017).[190] Empathy for others is one resource which can help with forgiveness. Trying to understand the other persons' situation. Prayer or meditations have been found to help with forgiveness, as this is a common practice in religion and spirituality.[191] However, this may not be possible where people have lost faith in their religious or spiritual beliefs following a traumatic incident or moral injury (see Religious or Spiritual Coping).

Protection and prevention in the workplace against the development of embitterment reactions is beneficial to the individual, the organisation and the wider community. "*anger and frustration at the organisation can*

---

[188] (Wier, 2017)
[189] (Wier, 2017)
[190] (Wier, 2017)
[191] (Wier, 2017)

produce significant and long-lasting emotional distress" (Mitchell et al., 2001:44). Dunn (2016) research into chronic embitterment in NHS Trusts, states the mental health of staff has a direct impact on the quality of care patients receive. However, the connection between good outcomes for patients and good mental health of staff is not being made.[192] Sensky et al. (2015) state, identifying embitterment and implementing interventions early on, could prevent escalation and entrenchment of symptoms. He goes on to state, that it is important for the organisation to follow their own policies and procedures to ensure 'procedural justice.' This may then prevent embitterment reactions.[193]

Religious and Spiritual Coping

Models of Moral Injury (such as MISS-M), include loss of religious faith as a significant factor affecting military veterans exposed to combat trauma. For example, witnessing events which challenge or shatter one's belief in God.

How could a benevolent, loving God allow atrocities to happen to innocents? Park et al. (2018) states, the interplay between religious or spiritual coping (RS coping) and conditions such as depression, posttraumatic stress and suicidality, is complex. The individuals' degree of faith or spirituality, negative or positive RS coping, and the degree of combat exposure may affect mental health outcomes. Negative RS coping is defined as spiritual discontent and struggle. Positive RS coping is defined as seeking spiritual support and viewing situations with spiritual benevolence. Research showed negative RS coping was associated with PTSD. However, the study also identified that *"those with high combat [exposure] and high positive [religious/spiritual] coping had the highest levels of PTSD symptoms."*[194] This finding may suggest, that individuals who hold

---

[192] (Dunn, Chronic Embitterment in the NHS, 2016)
[193] (Sensky, Salimu, Ballard, & Pereira, 2015)
[194] (Park, et al., 2018)

firm religious or spiritual beliefs are significantly more susceptible to PTSD, caused by Moral Injury and high operational exposure. Furthermore, this hypothesis could correlate with Linden and Maercker (2011) statement, that PTED is more likely attributed to those who are *"devoted persons with strict convictions and beliefs"* (p.85). This perhaps supports their findings, that the ability to adopt new beliefs and adapt to change can buffer individuals against the development of PTED. Park et al. (2018) results contradict each other within the study to some extent, stating: positive RS coping was not associated with PTSD symptoms, yet high combat exposure, with high RS coping resulted in higher PTSD symptoms. *"RS coping may have not only been ineffective in alleviating symptoms of PTSD but may actually have strengthened the influence of high combat exposure....combat exposure was significantly and positively associated with PTSD symptoms. Only high combat exposure was significantly positively associated with Perceived Posttraumatic Growth (PPTG),"* yet states, *"positive RS coping was significantly and positively associated with PPTG, but was not related to PTSD symptoms."*[195] Loss of faith in military veterans exposed to Moral Injury, was found to be more common than an increase in religious or spiritual views. Provision of spiritual care which could improve wellness for morally injured veterans is potentially lacking.[196]

Shame can create Narcissism

Perhaps the most significant symptoms of PTED and MI are feelings of betrayal, injustice, humiliation, shame, guilt, negative self-concept (low self-esteem) and revenge fantasy; as well as a persistent pursuit of justice and/or punishment of the person perceived as the 'wrongdoer.' Linden and Maercker (2011) state, people with PTED are less likely to seek help and are resistant to change, even aggressive, when faced with an opportunity to view a perceived injustice from another perspective.

[195] (Park, et al., 2018)
[196] (Williamson, Greenberg, & Murphy, 2019)

There may be a sense of self-righteousness. Embittered persons can create a toxic environment for those around them due to self-centred rumination on their needs and feelings. Dr Ramani, Clinical Psychologist and specialist in narcissism states, the rage of a narcissist has a shame-based origin. Shame elicits rumination on a plan for revenge against the person who triggered the shame.[197] Rotter (2011) states, *"narcissistic and paranoid personality disorders........involve a specific underlying vulnerability to traumatic stress and prolonged reactive embitterment."*[198] Krizan and Johar (2014) state, there are two types of narcissistic personality. The grandiose person with high self-esteem and low emotional distress, linked to a dominant character; and the vulnerable person who is introverted, has low self-esteem and high emotional distress. The vulnerable narcissist may be viewed as complaining, bitter and defensive. Other traits are suspiciousness, angry rumination, distrust, feelings of dejection and shame, acts of rage, hostility and aggression (including reactive and displaced aggression), vindictiveness, resentment and revenge fantasy.

Reactions to minor perceived provocations can result in disproportionate and misdirected anger.[199] Kohut (1972; cited in Krizan and Johar, 2014) states, *"The need for revenge, for righting a wrong, for undoing a hurt by whatever means, and a deeply anchored, unrelenting compulsion in the pursuit of all these aims...are the characteristic features of narcissistic rage in all its forms."* In summary, there is a potential cross-over between PTED or MI symptoms and the behaviour of people with vulnerable (not grandiose) narcissistic traits, including associated causes of rage (such as shame, perceived insults or humiliations).

---

[197] (Durvasula, 2020)
[198] (Linden & Maercker, 2011)
[199] (Krizan & Johar, 2014)

Emotional Intelligence

Emotional Intelligence is a concept coined by Mayer and Salovey in 1990. This model is used to explain the ability of one to assess the feelings and emotions of self and others; and convert this understanding into thoughts and actions in response. Daniel Goleman took up the mantle in 1995 and published a book on Emotional Intelligence (EQ), stating EQ was more important for success than IQ. He identified self-awareness, self-management, social awareness and social skills as core strengths in EQ. However, he was not able to explain how to develop EQ.[200] Mikolajczak et al. (2009), undertook research into the potential protective factor of Emotional Intelligence (EI) against self-harm and the promotion of emotion regulation. Individuals with strong EI trait were found to have good coping skills and ability to self-regulate emotions. This reduced the risk of self-harm practices. Furthermore, the suggestion was made that self-harm, versus EI is a "*choice of coping strategies.*" Rumination, self-blame and helplessness were identified as maladaptive emotions, adopted as coping strategies that positively correlated with self-harm.[201] Research has suggested self-harm is a strategy for self-punishment, to alleviate dissociative symptoms, prevent outward aggression to others and an expression of emotions such as anger, guilt, loneliness and self-hatred. Anger, aggression, withdrawal (loneliness), guilt and negative self-concept (self-hatred) are significant features in PTED, MI, PTSD and CPTSD. Therefore, research into EI as a protective factor against the development of these conditions and cognitions may be of benefit.

Mikolajczak et al. (2009), suggest the purposes of self-harm may be "*the avoidance of unwanted emotions (i.e. distract oneself from intolerable feelings), their materialization (i.e. make the emotional pain tangible) and/or their*

---

[200] (Golis, 2020)
[201] (Mikolajczak, Petrides, & Hurry, 2009)

alteration (self-harm may cause the releasing of endorphins that, in turn, produce analgesia and a sense of well-being)."

EI traits in personality relate to 1) adaptability and flexibility to change, 2) assertiveness in situations and the ability to 'stand up for oneself', 3) the ability to perceive and understand the emotions of oneself and others, 4) the ability to express feelings to others, 5) the ability to influence the feelings of others 6) the ability to control one's own emotions and not act on impulse or urges (emotional regulation), 6) the ability to maintain positive relationships, 7) Good level of self-esteem and confidence 8) Self-motivation and ability to cope with adversity 9) Good level of social awareness and social skills 10) ability to manage stress levels and pressure 11) the ability to empathise with others and their perspective 12) a cheerful personality and general satisfaction with life, and 13) optimism.[202] Mattingly and Kraiger (2019), reviewed works on the subject of training participants in the personal development of EI, to identify if EI can be taught. The research found only a moderate positive effect of EI training on individuals, regardless of the training model used.[203] Therefore assessing the EI of staff employed in people management roles (such as Human Resources and Occupational Health) or in supervisory positions, may be beneficial; particularly to bring balance to procedural matters and consideration for the individual at the centre of process and procedure.

Organisational safeguards and working practices

Chronic embitterment, feelings of injustice and moral injury are common experiences within the workplace (as discussed within this research). Sickness absence, operational effectiveness, budget spending, early ill health retirement, litigation, impact on clinical services and on mental

---

[202] (Mikolajczak, Petrides, & Hurry, 2009)
[203] (Mattingly & Kraiger, 2019)

health can all be significantly affected by the working practices of the organisation and individual employees. Advice and guidance for organisations on people management, systems and health and safety are widely available through regulatory agencies such as the Health and Safety Executive, Advisory, Conciliation and Arbitration Service (ACAS), Equality and Human Rights Commission and legislation such as the Equality Act 2010, Working Time Regulations and other employment policies. However, guidance, policy and procedure are only one small part of effective people management. The organisation and its employees need to work within shared and unwritten moral codes of right and wrong. They need to demonstrate competency, common decency, trustworthiness and emotional intelligence. Each individual in the organisation has a responsibility to do the right thing. Ones' intention and integrity are of importance for creating a sense of safety, security and trust in the workplace. Sensky et al. (2015), noted the importance of perceived procedural justice as a protective factor against the development of Burnout in staff.[204] Embitterment has been linked to Burnout.[205] Sinek (2014) states, *"Leaders who put a premium on numbers over lives are, more often than not, physically separated from the people they serve"* (p.102). He states, a 'command and control culture' increases stress levels which can push people to become self-centred for the sake of one's own preservation, over and above the needs of others. He states, when leaders give employees a noble cause, compelling reason or other moral code to pursue, this gives them the power to do 'the right thing' even if this means temporarily sacrificing personal comfort. When leaders prioritize their responsibility to provide care and welfare to employees over 'numbers', people will follow them. Employees will help leaders achieve their vision the right way, rather than taking short cuts or going against moral codes and values. Sinek states, when weak leaders only share the circle of safety and associated benefits with a select few and/or senior colleagues, others are aware of the lack of protection. They

---

[204] (Sensky, Salimu, Ballard, & Pereira, 2015)
[205] (Szczygiel & Mikolajczak, 2018) (Sensky, Salimu, Ballard, & Pereira, 2015)

respond by forming small tribes (cliques) of their own and mistakes are covered up, not exposed. A sense of insecurity replaces that of safety and cooperation. Therefore, this culture can result in moral breaches and injustice. Empathy for one another and cooperation are vital to safety and security within organisations. In frontline services employees are perhaps more likely to experience persistent levels of cortisol in their system due to repeated traumatic exposure and life threatening situations, as well as a sense of continuous threat from within the organisation (such as disciplinary, unsatisfactory performance procedure, ostracization and corruption). Cortisol is responsible for paranoia, the break-down of the immune system, aggression, self-centredness and lack of empathy for others. Sinek states, this *"makes us even more selfish and less concerned about one another or the organisation"* (p.56). He states, *"why add another degree of difficulty by fighting against each other when......already forced to struggle against the hardships of .... limited resources or other outside threats?"*(p.35). He goes on to state, that when we cooperate or look out for others, Serotonin and Oxytocin are released and the feelings we get from this chemical help us form bonds of trust, friendship and camaraderie. Feelings of safety increase, stress reduces, our desire to serve others is activated, as is our willingness to trust others. Poor leadership results in distrust, paranoia, aggression and selfishness. Cortisol is the chemical responsible for anxiety and stress which is released in response to potential danger. It is not meant to be a constant feature in our system. It can *"cause lasting damage if we have to live in a perpetual sense of fear or anxiety."* Cortisol blocks Oxytocin which enables empathy towards others.[206] The case studies in this research demonstrate the importance of the organisation supporting the individual and their needs, opposed to treating employees as a number or statistic. The study also highlights the impact of procedural justice or injustice on the individuals' mental health, as well as tempering standard operating procedure with consideration for the human being at the centre of process. As highlighted in the previous section, the level of EQ

---

[206] (Sinek, 2014)

(emotional intelligence) in staff working within people management roles (such as human resources, occupational health and supervision) is important for maintaining or increasing a sense of safety and security for colleagues in the workplace. The practice of EQ may also protect staff against moral injury and embitterment. Sinek states, "*We don't just trust people to obey the rules, we also trust that they know when to break them. The rules are there for normal operations. We trust the expertise of a special few people to know when to break the rules*" (P.74). For example, in an emergency situation and for the benefit and safety of others. He states, that in weak organisations "*too many people will break the rules for personal gain. In strong organisations people will break the rules because it is the right thing to do for others*" (p.73). This demonstrates how a breach of agreed rules, boundaries, values and morals may be tolerated or appreciated by the wider group when there is trust in the overriding intention behind the action or decision. Unfortunately, following the rules rigidly because of fear of disciplinary or job security may take precedence over achieving the task or doing what needs to be done in organisations with weak leadership.[207]

The next case study demonstrates how an organisation can potentially repair a damaged employer/employee relationship and provide appropriate support in the workplace.

Case Study 6 – First Responder

On 22nd May 2017, there was a terrorist attack on the Manchester Arena when people were leaving a concert being held there. A suicide bomber detonated a homemade device. 23 people died and 139 were injured. Over half the casualties were children. This officer had been involved in the aftermath of the Attack and was subsequently diagnosed with Chronic PTSD. The officer stated, "I think I had managed to stay in work

---

[207] (Sinek, 2014)

on pure adrenalin between May 2017 and June 2017. Issues in relation to the organisation, included their reluctance and refusal to record and recognise her psychological injury as an 'Injury on Duty' (IOD), lack of support and timely treatment. She stated, *"This was a really difficult time and a time when I became completely at odds with the Force."* The organisation finally agreed to record the IOD two years after the incident.

The researcher asked the officer to explain how she had been able to continue working for the police service when trust had been damaged. How did the organisation repair their relationship with you?

She stated, *"Once they had given me the IOD, I started to feel believed and that they were accepting some responsibility. I found out a few years later that frontline officers had been given an IOD within months of the attack, without needing to go before a panel which I found very unfair."* Once the IOD had been acknowledged, the organisation reimbursed the officer for the cost of private psychological assessments and treatment. They overturned their original decision to reduce the officers' pay to half, then nil after coming under pressure from a police charity who advocated for her. The charity supported her request to the organisation for medical redeployment to an alternative role; one which accommodated her needs and disabilities. She explains that, *"prior to this I was caught in a situation where I felt like a number and felt too unwell to do the inappropriate job they were offering me. The charity intervened directly to the Chief Constable and overturned their decision."* The officer had support from the Force Medical Officer (FMO), stating she had protection from the equality act 2010 due to her depression at the time. The FMO also supported the reinstatement of full pay and medical redeployment. The officer stated, *"this began some level of repair, as feeling believed was really important to me. You have to fight them on many fronts and get as many different sources of support as you can to make representations on your behalf."*

The officer stated, it was important that she was not 'pushed too hard' when she returned to work in a new role. She stated she still had extreme anxiety, memory loss and fatigue. She was thankful to be relocated to a department with previous experience of supporting colleagues affected by psychological injury. The organisation facilitated a phased return to work on reduced hours. The officer stated, "*I have a little satisfaction that under the NHS act, the organisation pays each month for my prescription medication. I feel like this is an admission of liability. It keeps me content that this is their way of taking some responsibility for what happened to me.*" The officer stated she was relieved to be told there were no expectations placed on her. The first few months in her new position were about seeing if the role suited her and her abilities. She stated this took some pressure off. The officer was placed under the supervision of a supportive Sergeant who was welfare focused and aware. "*She let me go to my remaining treatment sessions during work time without asking too many questions. She would offer me the opportunity to work from home if I was upset. All of these things helped me to trust my new unit and to work hard for them as soon as I was back to full strength. They also did a stress risk assessment with me but did this authentically and not as my previous Supervisor had done; as a paper exercise. My present unit has also treated me well during the Covid -19 period. I was very anxious in the early weeks of the virus hitting the UK. I didn't want to leave the house and was constantly worried about becoming infected. I have been told recently that due to my PTSD, the Coronavirus situation is a matching trigger due to my fear of death. I wrote an honest email to my Sergeant, who upon receipt contacted me and authorised my working from home and also issued me with a work tablet to access my emails. I am also given a welfare check by text each morning from one of the Sergeants on duty that day. I am feeling less like a number due to this support.*" However, staying in the organisation can be difficult and carries the risk of being retraumatising or triggering. This officer stated, "*The police environment surrounds you constantly with trauma, despair, death, and violence. I am not participating physically on the front line due to being non-operational now, but it is always there, just below the surface. You are exposed to information that you only get to know about when you are a Police Officer. I run my life at a slower pace now which I resisted at first, but it was forced upon me. I must live this way now, but I don't think on reflection that is such a bad thing. Covid-19 has been much easier for me than maybe for others, as I love that the world has slowed down.*

The researcher asked: Please explain how you were exposed to embittered others within the police; yet you chose a different path: The officer stated, "*I did not want to give them my suicide. They hide suicides and don't care.*" She stated, others had told her that the Home Office would laugh all the way to the bank if she resigned and did not get the pension she was entitled to, after paying into it for so many years. The officer stated, she knew her psychological injury had resulted from inadequate treatment from the organisation after the Arena attack. As such, she stated she was "*steadfast in having them admit this and give me my IOD status. I saw how ill many people had become, trying to get their forces to treat them with respect for the service they had given. This was never going to happen. I see now you are just a number. I knew that trying to tell them they were treating people inhumanely, sadly was futile. You have to decide to stay or go, and make it happen relatively quickly. You have a small window before you fall into the abyss of HR and Occupational health. You have to use the last piece of energy left inside you to use all sources at your disposal to fight. For me this was my GP, my EMDR therapist, my psychologist report with PTSD diagnosis, the Police Federation and police charities.*"

The researcher asked: What coping strategies did you use to not become embittered?: The officer stated, "*I learned from a police charity that you have to be proactive and either use your time off sick to get a new job or get treatment. I did both.*" The officer had a Curriculum Vitae written and paid for her own training and certification in Mental Health First Aid. She stated, she came to the realization that recovery was a long-term goal. Her marriage and relationship with her children would be damaged if unable to manage anger, heavy drinking and depression. She stated, 'the job' does not care about the impact on home life. Being able to identify the trauma which caused the onset of PTSD, opened up some avenues for access to free support specifically funded for the Manchester Arena attack. As a result, the officer received EMDR treatment which significantly reduced her experience of intrusive images. The officer stated, she accessed counselling through another police charity and "*constantly tried to understand what was wrong with me through my own reading and research.*" The officer has kept up with treatment (after three years) and stated, "*I hope to have a long life still ahead of me. I must not let my avoidance strategies get in the way of living the best life I can, being the best wife and mother. After all, my family did not ask for me to change due to just doing my job. I tried not to let myself be a victim. I knew I would go under if that happened.*" While the officer was off work, she accessed recreational therapy such as wood craft with a military charity, a sailing challenge on a voyage of recovery and joined a community choir made up of victims of the Arena attack.

She also volunteered at the Manchester Museum archiving memorial items left after the attack. The officer stated, "*all these activities and connection with others, helped me find my self-esteem again and allowed me to find my new self which I continue to do.*" The officer stated each treatment has helped her to get better, particularly private treatment. She recognises the need to 'hold back' and keep some boundaries in place when supporting others; stating, "*I cannot let myself be absorbed into someone else's pain again. I want to be emotionally unavailable and am aware that I have a tendency to completely put myself in another's shoes and try to rescue them. I did this after the bomb. I have a protection valve now that stops me doing that. An alarm bell goes off if I get too close professionally to anyone who needs a lot of support. I deal with this by signposting them to someone who can help.*" She recognises her personal limitations, where perhaps she did not consider her own welfare and self-care in the past. She also recognises personal limitations in trying to change the organisation. She stated, "*I select the amount of pain I let into my life now. I keep it to manageable loads. I see one of my roles now as helping others identify when they are affected by trauma and encourage them to ask for help when they need it. I think I have been given a gift in the role I am in, to help officers and tell them about Mental Health in a way that wasn't explained to me. I look after myself better now and practise self-care. I am much better now at asking for help."*

The researcher noted that this officer chose to adopt wisdom practices and emotional intelligence to counteract negativity in the environment and within herself. She spoke of being proactive and taking control of her situation. Not only was she determined to seek justice; she was also conscious that trying to change the culture and attitude within the organisation may be futile, unrealistic or unachievable. Therefore, she made a plan for staying in the organisation and a plan for leaving if it became necessary. This officer was open to the prospect of change, despite her long years of commitment and investment in the police service. She recognised her deeply held values, putting her family's needs and that of her own welfare and quality of life over and above her vocation and the organisation. Perhaps due to a new appreciation for life and time spent with loved ones, which can occur following trauma. She states she has hope; an antidote to feelings of helplessness, so often associated with chronic embitterment and moral injury. This officer has found meaning and purpose in her new role. A role where she can do her best to raise awareness of traumatic stress in other officers and one where she feels valued. The organisation was unsupportive for a length of time. Fortunately, they enabled the repair of the relationship with this officer to some degree. The actions taken by the organisation restored a sense of justice to this officer. She states, she feels the organisation has demonstrated responsibility for the Injury on Duty through their actions (such as paying for treatment and medication and reinstating full pay). This officer perceives the lack of support, intervention and timely treatment, as the main cause of the psychological injury and not the traumatic incident itself. *"dissatisfaction with organizational support predicted PTSD symptoms in police officers" (Carlier et al., 1997).* Because the organisation has now accommodated her individual needs in a supportive way; the perception of herself as 'just a number' may have been ameliorated. The organisation dynamically assesses the needs of this officer as and when they arise; rather than adopt a static risk assessment which does not allow for change and relapse. Both parties take a flexible approach. This officer rewards the organisation for their support with continued commitment, stating they *"helped me to trust my new unit and to work hard for them as soon as I was back to full strength."* Therefore, there was mutual effort and benefit. The officer describes her journey of Posttraumatic Growth (as in Tedeschi and Calhoun, 2004). She recognises the need to continue pushing through her distress and difficulties, such as avoidant behaviour, to confront those fears and anxieties in order to live her best life and to achieve. She states, she has regained self-esteem and is finding *"my new self which I continue to do."* This officer recognises the need to take control of her own future, health and family life. She understands that the organisation has a responsibility to support her and she has a responsibility to help herself. She has consciously avoided the mindset of victimization (a common feature in embittered persons). The officer stated this experience has given her a gift. The next section discusses possible treatments and therapies for PTED and MI.

CHAPTER 6

Treatment and Therapy

Dean et al. (2019) state, that treating Moral Injury (MI) with the same techniques used for PTSD since the Vietnam war is ineffective, because PTSD is driven by fear. MI is motivated by insults to one's moral code and core beliefs; symptoms not associated with PTSD.[208] However, Deprince (2001) found that betrayal predicted PTSD 'above and beyond' fear. Furthermore, that fear did not significantly predict PTSD arousal or anxiety. This finding could lead to a re-evaluation of appropriate treatment for PTSD.[209]

In relation to MI, Bryan et al. (2015) stated, that receiving forgiveness and understanding from support networks and the ability to forgive oneself, can inhibit feelings of guilt, shame, self-blame and difficulty with forgiveness and '*can block the pathway from perceived transgression to symptoms of posttraumatic stress disorder (PTSD).....*' [210] This could perhaps be interpreted as forgiveness, understanding and support from others having the effect of cutting off neural pathways between Moral Injury and the development of PTSD; thereby preventing or resolving PTSD symptoms altogether. Four years later, Koenig (2019) hypothesized that treatment specifically for MI in those with PTSD could help stabilize and manage PTSD symptoms and possibly even resolve the condition entirely.

---

[208] (Dean, Talbot, & Dean, 2019)
[209] (Deprince A. , 2001)
[210] (Bryan, Anestis, Bryan, & Anestis, 2015)

Furthermore, untreated MI could be rendering PTSD treatment ineffective and this is why the subject of Moral Injury is receiving so much attention.[211]

Litz et al. (cited in Molendijk, Kramer & Verweij, 2018), are not of the view that MI is a pathological issue that needs treatment. However, the opinion is that the resolution of MI is important for effective treatment of PTSD. The aim is to help people reach self-forgiveness and to accept their imperfections.[212]

PTED and MI are not currently recognized as clinical conditions, which may impact on research into any potential benefits of prescribed medication on associated symptoms. However, Zisook and Shear (2009) state, medication prescribed for depression may have a positive effect on prolonged grief disorder; for which, depression is a symptom.[213] Therefore, medication used to treat symptoms of PTSD, Anxiety and Depression, may have the potential to impact positively or negatively on symptoms of PTED and MI, which can be comorbid with these conditions. This may be another area of research to explore.

The US Department of Veterans Affairs have been testing interventions targeted specifically at MI in veterans. One such treatment is Adaptive Disclosure, which consists of eight sessions. The therapy assists veterans with talking about the event and its meaning. They are asked to have conversation with the person who has been lost, which is forgiving and compassionate in nature. Participating Marines showed significant reduction in PTSD symptoms.[214] The creators of Adaptive Disclosure, (Litz, Lebowitz, Gray and Nash, 2016) describe a therapy somewhat reminiscent of Gestalt therapy and the 'Empty Chair Technique, (first established in the 1940's by Fritz Perls) which, asks the person to have dialogue in the present with the person they imagine to be sitting in the

---

[211] (Koenig, 2019)
[212] (Molendijk, Kramer, & Verweij, 2018)
[213] (Zisook & Shear, 2009)
[214] (Maguen & Litz, 2020)

empty chair. One can express feelings towards the transgressor or lost person and explain the impact of the incident on them.[215] It is stated, to *'alleviate unresolved anger, pain, anxiety, resentment, and other negative feelings.'*[216] Though Adaptive Disclosure is presented as a new therapy specific to Moral Injury in military settings; Litz et al. (2016) state, this is a *"packaged and sequenced…hybrid of existing CBT strategies, exposure therapy, cognitive- based treatments (e.g Cognitive Processing Therapy – CPT), [and] techniques drawn from other traditions (e.g Gestalt, psychodynamic therapy, mindfulness)"* (p.8). Therefore; Litz et al., have taken existing therapeutic interventions and rebranded these under the name Adaptive disclosure. Where this therapeutic model may differ, is training *"care providers to understand, honor, and accommodate the military ethos and the unique phenomenology of war trauma"* (p.9). The aim of Adaptive Disclosure is to alter the perception of blame with forgiveness and compassion. The ethos being, *"1) pain means hope. Anguish, guilt and shame are signs of an intact conscience and self-and other expectations about goodness, humanity and justice; 2) goodness is reclaimable over the long haul and 3) forgiveness (of self and others) and repair are possible regardless of the transgression"* (p.18).[217] The researcher notes, that Litz et al. (2016) definition of Moral Injury, which informs the development of their programme Adaptive Disclosure, appears to intentionally omit the prospect that one may be on the receiving end of a morally injurious act, insult, humiliation, wrongdoing or injustice. Their book on Adaptive Disclosure focuses on witnessing, failing to prevent and perpetrating Moral Injury. It is perhaps naïve to suggest military personnel will not be directly affected by someone else's actions or behaviour. For example, in their model *"the experience of a service member who is angry and demoralized over betrayal by a trusted leader, whose ruthless and capricious decision led to the unnecessary death of civilians"* (p.20), may be morally injurious. However, there seems to be no provision for 'a service

---

[215] (MentalHealth.net, 2020)
[216] (PsychologyToday, 2020)
[217] (Litz, Lebowitz, Gray, & Nash, 2016)

member who is angry and demoralized over betrayal by a trusted leader, whose ruthless and capricious decision led to the preventable injury to the service member, which resulted in his/her loss of limb/or loss of career.' The researcher questions the reasoning or rationale for this decision.

Linden and Maercker (2011) on embitterment disorder, state that developing positive feelings and forgiveness towards one's transgressor may not be necessary to overcome feelings of revenge or emotional distress. Expressing emotions, thoughts of revenge and acknowledging them should be the goal of therapy. Suppressing emotions does not lessen their negative affect; it just changes the way the negative emotions are expressed, "*So feelings of anger and bitterness still burn within an individual and interfere with daily functioning.*" Furthermore, 'traumatic after affects' can only be eradicated when one gives up on rumination and desire for revenge. Revenge phenomena, MI and PTSD can be connected. Linden and Maercker (2011), suggest Wisdom Therapy (a new treatment specifically designed for PTED) and Emotion-Focused therapy as possible remedies; giving "*permission to fully feel and express what was previously not allowed or possible... validation of these feelings and acknowledgement of the extent of the violation*" (Linden & Maercker, 2011:97). The section on 'Predisposing factors and prevention' in this research, details examples of 'wisdom' skills and associated personality traits.

Those who are morally injured or embittered and find difficulty in forgiving may benefit from 'forgiveness therapy,' such as Enrights' forgiveness therapy or Worthingtons' REACH forgiveness model. Therapy aims to present the perpetrator as a 'wounded person' needing empathy and understanding, rather than a stereotypical 'bad' person.[218]

---

[218] (Wier, 2017)

Results of Enrights' forgiveness therapy have shown the amelioration of depression, anxiety, PTSD and Fibromyalgia in survivors of abuse.[219]

Sports and Recreational Therapy

Sail training for the relief of PTSD, Depression and Embitterment

A five day voyage of recovery was organised by a police charity for a group of officers suffering with (C)PTSD, Depression and embitterment reactions in association with the project 'Sailing Tectona.' The ship is a wooden sailing vessel with traditional rigging and sails. Everyone slept onboard, lived together, cooked and ate together and sailed the ship. The officers participating were the crew for the voyage. They learnt how to sail and navigate. Hoisting sails and raising the anchor took team work and good communication. For some, the challenge of overcoming sea sickness was also part of the experience. The voyage was transformational for the participants, as evidenced by their testimonials. The experience, aside from being positive and enjoyable; perhaps reframed world views, self-concept, self-esteem and feelings of value. The key ingredients seem to be kindness, support, cooperation, patience, encouragement, safety, time away from mundane and stressful normal life issues or responsibilities, regained meaning and purpose, value within the group (one which doesn't work without each individual), self-compassion, empathy for others and validation from others.

Sailing Testimonial: I am so happy to be able to talk about my experience during a week onboard Tectona. The ship is full of positivity and kindness, so much so I was worried to come off and join the real world again. I have never experienced anything like this before and thank all the staff on the Tectona, and the others who joined me for the week sailing. I have to admit that on the first experience of sailing I felt a sudden

---

[219] (Freedman & Enright, 2017)

dread and feeling of worry around what I have let myself in for. The next morning the feeling of togetherness and friendship quickly helped me snap out of that and begin to enjoy the week. I don't think there was anything which I disliked. Even being split up to do the daily tasks created a team atmosphere where everyone was happy to join in. Learning about the ship and how the sails work was great and to see what we achieved each day arriving in the stunning ports or the secluded beach, proved hard work paid off. It was good to be able to chat to others who have similar struggles and makes you realise you aren't alone. I normally struggle to sleep but this wasn't a problem on Tectona. It was as though symptoms and struggles I have at home had all disappeared whilst on board. Chats around the table at the end of the day brought positivity to the group and excitement for what's going to happen next. I had so many brilliant experiences, but I think my favourite part was waking up each morning and going up on deck to see the amazing views in each port. I really hope to sail on Tectona again and do many more activities with this fabulous bunch of people who became my friends overnight. I hope to use the positivity at home in my daily life and think about the momentum Tectona has given me to achieve targets and goals. Thank you to all the Crew who supported and guided us through the trip with patience and a sense of humour throughout.

Sailing Testimonial: I have CPTSD and find I struggle around groups of people. I decided to be open minded and take myself out of my comfort zone. Putting myself forward for the challenge was a positive in itself. One of my challenges was struggling with tying knots and feeling overwhelmed and unable to think clearly and logically....but all the crew were patient and supportive and encouraging. One of the ways I cope in general is to become insular and so by putting myself amongst a group of people I had never met, in a confined space was another challenge. It was good to prove I could do this and adjust to it. I enjoyed being part of a team working together to sail a tall ship out on the sea, being close to nature, seeing several pods of dolphins, being around supportive people who understand PTSD from lived experience, learning new skills, having fun and lots of laughs. The day to day sailing was done either in pairs or small teams and this provided opportunities to work together for a common goal and get physical exercise. It was lovely to observe fellow crew mates sharing how the voyage was helping them with their confidence and symptoms of PTSD. For me the main qualities were resilience, determination, perseverance and a sense of achievement. These are being carried over into my daily life. This was a unique opportunity and one I am grateful to have been involved in. This experience has left a strong bond between all of us and as we went back to our daily lives its lovely how we are staying in touch and giving each other support and encouragement via our social media group. A massive thank you to all who sailed on her, for making it such a memorable experience.

Sailing Testimonial: So, with some apprehension I signed up for the Sailing Challenge. It kept me going through some dark times leading up to the flight I needed to take to Exeter. After landing, one of the team kindly agreed to pick myself and another team member up from the airport. That was to start a great friendship between us that kept us going through the week onboard. I was nervous as I stepped off dry land and was taken by dinghy to the ship. We were shown to our bunks and that was to be the beginning of a brilliant week filled with camaraderie, laughter, challenges; and a real sense of achievement. Due to the patience of the crew and my fellow team mates, I soon started to say yes to the physical and mental requirements of sailing a tall ship and making sure we were all fed and the ship was clean. I had allowed myself to say no to speaking to people, leaving the house, answering the door, going food shopping and opening my mail for a while. This opportunity was make or break. I didn't think I would have the opportunity to test myself in such a safe and supportive environment again, so I gave it a go. My confidence started to grow with each task I completed. I was never made to feel an idiot and I started to take a chance on sharing my true self with the crew and team. I realised how much I had missed banter and having a laugh. Each day I started to find a little bit more of myself. Now I say yes to new experiences and am living the life I want with the bonus of learning from the dark times, and reflecting on the amazing sailing challenge I was lucky enough to experience.

Sailing Testimonial - I wanted to share what's been happening this week. My husband is determined to keep moving forward in his recovery since returning from the sailing challenge. He has been working with a therapist for a couple of months, undertaking graduated exposure therapy. He chose to visit a small café with me and sit outside with a coffee. We did this twice this week, which was amazing. He also chose to come to yoga. He has never been able to make it through the door before. Tonight, we are having a family BBQ which is unheard of. He rarely goes in the garden, as he would be scared he was being watched and investigated by the police while off long term sick. Some of these activities may seem every day to some people but for us they never happen. I can't quite put into words how I feel to look into his face and see him relaxed and happy. I'm so proud of him.

Charities offering recreational therapy

There are various charities, not for profit organisations and companies offering recreational and sports therapy for military and blue light services. These include the use of expeditions, bush craft and wild camping, photography, woodwork, art therapy, athletics, sail training and volunteering to name a few.

Yaghini (2020) states, meaning and purpose can be reclaimed by reframing existing skills developed in frontline services and utilising these in alternative environments. For example, matching military veterans to altruistic projects in underdeveloped countries where the veterans' skills can make a positive difference to humanity and conservation. This encourages individuals to take control of their own healing and recovery.

The work can reconnect individuals to feelings of empathy for others, compassion for self and decrease self-centred ruminations.[220]

Caddick and Smith (2014) refer to Carless et al. (2013) and team sport "*bringing me back to myself…to reconnect with aspects of their previous identity and sense of self that were highly valued in a military context.*" Benefits of sport and recreation for mental wellbeing in veterans with PTSD include, determination, coping, focus on ability (not disability), identity (sense of self and positive self-concept) and self-actualization (achievement).[221]

The officer in case study 1 with complex PTSD, depression, agoraphobia, anxiety and obsessive compulsive disorder stated: "*I have found solace in art therapy. My mind needs to be kept focussed otherwise I regress. My obsessive-compulsive disorder (although debilitating) helps me to a degree. I believe the only reason PTSD took so long to come out was due to having things such as sports and hobbies to obsess about over the years. The downside is that it's an obsession that my mind takes to the extreme.*"

The first Invictus Games were held in 2014 and the Duke of Sussex created the Invictus Games Foundation, with the aim of holding this event annually. "*The word 'Invictus' means 'unconquered'. It embodies the fighting spirit of wounded, injured and sick Service personnel and personifies what these tenacious men and women can achieve post injury. The Games harness the power of sport to inspire recovery, [and] support rehabilitation…*" There is a focus on ability, not disability. The last two lines of a poem by William Ernest Henley, adopted by the Games are "*I am the master of my fate, I am the Captain of my soul.*" The Invictus Games has been held in three countries since the initial games in London, 2014. The Hague was due to host the games in 2020 and the event has been cancelled due to the coronavirus pandemic. The Invictus Games Foundation have been granted funding for 'Beyond the Finish Line' research, into the impact of

---

[220] (Yaghini, 2020)
[221] (Caddick & Smith, 2014)

sports on the recovery of competitors. Posttraumatic Growth is another area receiving attention and is discussed in the next section.

CHAPTER 7

Post-Traumatic Growth - PTG

"That which does not kill us makes us stronger" - Friedrich Nietzsche. "I can be changed by what happens to me, but I refuse to be reduced by it" – Maya Angelou. Posttraumatic Growth was a term first coined in 1996 by Tedeschi and Calhoun. PTG is the concept of overcoming crisis through a process of struggle to reach positive outcomes - *"the idea that great good can come from great suffering is ancient"* (Tedeschi & Calhoun, 2004).[222] Posttraumatic Growth is often popularized by the metaphor of a caterpillar's metamorphosis and struggle to become a butterfly. Tedeschi and Calhoun (2004) state, PTG brings new perspectives on, and appreciation for life. Character, cognition and support are key factors in how one responds to trauma and opportunity for growth. One's history and wisdom combine with the process of PTG and this process never stops. The experience of anxiety, depression, sadness, guilt, anger and irritability are common following trauma and loss, however, may not be experienced in all cases. PTG is a process of adapting to negative life events. Tedeschi and Calhoun found that cases of growth far outweighed those resulting in psychiatric disorder, despite the major traumatic event(s). They state, that 'continuing personal distress and growth often co-exist.' PTG is 'change' in a person, improvement and positive outcome. Therefore, PTG is not the same as resilience to cope with crisis or optimism that all will end well. Tedeschi and Calhoun state, *"significant posttraumatic growth may require a significant threat or the shattering of fundamental schemas and may at times coexist with significant psychological distress."* Park et al. (2018) state, *"only high, and not moderate, combat exposure was associated with elevated Perceived Posttraumatic Growth scores*

---

[222] (Tedeschi & Calhoun, 2004)

relative to low exposure." The research suggested, that "*lack of findings* [for perceived posttraumatic growth in] *low levels of combat* [exposure] *may be due a significant amount of trauma being necessary in order to perceive one has grown from that experience.*"[223] PTG is of interest, when seeking to understand the opposing, negative response to the shattering of deeply held morals, values and beliefs, that is Moral Injury or PTED.

Linden and Maercker (2011), on the subject of PTED state, "*Some (few) people become wise in the course of their lives, others become embittered, and most of us become neither.*"[224] PTG is 'beating one's previous personal best' or as Tedeschi and Calhoun state, surpassing what was present before the crisis and adapting. People with good coping skills and resources may be less challenged by trauma and therefore, may be less likely to 'grow'. Tedeschi and Calhoun, propose that struggle is an essential part of PTG. Another model which may help explain this, is moving from the comfort zone to the fear zone, to the learning zone and finally to the growth zone. The comfort zone feels safe, familiar and controlled. One may leave the comfort zone of their own accord to seek growth and development, or there may be a catalyst which forces this to happen. The fear zone feels unsafe, unsure, out of control and fearful. This is the zone where one may make excuses for why they cannot do something, become avoidant and sensitive to the criticism of self and others. With perseverance and struggle, one may push on to the learning zone. This is where one becomes competent in their new skills and coping behaviour. Ones' comfort zone has expanded. This enables movement into the growth zone, where one sets goals and dreams, finds meaning and purpose and achieves aims and objectives.[225]

In the 'just world belief' hypothesis, people get what they deserve and deserve what they get. There are expectations as to how people will behave, the rules they comply with and how safe and secure one's world

---

[223] (Park, et al., 2018)
[224] (Linden & Maercker, 2011)
[225] (Saurel, 2019)

is.[226] Linden and Maercker (2011), use this hypothesis in relation to PTED, the shattering of beliefs, meaning and purpose and future orientation. Tedeschi and Calhoun relate PTG with a similar model called 'assumptive world', which is one's understanding of the world, why things happen, how to operate in the world and a sense of meaning and purpose. PTG *"is the individual's struggle with the new reality in the aftermath of trauma,"*[227] and finding new meaning and understanding of the world.

"Writer Reynolds Price (1994) described his paralysis from cancer this way: [Trauma forces a person] to be somebody else, the next viable you-a stripped-down whole other clear-eyed person, realistic as a sawed-off shotgun and thankful for air, not to speak of the human kindness you'll meet if you get normal luck" (cited in Tedeschi & Calhoun, 2004).

Trauma can strip one right back and undo a lifetime of conditioning; such as roles, rules and what one must do to fit in with society. When this conditioning is torn away, one sees the world and self with clearer vision. Re-engaging with society may feel like learning to walk and talk all over again. One may feel they no longer have anything in common with the people around them.

Following trauma, the mind can operate on auto-pilot, like a computer trying to process events. For example, intrusive memories and rumination. The programme keeps running. Tedeschi and Calhoun (2004) state, growth does not happen until one computes that living with the old system is no longer possible, *"disengagement from previous goals and assumptions"* occur and new systems, goals and meanings are adopted. PTG is a process that can take a long time.

A long period of distress may result in greater growth compared with a quick recovery. This is because the distress keeps the mental processes going. If recovery happens fast, this could be indicative of little disturbance to one's assumptive world or comfort zone. Sharing stories

---

[226] (Linden & Maercker, 2011)
[227] (Tedeschi & Calhoun, 2004)

of trauma and growth can create PTG in others vicariously, which is why peer support can be so valuable and important. Leading others with shared traumatic experiences to unite in a common goal, can bring change to society, attitudes, laws and culture.

For example, the socially unacceptable behaviour of drink driving, raising awareness of the dangers and laws brought in to deter or punish drink drivers.[228]

Linden and Maercker (2011) on PTED, Tedeschi and Calhoun (2004) on PTG, agree that wisdom is important for growth following trauma. An appreciation for the 'little things' in life, (like quality time spent with loved ones), openness to new experiences, adaptability to change and making new meaning in life can see people grow and develop in the aftermath of trauma, rather than succumb to embitterment.

Linden and Maercker (2011), and Dunn (2018) state, rumination on traumatic events may be a factor in the onset of embitterment; whereas Tedeschi and Calhoun (2004) state, rumination may be a necessary cognitive process for PTG.[229] Rumination may be helpful if reflective (processing and problem-solving) rather than brooding. One may "*React to painful experiences by reflection, learning, and growth, or by anger, disengagement, and bitterness.*" (Linden et al., 2011:70). Therefore, the type of rumination experienced may direct one to wisdom and growth or embitterment. Case study 6 is perhaps an example of PTG using wisdom, reflection, problem-solving skills and appreciation for life under ever present psychological distress in day to day life. The biology of the brain and how this may impact on posttraumatic growth, is discussed next.

---

[228] (Tedeschi & Calhoun, 2004)
[229] (Linden & Maercker, 2011) (Tedeschi & Calhoun, 2004)

Neurobiology and posttraumatic growth

Fujisawa et al. (2015) state, "*studies on PTG tend to focus on the psychological phenomena rather than on the neurological mechanisms, thus the neural mechanisms underlying PTG remain unclear.*" Their study into the 'neural basis of psychological growth following adverse experiences,' found that people with higher psychological growth after negative and stressful life events, have stronger activity within the rostral prefrontal cortex (rPFC) and superior parietal lobule (SPL) within the left Central Executive Network (CEN) in the brain. Furthermore, they discovered a positive association between PTG and the functional connectivity between the SPL and supramarginal gyrus (SMG), which is responsible for reasoning and understanding the mental states of others.[230] Participants were scored using the posttraumatic growth inventory scale, the impact of events scale for posttraumatic symptoms and the Beck depression inventory scale, as well as undergoing a magnetic resonance imaging (MRI) scan to record brain activity. Nakagawa et al. (2016), carried out research into the 'effects of post-traumatic growth on the dorsolateral prefrontal cortex after a disaster.' The study states, the dorsolateral prefrontal cortex (DLPFC), may be responsible for coping and resilience in cases of PTSD and brain activity that corresponds with PTG, may provide resilience against the development of PTSD. The study measured PTG in participants using the PTG inventory scale and MRI scans of regional grey matter volume (rGMV) in the Prefrontal cortex. PTG inventory scores, including scores for positively 'relating to others' following trauma, were significantly associated with the delta-rGMV in the right DLPFC. Nakagawa et al., concludes that the DLPFC seems to be responsible for brain activity relating to posttraumatic growth.[231] Therefore, the SMG and DLPFC may be important for empathizing with others, facilitating social interactions, seeking help, reappraisal of the

---

[230] (Fujisawa, et al., 2015)
[231] (Nakagawa, et al., 2016)

traumatic experience and understanding the event from the perspective of others. Studies into PTED, wisdom therapy and forgiveness therapy, have highlighted the positive effect of these cognitions on PTG and psychological recovery after distressing events. Neuroscience could potentially assist with measuring the effectiveness of various treatments for PTSD, MI and PTED using MRI scans and other measurements such as PTG inventory scale and PTED scale.

The next case study demonstrates potential posttraumatic growth for a former Royal Marine who experienced several significant and distressing life events.

Case Study 7

The researcher interviewed a former Royal Marine about a string of negative events he experienced, including his medical discharge and simultaneous disciplinary proceedings, the loss of his career, marriage and home. The interview was carried out via video link. He walked through the park and spoke on hands-free in the car during the interview. Keeping busy and active throughout, was a coping strategy which supported him to discuss emotive events.

When talking about his pursuit of becoming a diving instructor in the armed forces, he stated this was mutually beneficial. Being in this environment had a positive effect on him and reduced his symptoms of sensory overload. The role also enabled him to support others where there was a need for trained and specialized instructors. A medical event occurred following a scuba dive, which resulted in exploratory health checks. It transpired that he had a Patent Foramen Ovale (PFO – hole in the heart). This was to end his burgeoning diving career. The military would not fund an operation to repair the PFO. Nor could he obtain charitable funding. He took out a loan and raised money through a crowd funding page to cover the cost of the operation. Despite this successful medical procedure, the military would not allow him to continue as a diving instructor, stating it was not his primary role. He felt unsupported by the organisation. This had a negative impact on his mental health. He also had a torn ligament in his knee and was advised to take six weeks respite to enable recovery. At the time he was working as a physical training instructor (PTI). However, the officer in charge wanted him back at work for re-assessment. He was then moved to an office role. During the remainder of his career with the military, he stated he made the best of the roles he was given and looked for the positive benefits therein. He felt that no matter how much he tried to get ahead and get promoted, this was never supported by his employer and he was repeatedly knocked back.

The researcher asked: As an outside observer, I see recruitment advertisements encouraging people to enrol with the military, with slogans like 'this is belonging' and portraying an idea that you look after each other as a family. Is this true? He stated it used to be and the culture within the hierarchy has changed during his ten year career.

He stated he became "*switched on*" again when his wife became pregnant. He was hypervigilant and paranoid, in a similar way to being operational and on deployment. He felt protective towards his wife and child. The situation at home as new parents was stressful for him and his wife. In addition, he was working long hours and the culmination of this with lack of sleep had an impact on his mood and psychological symptoms. The relationship was breaking down with his wife. He was feeling frustrated with his employer. His wife encouraged him to seek medical discharge, believing his job was causing him to be unwell and concerns that their child could lose a father. He stated, losing his military family and career was the time when he needed her support the most. He left the marines because it was what she wanted, not because it was what he wanted. He stated, "*looking back it was the right decision. However, my wife left me very soon after the medical discharge that she pushed for. It was a kick in the nuts. I lost two families at the same time. My military family and my wife and child.*" He went on to describe how he was left with a void. He felt empty, like a hollow shell. He felt worthless, without value and abandoned. He spoke of giving years of service and going the extra mile for others at work, only to be cast aside without support or help when he needed it. He was unable to get treatment from the military. The NHS would not provide him with support while he was still serving. This left him in a kind of limbo in terms of recovery and resettlement.

During medical discharge he was subjected to disciplinary proceedings for taking a military vehicle without authorization for its use. He explained that he had signed the vehicle out and so it was not unauthorized. He had also taken the fuel card to pay for petrol. The MOD denied having a copy of the document which showed he had signed for the vehicle; yet were able to produce evidence that he had used the fuel card. He was threatened that if he did not plead guilty, the matter would be handed over to the civilian police and would likely result in a civilian conviction. He felt he had no choice but to agree to their terms and the situation was out of his control. He states, he became more paranoid during this period and felt the MOD were 'dicking' him [under surveillance] during the disciplinary proceedings. He had suspicions about a couple who approached him when he was out at the beach, asking him intrusive questions. His paranoia escalated to the point he would not leave the house, believing his movements were being watched. He stated, isolation and paranoia made his anxiety and depression worsen. The researcher asked: what do you think was the motivation for the disciplinary proceedings when you were undergoing medical discharge? He stated, there was speculation that the military police may be disbanded and needed to justify their existence by fabricating cases.

He spiralled downwards and turned to alcohol and substance misuse. He wanted to end his life and took an overdose. On one occasion he tried to cut his wrists but was found by someone who prevented this. He realized he needed to make a change. He said it was the thought of his son growing up without him and the lies people may tell him about his dad, that gave him the motivation to stop drinking, turn his life around and find a way to adapt. He describes his new partner as being very supportive and his rock.

He stated, he experienced many losses and despite his repeated attempts to achieve, he felt he was knocked back by others and life events time and time again. He stated, he gave ten years of service and was cast aside by the organisation when he needed help and he was considered 'broken'. He was evicted from his accommodation on base, three days before Christmas. The MOD would not extend his tenancy till after the holiday, which would give him time to get his life sorted out. He stated it was "*another kick in the bollocks.*" The charities supporting him, looked at caravan parks open over the winter for people who needed somewhere to live. He stated the people at Universal Credit were unhelpful. It was another system involving paperwork. The charities offered him help with food from the food bank.

He rebelled against conformity, grew a beard (which was not permitted in the Royal Marines) and took to a party lifestyle, including drinking heavily and substance misuse. He stated, he tried to fill the void and empty feelings with this lifestyle. He was the "*life and soul of the party.*" He explained that it was an artificial high. He had more energy to work when he was on a high. He stated, "*it's not something I condone.*"

He was spending his savings and had no income. He stated he needed a 'blow-out' after all that had happened, yet he knew his behaviour could not continue and he needed to make changes. He had support and guidance from two charities to get back on his feet and get organized. He stated it felt intrusive. They scrutinized his bank statements and queried what he was spending money on. He stated, this made him feel ashamed and "*made me feel like shit. It reined me in a bit, got me cooking again which I enjoy. I didn't like myself, didn't feel like treating myself to a nice meal, nobody wanted me, I had no self-confidence.*" He remembers living on take away meals, not feeling he was worth cooking for. One of the charities encouraged him to prepare his own meals to save money. He stated he used to berate himself. For example, "*Get a grip and sort yourself out.*" He stated, "*one thing I learnt is to be kind to yourself.*"

The researcher asked: so, it was uncomfortable or painful to have a microscope on your life and you needed someone to do that and highlight where you could turn things around. He stated "*yes.*" He said he went from doing nothing and being in a state of depression, to doing too much and starting his own businesses. He acknowledged he was not ready and would have been better off working for someone else and picking up a pay packet. He took on gardening work and set up a catering van. He also became a surfing instructor. He set up a gardening company and did odd jobs for people. Gardening was something he had always enjoyed, so decided to do this to bring money in. He was not aware of what his earnings were during this time. He stated, keeping busy with different jobs helped him cope with what he refers to as "*the wild west days.*" He would operate for a week on a high, then come down and slump into a depression. He stated he was not proud of his behaviour. The researcher asked: "so, keeping busy, the alcohol and substances were a way of blocking out the pain, filling the void and emptiness and were a means of escapism from reality?" He stated, "Yes." The researcher asked: "have you stopped that now?" He stated, "yes. *Seeing the impact of drugs on another person I was in contact with, made me realize I needed to stop.*" He stated, there was not a lightbulb moment that made him turn his life around. It was a process through support and help from the charities.

He did not want to work for the benefit of someone else again. He stated, "*I did not want to sell my soul to line their pockets. I struggled to ask for help. The charities would not pay for courses while I was in debt. I needed to sort it out.*"

There have been ongoing tensions between him and his former wife regarding his contact with their young child, including for how long, when and where visits take place. He stated, he does think it must have been difficult for her to live with him during his period of anxiety, depression and symptoms of hypervigilance when she also had a new baby.

The researcher asked: "did you feel angry or bitter about everything that has happened? He stated *"yes, super torn up, chewed up, spat out, super bitter. You cannot rely on anyone else. You have got to do it yourself."*

The researcher asked: "has your trust in people gone?" He stated, *"yes, everyone at the time."*

The researcher asked: "how do you feel now? Has the anger and bitterness subsided?" He stated, *"not really, it's still there. I tried to move on and forget about it. It is there every single f**king day. Maybe not every day, but frequently."*

The researcher asked: do you have to distract yourself to not think about what happened, such as using exercise?" He stated, *"That's how I medicate myself, 100% yes."*

The researcher asked: "do you use the anger and frustration as an energy source to motivate you and be productive?" He stated, *"exactly that. It is a driving force. It keeps me going."*

He stated, he has adopted mantras to manage his *"temper issues, anger issues and road rage."* One such mantra is *"Do good things, don't be a c**t"* and *"be nice, you don't know what other people are going through. I also say, pay it forwards. If you are nice to one person and they say what do I owe you? say pay it forwards and help others."* He stated, the one thing which helps him cope most of all is helping others.

He spoke of a song which means a lot to him because of the lyrics. He used to play it and sing loudly. Doing this was a release and would pull him out of feeling low. At this point, he became tearful at the memory of a very low point in his life. The researcher apologized for any distress caused by the interview. He stated, *"It is okay. If I can help one person with what they are going through, it is worth every bit of pain I'm going through. I'm a fighter.*" He stated, singing the song loudly helps him release his anger and aggression. This motivates him to get up and out. He stated, "*as long as I have a place to sleep, clothes on my back and food, I'm alright.*" He stated, he finds the Rocky films inspirational and motivational. He has started doing charity work. For example, supporting a boxing club and swimming in open water to raise money. He is progressing towards extended contact with his child as his behaviour and circumstances have changed.

In conclusion, the researcher noted this former Royal Marine has suffered multiple challenges and losses, which have resulted in a significant change in lifestyle, sense of safety and security. He feels his attempts to achieve professionally were repeatedly thwarted by his employer. He lost a vocation, as well as his identity and sense of worth or value. He felt he had no control over events and therefore, was powerless. He felt discarded and abandoned by the organisation, to which he gave service and commitment. He felt unloved and unworthy of love when he lost his military family, his wife and child. He lost confidence in himself. He lost the security of a home. His safety may have been compromised by excess alcohol, use of substances and episodes where he wanted to end his life. He is now self-employed, has a stable relationship and home. He still feels angry and bitter over events. However, he has demonstrated a conscious effort to show empathy to other people and his former wife. He recognizes other people may have difficulties of their own. He is moving forwards and working towards new goals and challenges, despite his persistent feelings of embitterment, moral injury, anger and depression. He alludes to experiencing PTED symptoms, such as normal effect when distracted, helplessness regarding negative and traumatic events, betrayal and loss of trust, hypervigilance, bitterness, rage and anger, negative self-concept and difficulty moving on from the past. Events had a significant affect on social, environmental, psychological and occupational aspects of his life. This in turn had a persistent and significant affect on his emotional and cognitive regulation, including anger, rage, embitterment and loss of trust in others. However, he has adapted and continues to work with change. He appears to be in the process of recovery and rebuilding safety and security. He states that he uses his psychological distress as a power source to be productive, which may indicate some posttraumatic growth.

The next sections of this book discuss the research project, ethical considerations, questionnaires and results.

Claire Carter

CHAPTER 8

Research project - ethical considerations and Distress Protocol

The purpose of the research project is to inform a book on moral injury, post-traumatic embitterment disorder and PTSD in frontline services. The aim of the research and the book is to provide affected people and groups with information and support, to explore the potential convergent validity between the concept of moral injury and PTED, and identify if they are comorbid with PTSD and therefore requiring specific treatment to assist with PTSD recovery. The research aims to encourage further research in this area and to highlight the possible impact on family members living alongside these proposed conditions.

An online questionnaire and face to face or telephone interviews were undertaken with first responders, armed service veterans and healthcare professionals. Participants were sought via charities and peers.

Data collection

Prospective participants were asked to read and sign a consent form prior to interview. The consent form provided a brief background on the researcher, the purpose and topic of the research, how their contribution will be recorded and used. The form states that contributions will be kept anonymous and the recordings will be destroyed shortly after publication of the research.

The researcher is required to only ask for information which is proportionate and necessary for the purposes of the research. Participants are at liberty to disclose or withhold any or all information. The focus of the interview and questions was on symptoms, day to day functioning, possible disability, the impact on life and relationships, treatment and recovery. The researcher is required not to ask questions directly about negative life events or traumatic incidents.

Participants were advised not to share information that is restricted, classified or confidential to another person (such as names and places).

The researcher is obligated to breach confidentiality where there is a disclosure of immediate risk of harm to the participant or another person.

Participants were advised that the interview will be recorded using a Dictaphone and that the recording will be deleted shortly after publication of the research.

Data collected on hard copies of the questionnaire, would be transferred manually by the researcher onto the online form for the purpose of collating the raw data in one place for analysis.

A hard copy of the online questionnaire would be taken to face to face interviews. It is optional for the participant to complete this if they have not already done so. No face to face interviews took place due to Covid-19 lockdown and were carried out via video link.

Online questionnaire

Page one of the questionnaire gives a brief background of the researcher and the purpose and topic of research. Participants were advised that information collected is anonymous.

Participants were thanked for their contribution and advised to exit the questionnaire at any time if they no longer wanted to continue or they were in distress. Participants had the option to skip any questions they do not wish to answer.

Participants were not asked to give details of upsetting or traumatic incidents. They were asked to state in approximately one word, the nature of the event, i.e. divorce, redundancy, combat, life-threatening situation.

A hard copy of the online questionnaire was available on request for participants unable to access it online, or if they preferred a paper copy. A stamped addressed envelope would be provided for returning the questionnaire.

Face to Face or telephone interviews

Participants were invited to ask any questions for further explanation prior to, during or after the interview.

The participant was asked to confirm that they have read and understood the consent form. The researcher or participant had the option of arranging for support If there was difficulty reading, understanding or signing the consent form.

The researcher and participant would agree on a venue for interview, taking into consideration privacy, travel, environment and potential triggers to symptoms or trauma. 04/04/2020 due to Coronavirus lockdown, face to face interviews took place via video call using WhatsApp for encrypted security.

The researcher was required to avoid the need to postpone, delay or cancel arrangements made with the participant for interview, as this could cause anxiety, distress or loss of confidence in the process.

The participants were advised that they can postpone, delay or cancel the interview at any time. This includes terminating the interview once it had begun.

Telephone interviews were arranged for a time when there were unlikely to be distractions or disturbances. Participants were advised that breaks can be taken during the interview if needed.

The participant was advised that they can withdrawal their contribution at any time prior to publication of the research. Their contribution would be deleted with immediate effect.

Participants were asked if support is in place for them during and after the interview. Information on where to get support would be provided to all participants and including assistance which is accessible 24/7 if required. This is also in recognition that there could be post-interview distress.

The researcher is not required to undertake any counselling during the interview. If distress became apparent, the researcher would offer a break, to stop the interview or distract the participant by changing to a non-threatening topic of discussion. The researcher exercised their discretion to proceed or terminate any involvement in the research if the participant became too distressed or there were concerns for their welfare.

The researcher ended the interviews with discussion on a non-threatening and unrelated topic to distract the participant and shift focus onto pleasant thoughts and emotions. This was to reduce risk of distress post-interview to the participant and family members (who could be affected vicariously).

The participants were provided with a draft copy of any quotes or case studies created from their interview. They were invited to make any amendments or correct any inaccuracies. Permission and consent was sought to publish the final copy. Consideration was given to post interview distress.

The participants were notified of when and where the research is published.

There was no financial reward for participants making contributions to the research. The need for reimbursing participant expenses was not necessary due to Covid-19 lockdown.
Charities and agencies were not obligated to assist and bear no liability. They were able to signpost their beneficiaries to the research project for their interest only. All participants were volunteers.

Researcher Ethics and distress protocol

The research was undertaken voluntarily by the researcher and therefore not in receipt of sponsorship or funding. Consideration was given to the expenses incurred by the researcher and the financial viability of the project.

The researcher may have been exposed to distressing or traumatizing material and content, in which case they had the option to contact a mentor or undertake clinical supervision (counselling) if required.

The researcher was mindful of the number of interviews arranged per day or per week, so as not to become overloaded and to have time in between interviews.

The researcher had a fully charged mobile, and contact numbers for support agencies with them if needed.

1st Research Questionnaire

This questionnaire includes both the PTED scale and MIES (Moral Injury) scale. The researcher aims to determine whether or not both constructs can be discriminated from each other. If participants positively identify with factors from both scales this may suggest convergent validity between constructs. Furthermore, the questionnaire seeks to understand if PTED and MI may be comorbid with PTSD or Depression and whether the type of incident relating to PTED and MI are exceptional, yet common negative events or significant enough to meet diagnostic criteria for PTSD.

PTED Scale
(Linden et al., 2009)
Please circle or tick 0,1,2,3 or 4 for each statement to select a response 'Not true', 'Hardly true', 'Partially true', 'Very much true', or 'Extremely true'.

In the past years I had to cope with a harmful life event that from my perspective was unjust or unfair:

That hurt my feelings and caused considerable embitterment
That led to a noticeable and persistent negative change in my mental wellbeing
That I see as very unjust and unfair
About which I have to think over and over again
That causes me to be extremely upset when I am reminded of it
That triggers me to harbour thoughts of revenge
For which I blame and am angry with myself

That led to the feeling that there is no sense to strive or to make an effort

That makes me to frequently feel sullen and unhappy

That impaired my overall physical well being

That causes me to avoid certain places or persons so as to not be reminded of them

That makes me feel helpless and disempowered

That triggers feelings of satisfaction when I think that the responsible party having to experience a similar situation

That led to a considerable decrease in my strength and drive

That made that I am more easily irritated than before

That makes that I must distract myself in order to experience a normal mood

That made me unable to pursue occupational and/or family activities as before

That caused me to draw back from friends and social activities

Which frequently evokes painful memories

Moral Injury Event Scale

MIES: Nash et al. 2013

Instructions: Please circle your response to the following statements to indicate how much you agree or disagree regarding your experiences at any time since joining the service. Do you 'Strongly Agree', 'Moderately Agree' 'Slightly Agree', 'Slightly Disagree', 'Moderately Disagree' or 'Strongly Disagree'

I saw things that were morally wrong

I am troubled by having witnessed others' immoral acts

I acted in ways that violated my own moral code or values

I am troubled by having acted in ways that violated my own morals or values

I violated my own morals by failing to do something that I felt I should have done

I am troubled because I violated my morals by failing to do something that I felt I should have done

I feel betrayed by leaders who I once trusted

I feel betrayed by fellow service members who I once trusted

I feel betrayed by others outside the [service] who I once trusted

I trust[ed] my leaders and [colleagues] to always live up to their core values

I trust myself to always live up to my own moral code

Additional questions:

What was the negative and harmful experience or event? For example, Divorce, redundancy, combat, death of colleague or family member or life threatening situation.

Do you have a diagnosis of PTSD and/or Depression? if yes, please specify

Did you seek help with the negative experience or event?

Do you believe there were ways you could find a solution to the negative experience or event?

Are you a first responder?

Are you an armed forces veteran?

Are you a healthcare professional?

Thank you for taking the time to complete this questionnaire.

"subjects who score an average of 1.6 or more on the PTED Scale are suspect to suffer from prolonged embitterment in an intensity of clinical relevance. In

regard to clinical practicability, and in order to increase the specificity, a mean total score of 2.5 on the PTED Scale is recommended as a cut-off score, i.e., a score ≥2.5 is indicating a clinically significant intensity of reactive embitterment." (Linden, 2009) [232]

MIES: "*Two items were reverse-keyed; scale scores are generated by reverse coding these two items and then summing across items, with a higher score being indicative of having experienced a greater intensity of events. We labeled the resulting scale the Moral Injury Events Scale*" (Nash et al., 2013). [233]

Results and analysis of Questionnaire 1

112 participants responded to the online questionnaire. Responses on the scale, which were partially true (2), very much true (3) and extremely true (4), were positively associated with PTED symptoms and cognitions. Responses on the scale, which were slightly agree (4), moderately agree (5) and strongly agree (6), were positively associated with MI symptoms and cognitions. The higher the number and weighted average, the more positive the results were.

Responses on the scale, which were 'not at all (0) and hardly true (1) were negatively associated with PTED symptoms and cognitions. Responses on the scale, which were slightly disagree (3), moderately disagree (2) and strongly disagree (1),' were negatively associated with MI symptoms and cognitions.

The lower the number and weighted average, the more negative the results were. 10.71% stated they had not experienced an unjust, unfair or harmful event which had led to feelings of considerable embitterment. 8.93% stated this was hardly true. 80.36% stated in the past years they had to cope with a harmful life event that from their perspective was

---

[232] (Linden, Baumann, Lieberei, & Rotter, 2009)
[233] (Nash, 2013)

unjust or unfair and that hurt their feelings and caused considerable embitterment. Of those, over three quarters of respondents (78.58%) stated this had led to a noticeable and persistent negative change in their mental wellbeing.

Over three quarters (79.46%) stated the experience had caused them to think about the unjust and hurtful incident over and over again. Over three quarters (78.38%) of respondents stated the incident frequently evoked painful memories (1 person skipped this question). These results signify a high proportion of participants with the symptom of rumination and intrusive memories. Over three quarters (76.79%) of participants stated they become extremely upset when reminded of what happened.

A significant number of respondents experienced revenge fantasy (48.22%), with 8.93% stating this was extremely relevant to them. Just under half of participants (47.32%) blamed, or were angry with themselves for what happened. This indicated a greater proportion of respondents attributing blame to others. Two thirds (66.67%) felt there is no sense to strive or make an effort, indicating a loss of motivation and drive or perhaps loss of meaning and purpose (1 person skipped this question). Over two thirds (71.17%) stated the experience frequently made them feel sullen and unhappy and experienced a decrease in strength and drive (1 person skipped these questions).

Nearly three quarters of respondents (73.87%) stated the incident had led to an impairment in physical wellbeing (1 person skipped this question). Over two thirds (71.17%) stated they actively avoided reminders of the incident and what happened (1 person skipped this question). Over two thirds (72.73%) of participants stated the incident made them feel helpless and disempowered (2 people skipped this question). Just over one third of respondents (38.18%) stated, they experience feelings of satisfaction to think of the responsible party having to experience a similar situation (a taste of one's own medicine, 2 people skipped this question). Over two thirds (72.72%) of participants stated they had become more irritable than they were prior to the incident (2 people skipped this question). Over two thirds (68.47%) of participants had to distract themselves to experience normal mood and affect (1 person skipped this question).

Over two thirds (70.09%) of respondents stated they are unable to pursue occupational or family activities as before (2 people skipped this question). This may be attributed to loss of meaning and purpose or decrease in strength and drive. Over two thirds (72.07%) of respondents stated the incident had caused them to draw back from friends and social activities (1 person skipped this question). The inability to pursue occupational, family or social activities may indicate symptoms of anhedonia.

In summary: On the PTED scale, persistent mental ill health, embitterment, rumination, avoidance, loss of meaning and purpose, feelings of helplessness, irritability, anhedonia, withdrawal and intrusive memories were all shown to be of significance among the majority of respondents. Responses to 16 out of 19 statements, had a positive weighted average equal to or greater than 2, indicating clinical significance. Revenge fantasy and self-blame were significant for just under half of participants.

On the MIES scale: Over three quarters (82.88%) of respondents stated they saw things that were morally wrong (1 person skipped this question). Just over half (54.95%) stated they strongly agreed with this statement. Nearly three quarters (72.98%) of respondents stated they were troubled by having witnessed others' immoral acts (1 person skipped this question). Just over two thirds (68.47%) of participants stated they had not acted in ways that violated their own moral code or values (1 person skipped this question). Two thirds (66.36%) stated they were not troubled by having acted in ways that violated their own moral code or values (2 people skipped this question). Under half (41.29%) of respondents believed they had violated their own morals by failing to do something that they felt they should have done (3 people skipped this question). This correlated with 41.28% of the same respondents stating they were troubled by this and just under half who blamed or were angry with themselves for what happened, on the PTED scale. Over three quarters (79.28%) of respondents stated they felt betrayed by leaders who they once trusted (1 person skipped this question). Over half of respondents (62.17%) stated they felt betrayed by fellow service members (1 person skipped this question). Over half (62.72%) of respondents felt betrayed by people outside of the service who they once trusted (2 people skipped this question). Over three quarters (87.39%) of respondents trusted their leaders and colleagues to live up to their core values (1 person skipped this question). Given that 79.28% felt betrayed by leaders they once trusted compared with 62.72% of betrayal by colleagues, this may indicate a higher expectation and responsibility on trusted leaders to be of higher morality.

Nearly all (94.6%) respondents stated they trusted themselves to always live up to their own moral code (1 person skipped this question). Therefore, 94.6% of respondents would be expected to say they had not violated their moral code or values. Just under one third (31.53%) claimed they had acted in ways that violated their own moral code or values. There were 111 responses to these two questions. However, there is a discrepancy of 26.13% between these sets of data (the belief one had acted in ways that violated their own moral code or values and simultaneously stating they trusted themselves to always live up to their own moral code). This may indicate the word 'values' having a significantly different meaning to moral code, as this is the variance in wording between the two questions. Perhaps some respondents believe they have breached their own personal values; yet maintained the moral code within the context of occupational culture. This may corroborate the researchers' definition and differentiation between values, morals and beliefs; how morals can be manipulated to fit the situation, beliefs can be altered through open-mindedness and education and values are intrinsic to the individual. Cognitive dissonance has been researched in relation to policing where an officer may have to take action required by the role (and law) whilst at the same time being in conflict with their own values.[234]

In summary, on the MIES scale a significant proportion of respondents felt betrayed by trusted others, more notably leaders and had been exposed to incidents they found to be morally wrong. Positive responses ranged in significance for over half of respondents or more, for the majority of statements, with a weighted average score greater than 3 (out of a possible high score of 6) for 7 of 11 statements. Negative responses were found in relation to self-perpetration/blame with under one third claiming they had acted in ways that violated their own moral code or values. Under half of respondents believed they had violated their own morals by failing to do something that they felt they should have done with a weighted average score of between 2.48 and 2.81 across all negative responses. There was a positive weighted average score of 4.72 to the statement 'I feel betrayed by leaders who I once trusted,' a score of 3.9 for the statement 'I feel betrayed by fellow service members who I once trusted,' a score of 5 (out of a high score of 6) for the statement 'I trust[ed] my leaders and [colleagues] to always live up to their core values' and a high score of 5.41 to the statement 'I trust myself to always live up to my own moral code.'

When asked 'What was the negative and harmful experience or event? For example, Divorce, redundancy, combat, death of colleague or family member or life threatening situation' 94 of 112 participants (18 declined to answer), stated the traumatic incidents relating to their responses were:

---

[234] (Carter, Duty of Care - Psychological Injury in Policing, 2014)

1) Whistleblowing, coverup, gaslighting, sudden deaths, dangerous situations, feeling that the rug has been pulled from under me leaving me unable to trust others and myself.

2) Bullying incident at work and being the subject of an investigation.

3) Numerous crime scenes involving death - threatened by criminals who wanted to kill me

4) Variety of different events including situations where my life was threatened or where my safety and security was.

5) Near drowning, loss of career, endless body recoveries, refusal of Ill Health Retirement.

6) Aftermath of terrorist incident resulting in many deaths.

7) Multiple Events: Dunblane Primary School Murders, Sexual Assault on duty by a colleague, fighting to keep my job after an injury OFF duty left me disabled

8) Bullied at work, racially abused, sexually harassed by colleague, further abused because I took him to a tribunal, took the lot to tribunal had to defend myself in a 25 day hearing as a claimant

9) Suicide

10) Death, my illness, mistreated at work because of illness and husband's illness

11) Badly assaulted at work (Police Officer)

12) Death of colleague. Plenty of other situations.

13) Death of family member plus court case failing in retrospective sexual abuse on me

14) I have been divorced and lost family and friends but these are life and although I felt sad I never felt like

any of the statements you have asked, but if I did I'm sure I could find the help required

15) Violent death of colleagues

16) Divorce, deaths of colleagues, interviewing of I.R.A. ASU members

17) Death of colleagues, attempted murder of myself
18) Ill Health Retirement process

19) Divorce

20) Cancer diagnosis

21)Near death experience (my heart stopped

during an operation)

22) Bullied by jealous younger bigger colleague

23) Death of friends, being shot, having a permanent disability

24) Death, serious injuries, divorce, life threatening situation.

25) Numerous life threatening situations whilst on active service (Police Officer) now retired

26) Murder of colleagues
27) Illness of family members

28) Depression

29) All of the

above (Divorce, redundancy, combat, death of colleague or family member, life threatening situation)

30) Death of babies, suicide, violence, assault

31) Combat

32) Limitations on my family's life/ having to move house overnight and putting additional stress on my family

33) Life threatening, death of a friend/family divorce

34) Violent Murder, Immolation, fatal road traffic collisions (multiple), cot

death

35) Death

36) Mislead into a job role

37) Murders, bombings, loss of colleagues, divorce

38) Combat and death of a family member

39) Child murders

40) Corruption and bullying at work

41) Sexual harassment at work, victimisation divorce and domestic violence

42) Family member troubles

43) Attempted Murder

44) Divorce,

deaths in family

45) Death of family member by suicide

46) All of the above (Divorce, redundancy, combat, death of colleague or family member, life threatening situation

47) Suicide

48) Terrorist incidents

49) Attacked by a dog on duty

50) Arrested

51) Life threatening event

52) Injury on duty as police officer

53) Rather not say

54) First at scene of a drowned 3yr old child

55) Psychological breakdown at work leading to over 18 months off, and a pending early ill health retirement with a chronic mental health disorder

56) Death of Son

57) Death of colleagues in combat

58) Severe bullying by more senior ranks

59) Crash involving a horse. A cat being kicked to death

60) Several life threatening events

61) Death

62) Multiple Life threatening situations

63) Multiple deaths of friends and colleagues in RUC

64) Life threatening situations

65) Divorce

66) Death of three colleagues

67) Abuse as a child

68) combat

69) Being seriously assaulted and sustaining life changing injuries on two occasions. Working the aftermath of the 7th July London bombings, working as a CSI on horrible cases, and having my brother shot twice and held hostage in a terrorist attack at Le Bataclan, Paris, and texting me whilst there was a man outside where he was hiding with a Kalashnikov gun

70) Multiple terrorist murders in N. Ireland

71) Life threatening situation

72) Death

73) Numerous incidents surrounding death via unnatural causes during time as a serving police officer

74) Multiple events during police service

75) Injury and sexual trauma

76) Life Threatening situations...(plural)

77) Combat, life threatening situation also redundancy

78) Detention in custody

79) bomb disposal incident

80) 10 Operational Tours

81) death of colleague

82) Not able to speak of what has occurred

83) Contradictory diagnosis of PTSD

Independent Medical Officer states I just had a bad marriage despite witnessing the death of 5 colleagues in two of the three landmine attacks I was previously involved in as a police officer in Northern Ireland

84) Injured on duty

85) Combat

86) Injury on Duty - road traffic

collision causing permanent disablement

87) Misconduct allegation

88) Work overload and then victim in a road traffic collision that was poorly investigated by colleagues leading to no further action. I have been cast aside as the problem, not part of the solution

89) Extreme bullying and harassment, negligence

90) Yes

91) battle and many other things

92) Injured on duty

93) Life threatening crash

94) Ill health retirement process.

There were 94 responses of which, half of those (47) identified 'death' (including 4 responses of 'suicide,' 1 response of body recovery, 1 response of fatal road traffic collision, 8 responses of 'murder' and 2 who stated 'all of the above). One third (31) of responses identified 'life threatening' situation(s) (including 4 responses of 'terrorism', 2 response of road traffic collision, 2 responses 'combat' and 2 who stated 'all of the above'). 5 responses identified physical injury or disablement, 3 responses identified 'abuse.' 12 responses identified 'divorce' (including 2 who stated 'all of the above'). 4 responses identified 'redundancy' (including 2 who stated 'all of the above'). 4 responses identified 'sexual abuse, assault or harassment'. 5 responses identified 'ill health retirement' and process. 4 responses identified 'bullying'. 2 responses identified 'loss'.

Over one third of respondents (36.36%) were armed forces veterans. Over three quarters (80.91%) were serving or retired first responders. 8.16% of respondents were healthcare professionals. Just under two thirds (64.55%) stated they sought help with the negative experience or event. Half of respondents (50.91%) believed there were ways to find a solution to the event.

The research concludes that the majority of participants met criteria for both PTED and Moral Injury. Therefore, PTED and MI could not be discriminated from each other. Over half of respondents, (56.25%) met criteria for experiencing an incident perceived as unjust or unfair which caused considerable embitterment, that led to a persistent and noticeable change in mental health, they saw things that were morally wrong and felt betrayed by trusted leaders. A smaller proportion (26.7%) were embittered, suffered persistent change to mental wellbeing and believed they had violated their own moral code or values. 4.46% of respondents met every parameter for both PTED and Moral Injury signifying severity of symptoms. From this small study, it appears there is a convergence between PTED and MI where both constructs are experienced by individuals, relating to the same incident(s) and responsibility is weighted towards trusted leaders or others, rather than to self. Over three quarters (81.91%) of 94 respondents stated the traumatic incident(s) relating to MI and PTED were predominantly (and significantly) of death and life threatening events. Four of the deaths related to family members, which may be taken as an exceptional, yet common negative life event. I death related to a family member who died from suicide. 42 deaths included violence or were duty related. 3 participants identified sexual trauma or assault. The research suggests PTED is present in trauma which meets criteria for (C)PTSD. Therefore, PTED may not be discriminated from PTSD based on the nature of the traumatic incident, as proposed by the construct which states 'an exceptional, yet common negative life event (such as divorce or redundancy). Just under half of respondents (43.64%) stated they had a diagnosis of PTSD. 17.27% stated they had a diagnosis of Depression. Just over a third (39.09%) had no diagnosis. However, these respondents may be affected by symptoms of posttraumatic stress or depression and be undiagnosed at the time of the research. Results indicate symptoms of PTED and MI can be comorbid with PTSD and Depression.

2nd Research Questionnaire

This questionnaire used statements and keywords relating to, or adapted from the ICD-11 diagnostic criteria for PTSD[235] and CPTSD,[236] the MISS-M scale for Moral Injury,[237] EMIS-M scale for Moral Injury[238] and the PTED diagnostic criteria.[239] It was noted prior to analysis that there was some crossover between these constructs. The amendment to the DSM-5 definition of PTSD will be taken into account during analysis, as the removal of "intense fear, helplessness or horror, according to DSM-IV— has.......proved to have no utility in predicting the onset of PTSD"[240] and ICD-11 states diagnostic criteria for PTSD as "Re-experiencing in the present – intrusive memories, flashbacks, nightmares, fear, horror." Recent research has identified that fear may not always be a driver in the onset of PTSD.[241] Therefore for the purposes of this research responses to 'fear' as a factor will be recorded and not necessary to include when analyzing potential convergent validity between constructs. Each criteria or factor is coded for later analysis of the responses to statements and keywords. Keywords are cross referenced to the statements for paired

---

[235] (WHO, 2019)
[236] (WHO, 2019)
[237] (Koenig, Youssef, Ames, & Oliver, 2017)
[238] (Currier, 2017)
[239] (Linden, Baumann, Rotter, & Schippan, 2007)
[240] (APA, 2013)
[241] (Freyd J. , 2019)

comparison and included to check the participants understanding. The aim of the questionnaire is to identify a possible convergent validity or discrimination between the constructs of Moral Injury, PTED, and CPTSD. The questionnaire includes demographics of age, gender, education, occupation, ethnicity and religious beliefs. Participants are asked to respond to the statements using a scale of 'strongly agree, Moderately agree, slightly agree, slightly disagree, moderately disagree, strongly disagree.' Responses, which were 'strongly agree, Moderately agree and slightly agree indicated a positive correlation with the statement; and therefore, with symptoms or cognitions of MI and/or PTED and/or CPTSD. Participants are asked to select any keywords offered, that they associate with the negative incident or themselves.

Considerations

Unlike PTED, there is not yet a diagnostic criteria which has been agreed upon for Moral Injury. Scales which do exist may vary. Many MI scales are designed for military use. Therefore, the research adopted two scales (MISS-M and EMIS-M) and common drivers (causes), symptoms and behaviour of MI. MISS-M does not factor avoidance as a behaviour in moral injury. EMIS-M at 11. 'I sometimes feel so bad about things I did/saw in the military that I hide or withdraw from others,' suggests avoidance through guilt or shame. There does not seem to be a measure for avoiding reminders to emotional or moral pain, such as activities, people and places which is noted by Currier et al. (2017) as present in both MI and PTSD. Similarly, suicidal ideation is not included in MISS-M or EMIS-M, yet Koenig (2019) has noted MI may increase risk of suicide.[242] He firmly states, "MI should not be conceptualized as a distinct syndrome." In contrast, PTED is a stand-alone construct which may be comorbid with other mental health conditions. MISS-M does not factor intrusive memories directly. Statement, M6 – 'Some things I did continue to bother me' and statements M11-13 'Troubled by or over' may suggest

---

[242] (Koenig, 2019)

persistent thoughts or memories about what happened. Threatening event(s) which are prolonged or repetitive and difficult or impossible to escape (as in ICD11- CPTSD) are perhaps more likely than not to be in conflict with one's beliefs, morals and values, even though this is not made explicit. The research has not sought to make this assumption in its findings. The 'catch-all' criteria of 'Difficulty with affect regulation' in ICD11-CPTSD, can cover a broad range of maladaptive, dysfunctional thoughts, emotional reactions and behaviour. Many of which can be found in MI and PTED. This has perhaps increased the convergence validity between CPTSD, MI and PTED.

One of the criterion for PTED, is that there is no obvious, prior mental health condition which could account for the disturbance in an individual. This is not a prerequisite for CPTSD or MI – Statement 10 in this research, "I'm not the person I used to be, I used to be happy, confident and fun before the incident," may suggest there are no other mental health conditions predating the negative or traumatic incident(s). It is noteworthy that statement 10 has also been cross-referenced with negative self-concept (in MI, CPTSD and PTED) and feeling defeated or diminished (in CPTSD).

Here follows a list of symptoms associated with ICD-11, diagnostic criteria for PTSD and CPTSD, diagnostic criteria for PTED and symptoms commonly associated with MI. Each factor is given a code, which is cross referenced with each statement in the research questionnaire, to ensure all factors have been accommodated.

ICD-11, PTSD (Coding CP1-3)

Re-experiencing in the present – intrusive memories, flashbacks, nightmares, fear, horror, overwhelming emotions, physical sensations (CP1)

Avoidance of traumatic reminders – thoughts, memories, activities, people (CP2)

Persistent sense of current threat – hyperarousal, hypervigilance, startle reaction (CP3)

ICD-11, CPTSD (Coding CP4-11)

Threatening event(s) (CP4)
Prolonged or repetitive (CP5)
Difficult or impossible to escape (CP6)
Severe and persistent:
Problems with affect regulation (CP7)
Negative Self-Concept - Beliefs about oneself as diminished, defeated or worthless (CP8)
Feelings of shame, guilt or failure (related to the traumatic event) (CP9)
Disturbances in relationships - Difficulties in sustaining relationships and feeling close to others (CP10)
Significant impairment in personal, family, social, educational, occupational or other important areas of functioning. (physical, spiritual) (CP11)

PTED (Coding TED1-21) Core diagnostic criteria

Exceptional negative life event(s) (TED1)

Patients know about this life event and see their present negative state as a direct and lasting consequence of this event (TED2)

Patients experience the negative life event as 'unjust' and respond with embitterment and emotional arousal when reminded of the event (TED3)

No obvious mental disorder in the year before the critical event. The present state is no recurrence of a pre-existing mental disorder (TED4)

Impairment: performance of daily activities and roles is impaired (TED5)

PTED Additional signs and symptoms

Violation of basic values and beliefs (TED6)

Victim (TED7)

Emotional arousal when reminded of the event – normal affect when distracted (TED8)

Helpless to cope with the event or cause (TED9)

Self-blame – for not preventing it, or not being able to cope with it (TED10)

Intrusive memories – feel it important not to forget (TED11)

Suicidal ideation (TED12)

dysphoria, aggression, downheartedness (TED13)

(Avoidance) phobic symptoms in respect to the place or to persons related to the event (TED14)

Drive is reduced and blocked. Or unwilling (TED15)

Duration: longer than 3 months (TED16)

Revenge phenomenon (TED17)

Hopelessness (TED18)

loss of trust (TED19)

Difficulty with forgiveness (TED20)

Uncertain whether they want wounds to heal (TED21)

Moral Injury (Coding M1-18)– MISS-M/EMIS-M scale

Perpetrating, failing to prevent, bearing witness to, or learning about acts that transgress deeply held moral beliefs and expectations – This is expressed as a 'betrayal of morals, values or beliefs in the questionnaire (M1)

lasting psychological, biological, spiritual, behavioural, and social impact (M2)

Self-blame or condemnation (M3)

Difficulty forgiving (M4)

Betrayal (M5)

Guilt and Shame (M6)

Violated morals (M7)

Loss of religious faith (M8)

Loss of hope (M9)

Loss of trust (M10)

Loss of meaning and purpose (M11)

Negative self-concept (M12)

Revenge (M13)

Anger (M14)

Self-sabotage (M15)

Avoidance of triggers to moral

Suicidal ideation (M18)

and emotional pain (M16)

Continue to be bothered or troubled by the incident (M17)

Clusters

Cluster 1 potential convergence for CPTSD, PTED and MI: negative self-concept, self-condemnation, difficulty with relationships, affect regulation (R), Significant impairment in important areas of life and functioning, persistent effect, negative traumatic event
Statements: 1,4,5,7,8,9,10,11,12,13,14,16,17,18,19,20,21,22,25,26

Cluster 2 potential convergence for PTED and MI: betrayal, violation or breach of values, beliefs or morals
Statements: 15

Stand-alone statements:
CPTSD, 2,3,6,23,24: Duration of threatening incident, repeated threatening incidents hyperarousal and hypervigilance, nightmares

Keywords - Coding 1-37

Fear (1)

Unforgiving (2)

Betrayal (3)

Injustice (4)

Victimized (5)

Bitterness (6)

Distrust (7)

Hopelessness (8)

Helplessness (9)

Loss (10)

Traumatic (11)

Shattered beliefs (12)

Immoral (13)

Unfair (14)

Revenge (15)

Wrong (16)

Pointless (17)

Threatening (18)

Blame (19)

Self-blame (20)

Guilt (21)

Shame (22)

Loss of control (23)

Overwhelming (24)

Failure (25)

Rumination (26)

Nightmares (27)

On alert (28)

Avoidance (29)

Defeated (30)

Withdrawn (31)

Changed (32)

Impaired (33)

Suicidal (34)

Physical

discomfort (35)

Self-destructive

(36)

Troubled (37)

Final version of questionnaire Statements, results and cross referencing with CPTSD, PTED, MI, & keywords

No.	Statement	CPTSD	PTED	MI	Results	Keywords
1	I keep replaying the incident(s) over and over in my mind (Rumination, intrusive memory, flashback)	CP1	TED11	MI7	93.18% Weighted Average 3.86	Rumination 31.82%
2	When I am reminded of the incident(s) I get sensations in my body (hyper-arousal, physical	CP1			93.18% Weighted Average 3.90	Physical Discomfort 45.45%

	sensation)				
3	I struggle to sleep because of recurring bad dreams (nightmares)	CP1			82.95% Weighted Average 3.53	Nightmares 72.73%
4	I prefer to keep busy so I have less time to think (Avoidance, normal affect when distracted)	CP2	TED8 TED14	M16	86.36% Weighted Average 3.73	Avoidance 64.77%
5	There are places or people I avoid because it hurts to be reminded of what happened (avoidance)	CP2	TED14	M16	87.5% Weighted Average 4.06	Avoidance 64.77%
6	I feel on edge for no reason, I can be jumpy (hyper-arousal, persistent sense of	CP3			90.91% Weighted Average 4.05	Threatening 45.45% On alert 65.91%

	threat)					
7	My way of life was under attack. I felt I would lose what was important to me (threat to security, values and beliefs, negative life event)	CP4	TED1 TED6	M11 M8 M10 M19	88.64% Weighted Average 3.94	Threatening 45.45% Traumatic 84.09%
8	I couldn't see a way out, I felt powerless (inescapable, powerless, helpless, hopeless, victim)	CP6	TED1 TED7 TED9	M9	94.32% Weighted Average 4.09	victimized 30.68% Hopelessness 55.68% Helplessness 64.77%
9	I sometimes lose control of myself, I get angry over little things (affect dysregulation)	CP1, CP7	TED8	M14	94.32% Weighted Average 4.22	Loss of control 47.73% Overwhelming 69.32%

10	I'm not the person I used to be, I used to be happy, confident and fun before the incident (defeated, diminished, negative self-concept, no previous MH)	CP8	TED2 TED4	MI2	96.59% Weighted Average 4.36	Changed 76.14% Defeated 23.86%
11	I have no fight left in me, I can't see the point in trying anymore (loss of meaning and purpose, loss of drive, dysphoria, affect dysregulation)	CP7	TED15	MI1	75% Weighted Average 3.24	Loss 51.14% Pointless 28.41%
12	Experiences have taught me that it is only a matter of time before	CP10	TED19	M5 MI0	85.23% Weighted Average 3.63	Betrayal 43.18% Distrust 60.23%

	people... will betray my trust (difficulty with relationships, loss of trust, betrayal)					
13	I find it difficult to keep a job for long, I struggle to work with others (significant impact on occupation, loss of resources, difficulty with relationships, avoidance)	CP10 CP11	TED5	M2 M1 6	60.92% Weighte d Average 2.86	loss 51.14% Impaired 28.41%
14	I struggle to attend family occasions or celebrations (significant impact on personal, family and social areas of life,	CP11	TED5	M2 M1 6	82.77% Weighte d Average 3.54	Withdrawn 62.50% Impaired 28.41%

	avoidance)					
15	what happened was unfair, it was an injustice that went against my….. values, morals and beliefs (unfair, unjust, immoral, violation of beliefs, morals and values)		TED3	M1 M7	84.10% Weighted Average 3.92	Injustice 71.59% Shattered beliefs 34.09% Unfair 57.95% Immoral 25% Wrong 47.73%
16	I often fantasize about getting revenge to make myself feel better (revenge, affect dysregulation)	CP7	TED17	M13	56.82% Weighted Average 3.01	Revenge 31.82%
17	I struggle to do normal every-day tasks	CP11	TED5	M2	82.96% Weighted Average	Impaired 28.41%

					3.45	
18	I feel ashamed and guilty for not being able to cope with what happened (self-blame, self-condemnatio n, negative self-concept)	CP8 CP9	TED9 TED1 0	M3 M1 2 M6	94.32% Weighte d Average 4.00	Blame 35.23% Self-blame 46.59% Guilt 53.41% Shame 48.86%
19	I find it difficult to forgive those responsible for what happened (embitterme nt, difficulty with forgiveness, affect dysregulation)	CP7	TED3 TED2 0	M4	85.23% Weighte d Average 3.93	unforgiving 26.14% Bitterness 54.55%

20	At times I think about ending my life (suicidal ideation, affect dysregulation)	CP7	TED1 2	MI 8	63.63% Weighte d Average 2.83	suicidal 45.45%
21	I lost faith in my spiritual beliefs	CP11	TED6	M8 MI	59.09% Weighte d Average 2.85	Shattered beliefs 34.09%
22	Life feels pointless (loss of meaning and purpose, dysphoria, dissatisfactio n with life, affect dysregulation)	CP7	TED1 3	MI I	60.23% Weighte d Average 2.80	Loss 51.14% Pointless 28.41%
23	I experienced a threatening incident which lasted a very long time	CP4			71.59% Weighte d Average 3.27	Threatening 45.45% Traumatic 84.09%

24	I repeatedly experienced incidents that made me feel threatened	CP5			84.09% Weighted Average 3.78	Threatening 45.45% Traumatic 84.09% Fear 67.05%
25	Sometimes I am self-destructive and sabotage my own progress (affect dysregulation, self-punishment, embitterment, dysphoria)	CP7	TED20 TED3	MI 5	73.87% Weighted Average 3.26	Self-destructive 35.23% Failure 57.95%
26	I have had these thoughts and feelings for over 3 months (PTED criteria, affect dysregulation, impairment)	CP11	TED16 TED5	MI 2	97.73% Weighted Average 4.49	Impaired 28.41% Troubled 63.64%

There were 88 respondents to this research questionnaire.

Occupation of respondents to questionnaire 2

First Responder (Retired) 43.18% First Responder (Serving) 29.55%, Armed Forces Veteran 15.91%, Armed Forces Serving 1.14%, Healthcare Professional (Retired) 2.27%, Healthcare Professional (Serving) 3.41%

Diagnosis of respondents to questionnaire 2

PTSD 55.95%, Complex PTSD 30.95%, Anxiety 52.38%, Depression 63.10%, Personality Disorder 2.38%, Adjustment Disorder 3.57%, PTED 0%, Moral Injury 2.38%

Other (please specify) 10.71%:

GP states I meet criteria for PTSD but not diagnosed
I feel it was/is PTSD. But if they tick that box they have to help deal with it.
Depression and anxiety is easier for them to say it's Your problem.
Chronic PTSD
CRPS, thrombosis
Dysthymia
Disassociation
PTSR-Post Traumatic Stress Reaction
Phobic anxiety??? What the f**k???
Agoraphobia, OCD

Age and gender respondents to questionnaire 2

18-24 0%, 25-34 2.27%, 35-44 15.91%, 45-54 47.73%, 55-64 29.55%, 65 plus 4.55%

Male 72.73%, female 26.14%, other (Trans female) 1.14%

Ethnicity responses to questionnaire 2

White – British 94.25%, Black or Black British - African

0%, White – Irish 1.15%, Black or Black British - Any other Black background

0%, White - Any other White background 3.45%, Asian or Asian British - Indian

0.00%, Mixed - White & Black Caribbean 0%, Asian or Asian British - Pakistani

0%, Mixed - White & Black African 0%, Asian or Asian British - Bangladeshi

0%, Mixed - White & Asian 1.15%, Asian or Asian British - Any other Asian background 0%, Mixed - Any other Mixed background 0%, Chinese 0%, Black or Black British – Caribbean 0%, Other ethnic group 0%

Analysis of Questionnaire 2

An average of 80.93% of participants experienced symptoms shared with PTED, MI and CPTSD (cluster 1: 20 statements). The lowest positive response of over half of participants (56.82%) was for 'revenge'. This indicates a significant comorbidity or convergence between CPTSD and the constructs of PTED and MI. 84.10% of respondents stated, "What happened was unfair, it was an injustice that went against my values, morals and beliefs;" demonstrating a significant correlation between the causation of both MI and PTED (cluster 2 - statement 15). A significant number (84.54%) of participants responded positively with the five statements associated with CPTSD (those which discriminated from MI and PTED). This further suggests that a significant number of respondents affected by PTED and MI are also affected by CPTSD; and PTED and MI could not be positively discriminated against each other. Therefore, PTED and MI appear to be fundamentally the same.

Hayes et al. (2012) states, "*The hallmark symptoms of PTSD involve alterations to cognitive processes such as memory, attention, planning, and problem solving.*"[243] Linden and Maercker (2011) state, that the ability to problem solve can be a protective factor against embitterment and rumination (PTED).[244] The damage caused to the brain, affecting the area responsible for problem-solving functions in people with PTSD may account for the convergence between PTED, MI and PTSD. Furthermore, this may explain why chronic embitterment may be difficult to treat. This research calls into question whether there is sufficient discrimination between the constructs of CPTSD, MI and PTED. It appears the symptomatology for all three constructs are the same, even if presented somewhat differently; with the exception of causation (such as fear, physical threat or an injustice or betrayal). For example, as discussed in the comments on 'considerations,' CPTSD criteria incudes 'difficulty with affect regulation' and this could cover a broad range of distorted cognition and emotional behaviour found in MI and PTED. Just over two thirds of respondents indicated fear (67.05%). A higher number of respondents (71.59%), positively indicated 'injustice' in relation to the traumatic incident. In comparison, only 25% identified the incident as 'immoral' which was expected to be greater for moral injury. The keyword 'wrong,' was more positively indicated than 'immoral' by 47.73% of respondents. Just over half of respondents (57.95%) felt the traumatic incident was unfair. Approximately one third of respondents (34.09%) indicated the traumatic incident had Shattered their beliefs. A significantly greater number of respondents (84.09%), positively associated the incident with being traumatic rather than 'threatening' (45.45%).

In conclusion, this data supports other research (such as Freyd, 2019) which suggests fear in traumatic experience is not more prevalent than other causes of PTSD (CPTSD). Nor can the symptomatology of PTED be ascribed only to exceptional, yet common negative life events because of the convergence found with CPTSD. The majority of respondents attributed their symptoms, thoughts and feelings to traumatic incidents

---

[243] (Hayes, VanElzakker, & Shin, 2012)
[244] (Linden & Maercker, 2011)

which meet the criteria for PTSD in DSM-5 and 86.9 % of respondents have a diagnosis of (C)PTSD compared with 3.57% diagnosed with adjustment disorder (a classification to which PTED belongs). A retest of the validity of this research questionnaire would be beneficial with a better spread across organisational cultures (frontline services). While there were significant positive responses to statements, the researcher noted a lack of convergence between statements and corresponding keywords. This may indicate a reluctance to associate with certain words which one perceives as weakness, shameful or demeaning. For example, the admission of fear, failure, defeat, being unforgiving, bitterness, blame and so on. Respondents were more comfortable to label their experience as an injustice than to say the event was immoral. This may indicate a higher proportion of traumatic experiences which transgress shared norms and values (such as rules and ethics), opposed to morals which can be subjective and a personal perspective.

This finding positively correlates with research questionnaire 1, indicating there may be a different perception on morals versus values and how participants respond to statements accordingly.

3rd Research Questionnaire

The purpose of this questionnaire is to identify prevalent perceptions of the cause of traumatic incident(s) and psychological injury (PTSD). Moral Injury (MI) and PTED share features of injustice, blame and comorbidity with traumatic experience. Moral Injury and chronic embitterment have been found to maintain PTSD symptoms. Research has hypothesized that MI and PTED require different treatment to PTSD. PTSD may be resistant to treatment until MI and embitterment symptoms are resolved. This research aims to understand 1) what proportion of psychological injury (traumatic) is personally perceived as being attributed to 'blame', compared with attributed to the traumatic experience, 2) what impact does social or institutional culture have on this perception? For example, are there differences in the perception of blame between military and first responder culture? 3) Does the psychological process of attributing blame have a causal effect on the development of PTSD and 4) is blame (including self-blame) the missing link as to why some people develop PTSD following traumatic experience and some do not?

The following questions were asked of First Responders, Military personnel and Healthcare professionals (serving and retired). There was an option for 'other':

1) Which of the following apply to you? (you can select more than one) First Responder (serving), *First Responder (retired), Military (serving), Military (retired), Healthcare professional (serving), Healthcare professional (retired), other*
2) Have you experienced a traumatic incident(s)? *Yes/No*
3) Did the traumatic incident(s) occur on duty? *Yes/No/Not applicable*
4) Do you believe someone was responsible for the traumatic incident? *Yes/No/Not applicable*
5) Do you believe someone is accountable for the traumatic incident? *Yes/No/Not applicable*
6) Do you believe someone is to blame for the traumatic incident? *Yes/No/Not applicable*
7) Do you have a diagnosis of PTSD (or Complex PTSD)? *Yes/No*
8) Do you have symptoms of PTSD and no diagnosis? *Yes/No*
9) Who or what do you believe is the cause for the development of your psychological injury? (select all that apply) *Traumatic incident, Organisation (employer), Offender, Supervisor/line manager/senior manager, Accident, Fate or luck, Colleague or peer, Enemy forces, Self, Friendly forces, Natural event or disaster, Covid-19, Other*
10) Do you believe someone is responsible for causing your psychological injury? *Yes/No/Not applicable*
11) Do you believe someone is accountable for causing your psychological injury? *Yes/No/Not applicable*

12) Do you believe someone is to blame for causing your psychological injury? *Yes/No/Not applicable*

13) Do you believe the traumatic experience is the cause of your psychological injury? *Yes/No/Not applicable*

14) Do you believe someone is to blame for your psychological injury and can you name the reasons why? *Yes/No/Not applicable*

15) Do you believe someone could have prevented the traumatic incident? *Yes/No/Not applicable*

16) Do you believe someone could have prevented the development of your psychological injury? *Yes/No/Not applicable*

17) Do you believe someone had an obligation to prevent the traumatic incident? *Yes/No/Not applicable*

18) Do you believe someone had an obligation to prevent the development of your psychological injury? *Yes/No/Not applicable*

19) Do you believe the person(s) to blame had the intention of causing the traumatic incident? *Yes/No/Not applicable*

20) Do you believe the person(s) to blame for the development of your psychological injury intended this to happen? *Yes/No/Not applicable*

21) Do you believe the person(s) to blame for the traumatic incident had the capacity and the resources to prevent this from happening? *Yes/No/Not applicable*

22) Do you believe the person(s) to blame for the development of your psychological injury had the capacity and the resources to prevent this from happening? *Yes/No/Not applicable*

23) What is your gender? *Male/Female/Other (please specify)*

24) What is your age? *18-20, 21-29, 30-39, 40-49, 50-59,60 or older*

25) What is the highest level of school you have completed? *Primary, some secondary but no qualifications, secondary school qualifications, some college but no qualifications, college with qualifications, under or post-graduate degree, none of the above*

26) Which race/ethnicity best describes you? (Please choose only one.) *White/White British, Black/Black British, Asian/Asian British, Mixed race, rather not say, another race or ethnicity (please specify)*

Results and analysis of questionnaire 3

64 participants completed the online questionnaire. 100% of respondents had experienced a traumatic incident. Nearly all (98.44%) of these occurred on duty. Only four respondents were not affected by PTSD symptoms.

There was a slight variance in the perception of responsibility and blame, compared with accountability for the traumatic incident. Over three quarters (78.13%) of participants believe someone was responsible and to blame for the traumatic incident. A greater proportion of the respondents (82.81%) believe someone is accountable for the traumatic incident. This demonstrates the importance of interpreting the meanings of different types of 'blame.' Accountability may be construed as blame or responsibility, which can be proven with evidence and where a breach goes against an expected norm or written rule. Responsibility and blame may hold subjective and personal meanings, such as an offense or humiliation caused, immoral behaviour, a feeling that an incident is someone else's fault, even if this cannot be proven. 17.19% of respondents believe someone is to blame for their psychological injury but cannot name the reasons why. This could indicate moral dumfounding, where one feels something is wrong and cannot back this up with logical reasons.

In order of significance, respondents believe the following factors are responsible for the development of their psychological injury: Over two thirds of respondents (68.75%) stated 'The organisation.' The same proportion (67.19%) stated 'the traumatic incident.' Just over half (51.56%) stated supervisor/manager/senior manager and 'offender.' 18.75% stated 'accident' and 'colleague or peer.' 15.63% stated 'self.' 14.06% stated fate or luck.' 7.81% stated 'enemy forces.' 6.25% stated 'friendly forces' and 'other' (unspecified). 4.69% stated 'natural event.'

29 participants are serving first responders, 26 participants are retired

first responders, 11 respondents are military veterans, 3 participants are serving healthcare professionals and 2 are retired healthcare professionals. One respondent selected three occupations and 8 military veterans selected a second occupation. This may explain the higher response to 'offender' being identified as responsible for the development of psychological injury, compared with enemy forces or friendly forces (which are terms used in the military).

51.56% believe someone could have prevented the traumatic incident. 67.19% of respondents believe someone had an obligation to prevent the traumatic incident. 35.94% of respondents believe the person(s) to blame had the intention of causing the traumatic incident. 62.50% of respondents believe the person(s) to blame for the traumatic incident had the capacity and the resources to prevent this from happening. Participants appeared more likely to believe the traumatic incident was not intentional. Between half to just over two thirds of respondents believed the traumatic incident was preventable, those responsible had the capacity or resources to prevent the incident and they were obligated to do so.

A significantly higher proportion of respondents, (for which 92.19% believe the traumatic incident is the cause of their psychological injury) believe that despite the traumatic incident their psychological injury was not inevitable. 87.50% believe someone could have prevented the development of their psychological injury. 92.19% of respondents believe someone had an obligation to prevent the development of their psychological injury. 81.25% of respondents believe the person(s) to blame for the development of their psychological injury had the capacity and the resources to prevent this from happening. Over three quarters (76.56%) of respondents believe someone is responsible for causing their psychological injury. Over three quarters (79.69%) of respondents believe someone is accountable for causing their psychological injury. Over three quarters (76.56%) of respondents believe someone is to blame for causing their psychological injury. Over two thirds (70.31%) of respondents believe the person(s) to blame for the development of their psychological injury did not intend this to happen. 81.25% of respondents believe the person to blame had the capacity and resources to prevent the injury.

Nearly all (98.44%) respondents stated the traumatic incident(s) was work-related and data shows significant positive responses indicating obligation, capacity, preventability, blame, responsibility and accountability. This suggests the overwhelming belief that the organisation and/or senior staff are to blame for their psychological injury and were negligent or incompetent in not providing the necessary resources (such as treatment and support), to prevent the development of psychological injury.

On balance, the development of psychological injury was attributed to others with responsibility, obligation and capacity over and above the traumatic incident. Therefore, posttraumatic blame appears to be a significant feature of traumatic experience in frontline service and the development (and possibly maintenance of) psychological injury.

70.31% of respondents were male. 28.13% were female and 1.56% other (unspecified). Respondents aged 30-39 are 7.81%. Half (50%) are 40-49 years of age. A quarter are 50-59. 17.19% are 60 years of age or over.

One respondent stated they had no level of education or qualifications. Under half of respondents (43.75%) have under-graduate or post-graduate education. One quarter have a college education with qualifications. 29.69% of respondents had a maximum of secondary school education and qualifications.

95.31% of respondents are white British. A greater proportion of respondents were male, white British and first responders. There are cultural differences between frontline organisations, work environments and type of traumatic exposure. A wider study with more participants across occupational and organisational frontline settings would be beneficial. Capturing any variance in perception of blame across length of service and levels of resilience to trauma, posttraumatic growth or recovery may also be of interest in further research.

Potential synthesis between Moral Injury (MI) and PTED constructs

The PTED scale has been proven to be robust. It has a suggested score for clinically significant levels of embitterment. This can assist medical professionals to identify candidates for treatment.[245]

Koenig et al. (2019) states, there "*is no measure of MI that uses gold standard methodology here.*" Development of more robust measures are needed.[246] Moving on from the MIES (Moral Injury Events Scale),[247] Koenig developed a scale which measures symptoms as well as the original factors of betrayal, perpetration other and perpetration self. It is for military use.[248] He states, the scale MISS-M, is a "*valid measure for assessing symptom severity in clinical practice.*"[249]

Robust measurement of MI and PTED, and official recognition may be necessary for evolving services, diagnosis and treatment. MI and PTED, appear to be comorbid with PTSD. Linden and Maercker (2011) state, rumination and revenge phenomenon found in PTED can maintain PTSD symptoms. PTSD has proven to be resistant to treatment. Research suggests that MI focused treatment has shown to significantly reduce PTSD symptoms and increase post-traumatic growth.[250]

MI measures are predominately concerned with military experience,

---

[245] (Linden, Baumann, Lieberei, & Rotter, 2009)
[246] (Koenig, 2019)
[247] (Nash, 2013)
[248] (Koenig, 2018)
[249] (Koenig, 2018)
[250] (Maguen & Litz, 2020)

though it is now being acknowledged as occurring within civilian populations, such as healthcare and first responder roles, intimate abuse and learning about someone's trauma.[251]   Koenig et al. (2019) state, *"research should seek to identify and treat noncombat veterans, civilians in high-risk professions (physicians, nurses, police, firemen, other first responders), and those with a history of trauma (abuse, rape)."*[252] PTED has been found in general populations and traumatized groups resulting from common yet negative life experiences, a prone personality to embitterment (where there is no known trigger event) or comorbid with other conditions.[253] Therefore, both PTED and MI can be found in non-military populations. This research has found PTED within high risk roles, which expose individuals to significant trauma and correlating with both low level and severe traumatic experience.

Both MI and PTED factor a shattering of deeply held beliefs, morals and values. Unlike the MISS-M scale,[254] the PTED scale[255] does not differentiate between a ruptured value or belief which is psychological, spiritual or religious. MISS-M seeks to identify the perpetrator of moral transgression as self, or someone in a position of trust, power or authority - namely God, Leaders or peers. The PTED scale appears to only present one statement, which could indicate self-perpetration – (7) 'For which I blame and am angry with myself'. However, this could be interpreted as the individual thinking or feeling they should have done something to prevent the negative incident. Linden et al. (2007) states, 'victims' may blame themselves for not being able to cope with what's happened or not preventing the event.[256] This may be convergent with the MI factor of bearing witness to harm or failing to act to prevent harm. Factor (12), 'That makes me feel helpless and disempowered' in the

---

[251] (Barnes, Hurley, & Taber, 2019)
[252] (Koenig, Ames, & Bussing, 2019)
[253] (Linden & Rotter, 2018)
[254] (Koenig, 2018)
[255] (Linden, Baumann, Lieberei, & Rotter, 2009)
[256] (Linden, Baumann, Rotter, & Schippan, 2007)

PTED scale, could correlate with feeling unable to prevent harm or it could suggest the harm was inflicted by someone else.

MISS-M statements explore the individual's sense of meaning and purpose in life. The PTED scale has three statements which may allude to a loss of meaning and purpose, as well as hopelessness – (8) 'That led to the feeling that there is no sense to strive or to make an effort', (14) That led to a considerable decrease in my strength and drive, and (17) 'That made me unable to pursue occupational and/or family activities as before.' Linden and Maercker (2011), regarding PTED, highlights the embittered persons' loss of future orientation, loss of meaning and purpose and losing the resources to achieve one's aims. Their research identifies feelings of betrayal, a loss of trust and a personality trait of cynicism. MISS-M asks participants to respond to statements on a 1-10 scale of severity. Statements include factors such as trust, betrayal and future orientation. For example, (M23) – Most people are trustworthy. (M1) – Feel betrayed by leaders once trusted. (M30) – I have discovered a meaningful life purpose.

Koenig's (2018) model of MI, acknowledges the psychological and spiritual/religious symptoms. MISS-M refers specifically to a loss of religious faith or hope. Koenig perhaps alludes to a loss of faith in people by exploring the individuals' loss of trust in others and self, as well as a loss of hope in one's future, meaning and purpose. The PTED scale doesn't explore religious or spiritual contexts.

MISS-M directly identifies feelings of guilt and shame. The PTED scale potentially alludes to this emotional response at, (4) 'About which I have to think over and over again,' (5) 'That causes me to be extremely upset when I am reminded of it', (7) 'For which I blame and am angry with myself.' However, I suggest this is one possible interpretation and the PTED statements (4) and (5) could be trauma responses, such as intrusive memories or reexperiencing or as Koenig (2019) states, *"the event happened because of the way I acted"* or *"the sort of person I am,"* *leading to guilt or shame'*.[257] MISS-M identifies survivors guilt.

Perhaps the only potential correlation between revenge phenomenon found in PTED with MISS-M, is the statement (M7), ' It bothers me that I enjoyed hurting/killing people'. There is a connection between desire for revenge and vengeful acts. However, Linden and Maercker (2011) highlights that there are no clear figures to show what proportion of revenge fantasy becomes acted out in reality. He does identify homicide-suicide as a potential factor in PTED and that access to weapons could increase the risks.[258] EMIS model of MI (Currier et al., 2017) identifies a desire for revenge as a feature of MI.

MISS-M uses statements directly related to difficulty forgiving self or others. However, it seems to omit forgiveness of leaders, peers and those outside military service. Forgiveness of God and Self appear to be the only perceived transgressors identified in this context. The PTED scale doesn't appear to factor difficulty with forgiveness, yet Linden and Maercker (2011) state, that forgiveness as a personality trait can be a protective factor against the development of embitterment and revenge phenomenon; though forgiveness is not necessary for overcoming trauma. He explores forgiveness as an opposite to embitterment. He highlights that being able to view the negative incident from various perspectives, including constructive criticism of self can help with recovery, as well as having good self-esteem.[259] MISS-M explores factors of self-condemnation and difficulty with forgiveness, including self-blame, critical self, self-esteem and post-traumatic growth. For example, (M45) 'I certainly feel useless at times' and (M39) 'Learning from bad things I've done helps me get over them.' (M35) – I have forgiven myself for what happened.

---

[257] (Koenig, 2019)
[258] (Linden & Maercker, 2011)
[259] (Linden & Maercker, 2011)

"PTED is not defined by the critical event, but by a psychological process (violation of basic beliefs) and by the type, severity and course of psychopathology (embitterment, intrusive thoughts, irritability, dissociation, phobic avoidance)" (Linden et al., 2007)

PTED is defined as a disorder. MI is thought to be a dimensional problem and not a mental disorder.[260] However, Barnes et al. (2019) states, it has a *'profound affect'* on one's ability to function in many areas, such as emotional, psychological, behavioural, social, and spiritual. PTED is also identified as a multi-dimensional condition with biological, social, psychological and emotional factors. PTED has been explored in relation to personality traits, comorbid conditions, political conflict, relationship issues, social pain, terminal illness and the workplace.[261] One of the criteria for PTED is that the individual has *"No obvious mental disorder in the year before the critical event. The present state is no recurrence of a pre-existing mental disorder"* (Linden et al., 2007). This is important for the purpose of discriminating PTED from other conditions. However, Linden highlights the difficulty in assessing whether there are pre or comorbid conditions, such as personality disorder.[262] Whereas MI has been found to be commonly comorbid with PTSD.[263]

Unlike the PTED scale which suggests a clinically relevant score of >2.5,[264] MI scales at this time have not identified a clinically significant cut-off score.[265] Linden et al. (2007), identified an average duration of symptoms of 31.7 months and impaired daily activities,[266] which suggests meeting the Equality Act 2010 definition of disability. Therefore, it may be plausible that those affected by MI could also be protected under the Act in the UK depending on the duration of dysfunction. There is no need to

---

[260] (Barnes, Hurley, & Taber, 2019)
[261] (Linden & Maercker, 2011)
[262] (Linden, Baumann, Rotter, & Schippan, 2007)
[263] (Barnes, Hurley, & Taber, 2019)
[264] (Linden, Baumann, Lieberei, & Rotter, 2009)
[265] (Koenig, 2019)
[266] (Linden, Baumann, Rotter, & Schippan, 2007)

have a clinically recognised diagnosis to meet the definition of disability, rather symptoms have a substantial effect on normal day to day functioning which lasts at least 12 months, is likely to last at least 12 months or is recurring.[267] PTED and MI have both been found to increase the risk of suicide.[268]

MI and PTED appear to share significant core factors, such as a trigger event or experience considered morally wrong and unjust, which significantly challenges or shatters one's deeply held beliefs, morals or values. MI and PTED can feature feelings of betrayal, anger, shame, guilt, hopelessness, avoidance, withdrawal from others, difficultly forgiving, self-blame, loss of trust, loss of meaning and purpose, loss of resources and can be post-traumatic in nature.

Dean et al. (2019), describes MI as an insult to one's morality.[269] Linden and Maercker (2011) describe PTED as resulting from an insulting event.

PTED seems to place the responsibility on the individual, such as their personal perception on the event, how they assimilate what has happened, their coping skills (such as ability to problem solve), their pre-morbid character (such as cynicism, strict beliefs and high standards) and their personality (such as open-mindedness, wisdom and adaptability to change).[270] MI appears to place the responsibility onto external factors, such as 'broken systems',[271] high impact job role or history of abuse.[272] Both PTED and MI acknowledge the multi-dimensional factors which are external (i.e. societal, environmental, work related systems) and personal (i.e. behavioural, psychological).[273] MI also identifies spiritual factors,

---

[267] (Equality Act 2010 Guidance; The Definition Of Disability, 2011)
[268] (Linden & Maercker, 2011) (Koenig, 2019)
[269] (Dean, Talbot, & Dean, 2019)
[270] (Linden & Maercker, 2011)
[271] (Dean, Talbot, & Dean, 2019)
[272] (Koenig, Ames, & Bussing, 2019)
[273] (Linden & Maercker, 2011)

including religious beliefs.[274] The onset of PTED appears to be influenced by these dimensional factors, which can impact on one's resilience. MI appears to affect ones' functioning in these areas of life.[275]

MIES *"demonstrates only small to moderate correlations with other indicators of psychopathology, indicating that it is a relatively distinct construct." (Bryan et al., 2015).* [276] *"Discriminant validity was demonstrated by relatively weak correlations with other psychosocial, religious, and physical health constructs" –* (Koenig et al., 2017, The Moral Injury Symptom Scale-Military Version)[277] It is unclear whether MI construct has previously been compared with that of PTED, prior to this research study.

Summary

PTED and Moral Injury may be of great interest in the pursuit of bringing relief to those who are affected by trauma. Perhaps these conditions should be viewed as co-morbid with PTSD in many cases. PTSD treatment may be more effective if MI and PTED are addressed first; much like co-morbid alcoholism or drug abuse which needs to be overcome prior to, or in conjunction with PTSD treatment. We know that people need to feel safe and secure before effective trauma treatment can begin.[278] It appears that PTED and MI constructs largely share the same symptoms and cause. Deeply held values, beliefs and morals are challenged or shattered. Symptoms include anger, sense of betrayal or injustice, shame, guilt, self-blame, negative self-concept, rumination, revenge fantasy, suicidal thoughts and feelings, loss of trust, loss of meaning and purpose and difficulty with forgiveness. It seems MI is now being observed in civilian populations which could bring the synthesis between PTED and Moral Injury still closer.

---

[274] (Koenig, Ames, & Bussing, 2019)
[275] (Barnes, Hurley, & Taber, 2019)
[276] (Bryan, Anestis, Bryan, & Anestis, 2015)
[277] (Koenig, Youssef, Ames, & Oliver, 2017)
[278] (Herman, 1997)

4th Research Questionnaire

The researcher asked respondents working in frontline services to detail covert acts of retaliation. This was to further understand revenge phenomenon associated with PTED, MI and PTSD. The aim was to explore alternative types of revenge, other than revenge fantasy or violent acts of revenge (such as homicide-suicide) which tend to be the focus within these constructs. The researcher was interested to know if covert retaliation within hierarchical organisations offered some relief to feelings of helplessness, powerlessness, subordination, humiliation and injustice; including where procedural justice is not attainable (such as through grievance procedure). Initially, respondents were confused by the term 'covert retaliation or revenge.' Therefore, the researcher amended the questionnaire to 'sneaky, underhanded retaliation.' Insufficient responses were acquired (Eleven), to make this research valid. However, the data obtained is still of interest and perhaps worth further research and exploration in the future.

1. What act(s) of sneaky, underhanded retaliation against colleagues or senior officers have you done to get back at them for poor decisions, poor leadership, unjust behaviour, humiliation or because you felt it was the only way you could get revenge? For example, an act of sabotage.

Respondents stated:

1) Driving the patrol car round in reverse gear to get around mileage restrictions

2) None, I was too unwell and just told my Supervisors they were not allowed to phone me or do home visits and my Fed Rep did home visits. I then got medically redeployed out of the department

3) Three respondents stated None. One stated, I have done it the right way at my expense

4) Telling an officer, if you want your land rover which is not roadworthy to sign for it, after

ordering me he wants it now

5) I reported my inspector to the anonymous national complaints number. He constantly used bullying and coercive behaviours and threats to transfer me if I ever disagreed with him. He belittled staff in front of a female visitor (civilian), by telling the visitor that this officer was the Rolf Harris of the section In front of the officer and the whole office staff. After being bullied for 18 months I was so outraged I reported him to the complaints line. He was investigated and eventually transferred

6) Whilst suffering from a very nasty cold, deliberately went and used the telephone in my bosses office. I might have sneezed, oh and snorted a bit. He had 10 days off work with a cold he developed a short time later

7) Doing a bad job to make them look bad, following orders knowing the outcome would fail, bad mouthing them to others

8) Bullying and harassment complaints, before lodging tribunal papers on them and slating them on twitter

9) Refused all overtime and withdrew from all specialisms that I did voluntarily.

2. What stories of sneaky, underhanded retaliation or revenge have you heard about which happened in your organisation?

Respondents stated:

1) Punishment postings, applications blocked or paper sifted, picked for unpleasant duties

2) None I can remember

3) I suffered discrimination because I refused to join the Masons...politely. I couldn't afford it, and I do not believe in "God". I qualified Sergeant, Inspector, and passed a Course to be an Instructor, and was used as such for several years. When I declined a training Post

that involved travel 40 miles each way daily, I politely declined - to be told "You will do what you are ordered to do". So I resigned after 11years of impeccable service (I have the certificate). Later told by a Mason that I had been "Black-balled"... which many disagreed with but kept quiet. They had their revenge alright.

4) Giving any officer a map

5) Usually tea contamination. Moving stuff around on desks. Low level stuff really. When senior officers had personal toilets, using them on nights and not flushing was popular. Almost hangable being caught on the Div Commanders toilet!

6) A lot of officers reporting each other. Sergeants setting up traps to stick officers on

(disciplinary). Fake reports of racism or sexual harassment to get back at officers

7) Enlisting them onto free offers that humiliated them, sex sites, free sex aids, gay sex sites, wigs, inappropriate covert medication (such as laxatives in tea), spitting in drinks, sending partners comments stating they were cheating

8) Getting them back in long grass ... they may have won a battle but I won the war...went above their head direct to Chief Constable

9) Sickness, fairness at work and bad apple

10) Punishment moves like into custody, moves across county making getting to work difficult.

3. Would you say these types of retaliation or revenge are culturally accepted or commonplace within your organisation?

Nearly two thirds (63.64%) of respondents stated 'yes.'

4. Is sneaky, underhanded retaliation or revenge the only way to realistically get a feeling of justice or regain a feeling of personal power as a subordinate in a hierarchical organisation?

Nearly three quarters (72.73%) of respondents stated 'yes.'

5. If you answered yes to question 4, please explain why

Respondents stated:

1) The organisation hates to be challenged in any way, even when it is wrong, and will not let things lie. Openly challenging wrong doing is career suicide

2) Justifying your authority correct, but going about it the wrong way

3) There is no recourse through normal complaints channels as in the long term it can derail your career for future

4) I do not feel this way, I spoke out against it however this led to me being ostracised from the team. I believe others use this type of tactic as many officers stick together and some are protected by higher ranks or tick certain boxes

5) There was no other way to fight against the culture or bully

6) Can't let the bastards grind me down ... once they **** up on service policy I hammer it back at them

7) Middle management are incompetent and do not reflect COG thinking in assisting officers

8) Doing it the right way causes the complainant more difficulties than the person who is wrong, it takes far too long.

6. Did the act of retaliation or revenge bring you satisfaction or sense of relief?

Over half of respondents (54.55%) stated 'yes.' Just over one third (36.36%) stated 'not applicable.'

7. In which frontline service did these (allege revenge happen?

Police service 81.82%, Armed forces 18.18%, Fire s service 0%, Prison service 0%, NHS hospital 0%, C 0%

8. What is your gender?

Male 90.91%, Female 9.09%, Other (please specify) 0%

9. What is your highest level of education?

High school 0%, College 36.36%, Undergraduate 9.09%, post graduate 54.55%, N/A 0%, Other (please specify) 0%

10. What is your age?

Under 18 - 0%, 18 – 29 (9.09%), 30 – 44 (0%), 45 – 59 (63.64%), 60+ (27.27%)

In summary, there were insufficient responses to this online questionnaire and some respondents did not seem to understand some of the questions, given their answers. Therefore this research cannot draw any conclusions. However, some of the examples given are interesting for exploring revenge in embitterment or MI as forms of covert retaliation within hierarchical organisations, when overt revenge is not possible. Revenge phenomenon has been discussed in research as being purely cognitive and fantastical or perhaps the rare extreme of openly or violently enacting revenge. This research suggests covert retaliation or revenge is another coping mechanism for overcoming feelings of powerlessness, injustice and humiliation.

Following on from the literary review and research results, the researcher presents a new theory of posttraumatic blame, associated with trauma and significant negative life event(s) in the next section.

Claire Carter

CHAPTER 9

Posttraumatic-Blame Theory

The researcher posits a new theory called Posttraumatic-Blame (PTB) (2020) associated with (C)PTSD and a potential definition of Moral Injury. PTB may or may not result from 'persistent distorted blame of self or others about the cause or consequences of the traumatic event(s)' (as in DSM-5 diagnostic criteria, D3 for PTSD). In order to define PTB or blame as 'distorted,' a medical professional would need to make a judgement that there is no foundation, justification, rationale or evidence to support the patients' blame attribution(s). This would neither be a realistic expectation or an ethical one; and certainly not within the remit of a clinical practitioner. The only achievable measure, is the patients' perception and belief that the attribution of blame is appropriate. The researcher suggests criteria D3 within the DSM-5 definition is amended and the word 'distorted' removed; to instead state 'persistent blame of self or others about the cause or consequences of the traumatic event(s). PTB can be a persistent cognition contributing to dysfunction, and therefore may be considered pathological in nature. A morally injurious element within the traumatic experience may lead to Posttraumatic-Blame. PTB may present as unreconcilable embitterment, anger, disappointment or sadness and victimization. PTB may include factors such as betrayal, Institutional betrayal, injustice and Moral Injury.

For Posttraumatic-Blame to apply, there must be 1) a traumatic incident 2) for which one perceives a person(s) or organisation responsible for failing to prevent physical injury or the development of psychological injury or loss suffered.

The individual makes a cognitive assessment of the traumatic incident, the participants (including self) and whether the incident and associated consequences (such as psychological injury, loss, change) could have been prevented. Participants are assessed for negligence (intentional or unintentional) and whether they had the capacity to prevent the incident (i.e. the resources were available to prevent the incident, the participant(s) had mental, emotional and physical capability, the participant(s) had knowledge or experience which could have informed their behaviour). The outcome of the assessment is that the participant(s) is assessed as responsible. For example, they had capacity, were in a position of authority or in a trusted position, and were negligent. To summarize; the person(s) or organisation is perceived as 1) responsible and/or 2) accountable and/or 3) negligent and/or 4) has capacity and/or 5) the incident and/or injury is perceived as preventable.

The psychopathology (psychological process) of PTB is hypothesized as including (and not limited to):

A) Injustice or wrongdoing – the perception of which shatters previously held beliefs about life, people or systems

B) Future Disorientation – the disruption to deeply held values and norms disorientates the individual and affects the ability to visualize or plan for the future, or understanding what the future means without previously held beliefs. One's values and morals may stay intact. The individual may wonder how they will be able to coexist in a world which does not share their values and morals (as they once believed). An unimagined future results in a loss of meaning, purpose and motivation in life.

The individual may experience anxiety about the future. Anhedonia (loss of pleasure or enjoyment) may be attributed to this loss of future orientation, meaning and purpose

C) Disordered Cognition and Emotional Dysregulation – the individual becomes locked in a mental and emotional state of distress. Thoughts and feelings are in disarray as one attempts to make sense of the traumatic incident, responsibility, accountability, why and how the incident happened, 'what if?' or 'if only…' attempts to process loss, grief, feelings of guilt or shame, altered future or significant life change and feelings of vulnerability or insecurity.

The individual may attempt to organize thoughts and feelings through a process of rumination, replaying thoughts, feelings, memories and events. The aim of this rumination is coming to an understanding, solve problems, find a resolution or determine a course of action. The goal of the individual is to regain a sense of personal control, security, safety and future direction. The persistent pursuit for 'justice' may be an attempt to reassert the individuals' beliefs about how people and the world operate or behave; to re-establish beliefs which were shattered, rather than adopt new beliefs or accept change. This may appear to be productive or solution focused. However, justice may not be forthcoming and even if achieved, justice cannot undo what has happened. The persistent pursuit of justice can entrench and exacerbate symptoms (such as rumination on events). Therefore, problem-solving should focus on posttraumatic growth (with or without the pursuit for justice). Three possible pathways may emerge 1) reflection, acceptance, positive problem-solving and posttraumatic growth, 2) rumination, unacceptance, a focus on anger and action directed to others (which may include revenge fantasy), resistance to change one's position or adapt to circumstances 3) rumination, unacceptance, a focus on grief, sadness or victimization and a resistance to change or adapt (which may correlate with depression)

D) Organized Cognition, Emotional Regulation and Future Orientation – The goal is for the individual to reach a new understanding of life, people, systems and the world; to change and adapt to new beliefs, meaning, purpose and lifestyle. The individual assimilates the traumatic experience into their new understanding.

In summary: the proposed psychopathology of PTB is A) Perception of injustice or wrongdoing B) Future Disorientation C) Disorganized Cognition and Emotional Dysregulation D) Organized Cognition, Emotional Regulation and Future Orientation –(no longer pathological).

Symptoms of PTB may include: i) embitterment ii) anhedonia iii) guilt or shame iv) grief v) resistance to change vi) victimization vii) anger viii) revenge fantasy ix) future disorientation x) rigid perceptions xi) persistent negative rumination xii) difficulty problem-solving.

Difficulty with forgiveness has not been included. PTB focuses on the individual's reluctance to change and adapt to new beliefs or lifestyle which may present as difficulty with forgiveness. For example, the inability to forgive may allow for the avoidance of change, as with rigid perceptions, and persistent feeling of victimization. Furthermore, embitterment is, by nature, unforgiving and is a named symptom in PTB. Therapeutic focus on 'acceptance of an altered self' and how the altered self 'fits' with altered beliefs and altered future is suggested, as well as support with change, grief and loss. In conclusion, Posttraumatic Blame is characterized and defined as:

Criteria A

A traumatic incident occurs for which:

1) one perceives a person(s) or organisation responsible for failing to prevent i) physical injury and/or ii) the development of psychological injury and/or iii) loss suffered

Criteria B

The person(s) or organisation is perceived as 1) responsible and/or 2) accountable and/or 3) negligent and/or 4) has capacity and/or 5) the incident or injury is perceived as preventable

Criteria C

Symptoms of PTB may include:

i) embitterment ii) anhedonia iii) guilt or shame iv) grief v) resistance to change vi) victimization vii) anger viii) revenge fantasy ix) future disorientation x) rigid perceptions xi) persistent negative rumination xii) difficulty problem-solving

The psychopathology of PTB is:

1) Perception of injustice, breach of values and norms, or wrongdoing

2) Future Disorientation

3) Disorganized Cognition and Emotional Dysregulation

4) Organized Cognition, Emotional Regulation and Future Orientation – (no longer pathological).

Therapeutic focus

Suggested therapeutic focus is on loss, acceptance, problem-solving skills and change or adaptation, including Posttraumatic Growth, altered self, altered beliefs, future direction, focus on capabilities (not disabilities).

Definition of Moral Injury (Seggie, C.)

'A breach of one's expectations of self or others in accordance with roles and responsibilities, which challenges one's beliefs about safety, security and functional norms and leads to embitterment and Posttraumatic Blame.'

Normal and pathological blame

This research has explored blame as a multi-faceted symptom. For example; 1) as a major precursor to the development of PTSD, chronic embitterment, PTED or Moral Injury and 2) as a minor symptom, which interacts alongside other PTSD, PTED and MI symptoms within a cluster. Blame can exist as a singularity, experienced in everyday life and everyday situations. However, this research is interested in blame as a persistent and damaging, yet functional symptom resulting from exceptional traumatic experience. Posttraumatic-blame can be enduring, so as to maintain PTSD symptoms (such as hyperarousal, hypervigilance, intrusive thoughts or memories) and symptoms of chronic embitterment (such as anger, rumination and revenge fantasy). Therefore, blame may become pathological within the context of PTSD and other conditions. The researcher posits that blame may serve (in part) as a function for ordering thoughts, feelings and beliefs about the traumatic incident(s). The process of understanding why or how the traumatic incident(s) occurred (such as why or how did this happen) and involves the process of determining who and what. For example, what happened, what could have been done differently, who had responsibility, who behaved wrongly. Subsequently, blame may or may not be attributed to self or other(s). Once blame has been attributed, a resolution may be necessary in order to re-evaluate the incident and find acceptance (assimilation), compassion and empathy for self and others. This process may need to happen before PTSD treatments can be effective in some individuals (as identified in research into PTED and MI, comorbid with PTSD).

The next case study demonstrates the application of posttraumatic blame theory.

Case Study 8

Arrangements were made with this veteran for a video call with his wife present for support. Initially, the video call was to explain the purpose of the research project and book, advise the case study would be anonymous and how his information would be handled and kept safe. The call was also for the veteran to gauge potential rapport with the researcher. The veteran agreed to continue with a video interview during the call. The veteran recounted his experiences factually and chronologically, as if a linear narrative was necessary for memory recall. Emotions were not verbalized, though at times he became tearful and distressed when particular memories or thoughts came to the fore. The interview was drawn to a close with discussion of other topics which helped shift onto neutral or happy thoughts and feelings. A copy of the case study was sent to the veteran and his wife for approval and consent for publication.

This case study is used to demonstrate Posttraumatic-Blame Theory. A military veteran (Sergeant) of 26 years' service, participated in a video interview with the researcher. The purpose of the interview was explained and verbal consent was given. His wife was present throughout in a supportive role. This veteran had been involved in various conflicts and high risk situations, including Northern Ireland and the Gulf war. He attributes his PTSD to two traumatic incidents, on home-soil and in the workplace. Furthermore, he attributes the onset of his PTSD to the negligence of 'others' who he believes had responsibility, trust, authority and capacity to prevent the traumatic incident(s). This veteran described his relationship with military service positively and was clear that he received support from colleagues and peers in service in relation to the two traumatic incidents.

Despite supportive others, he feels unable to 'move on' from the injustice or wrongdoing which significantly impacted on him, his health and his day to day functioning.

This veteran has a diagnosis of CPTSD and symptoms linked to experiences in the Gulf war, stating he has gaps in memory and flashbacks (including smells and images). However, he attributes the onset of posttraumatic symptoms to incident 1 which was prior to the Gulf war.

Incident 1: A false allegation was made by an individual against the veteran, claiming he had an intimidating character. He had supportive colleagues around him and witnesses prepared to attend the hearing. There was a lengthy and stressful investigation which the veteran believed to be unjustified. He found the process to be unfair as his witnesses were not allowed to attend and he did not have representation at the hearing. Yet, the opposition had both. The man who made the allegations had a history of making allegations against others. The veteran is of the opinion, the man was attempting to use these situations to further his career and promotion. He felt very hurt by the allegations, which knocked his confidence and made him question his abilities as a supervisor. He was also concerned about the impact on his own career progression. However, promotions had been 'frozen' at the time due to the climate within the organisation. The veteran was cleared of any wrongdoing. A colleague of rank told him after the hearing, the case could have been thrown out, if he had gone to see him. The veteran did not seek representation for the hearing or help from this colleague; as he believed he had done nothing wrong, there was no case to answer and the case would not proceed. He had faith in the system and process. There were colleagues who had overheard information that could have potentially ended the case before it got started. They did not come forward. The veteran felt let-down by them, calling them cowards for watching a friend be subjected to an injustice and a stressful process. The researcher noted the potential for the veteran to have deeply held values, morals and beliefs shattered. He suffered a loss of faith in justice, process and colleagues, as well as a loss of trust. He experienced negative self-concept; questioning his abilities and style as a supervisor. There are individuals he blames for this injustice and he is unable to 'let it go.' He attributes this incident as the onset of posttraumatic symptoms.

He believes the incident could have been prevented by those who had the capacity (opportunity, knowledge/information), the obligation (as friends and colleagues), and the responsibility (those in authority to do the right thing). He believes others had it within their power to prevent the stressful experience.

Incident 2: The sergeant raised concerns to colleagues (also supervisors) about the attitude of an individual under his charge. Their opinions were, that this was just his character. However, the sergeant felt there were reasons for the soldier's behaviour. He did not know what those reasons were. The soldier appeared withdrawn from others and only connected with one person who he got on well with. The sergeant asked to meet with the soldier in the presence of a colleague (after his experience with incident 1). He wanted a witness to the conversation to safeguard himself against any allegation. The soldier stated he had no issues. The sergeant, invited his feedback should he experience any problems (including with his management style). The sergeant had email correspondence with line managers who had knowledge of this soldiers' mental health condition (PTSD), and did not communicate this to him as direct supervisor. An incident occurred in an outside area, where no one was present. The sergeant was aware of the soldier approaching him. He had not long furnished the soldier with his weapon and knew it was loaded with ammunition. The soldier was aggressive as he approached the sergeant, shouting "what did you just call me; a paki?" The sergeant had not uttered anything to the soldier and stated so. The soldier was volatile, angry and seemingly looking to manifest an argument. He put his rifle under the sergeants' chin. The sergeant was in fear for his life and believed the soldier could have killed him any second. He managed to get away to the control room where colleagues were working. The soldier pursued him. His rifle was wrestled off him and he was subdued. The sergeant was grateful to have the support of his colleagues and the military police in the way the incident was handled. However, the sergeant was told the soldier had been relocated to the same residential area where he and his family lived. This news escalated his fears for his safety and that of his family. The sergeant did not know if he would target them. He was still unaware at this point that the soldier was suffering with PTSD. The sergeant stated he believes it was this incident which escalated his posttraumatic symptoms to full diagnostic PTSD.

The sergeant subsequently attended a programme for soldiers affected by PTSD. He arrived, to find the soldier who had threatened his life, sitting opposite him. The sergeant reconciled with the soldier, understanding now that his actions and behaviour had been due to PTSD. He stated they got on well together. The sergeant expressed blame for the traumatic incident on colleagues who had knowledge of the soldiers' difficulties and did not communicate this. He believes them to be responsible for failing to provide appropriate welfare for the soldier (such as with a phased return to duty). The sergeant did not blame the soldier for the traumatic incident, even though it was the soldier who threatened his life. This demonstrates the attribution of posttraumatic blame for his psychological injury, on both the incident and persons with a duty of care to the soldier and the sergeant. Blame was not attributed to the aggressor (soldier), as he was perhaps assessed as not having mental and emotional capacity and possibly was not stable enough to prevent his actions. Though the soldier is responsible for his behaviour, he did not have control over the regulation of his thoughts and feelings. Those with a responsibility for his welfare and that of colleagues were assessed as having the capacity to prevent the incident.

The next section draws conclusions on the reviewed research, answers the questions posed in the Thesis at the beginning of the project, and suggests questions for further research which have arisen from the review. The book closes with some final words from the author.

CHAPTER 10

Summary, Conclusions and further questions

Summary

(1) Do Moral Injury (MI) and PTED share the same symptomatology? (2) Do MI and PTED share the same type of triggering event or causation?

This research proposes that MI and PTED are fundamentally the same construct in relation to symptomatology and causation. A morally injurious or unjust act occurs and embitterment reactions result (such as blame, negative self-concept, anger, revenge fantasy, guilt, shame, loss of meaning and purpose, loss of trust, sense of betrayal, helplessness).

(3) Are MI and PTED comorbid with PTSD and do they share the same triggering event?

Chronic embitterment and MI are significantly present in research respondents with a diagnosis of PTSD, Complex PTSD or those who appeared to meet the criteria for these conditions on research questionnaires and case studies. Researchers have identified MI as often comorbid with PTSD. Sabic et al., (2018) and Lehrner & Yehuda, (2018) identified significant cross-over between PTED and PTSD symptoms. Research into secondary trauma to a primary event may be beneficial; potentially connecting embitterment or MI to the index trauma. For example, a life threatening incident is the primary event. The negative response of others to this event comes as a 'secondary assault' (such as in the theory of institutional betrayal). The second assault triggers the onset of embitterment reactions and attribution of blame. Therefore, this research hypothesizes that the cause of PTSD (life-threatening event) and MI/PTED (injustice) are different, yet the triggering event may inextricably link these constructs together. Furthermore, this research posits that there is not sufficient means by which to discriminate PTED and MI from PTSD as separate standalone constructs.

(4) Do MI and PTED have specific recommended treatment options and are they the same?

Research into treatment options are in their infancy. Trials are underway for Wisdom Therapy for PTED and Adaptive Disclosure Therapy for MI. Early outcomes appear to be positive. Forgiveness Therapy may also be beneficial for both.

(5) Do we need these two separate classifications?

This research proposes that MI and PTED are fundamentally the same; though one model is a disorder and the other still unspecified. PTED is a stand-alone construct. One might consider MI a syndrome relating to PTSD. Both are psychosocial constructs which may impact on biological, psychological, social and spiritual areas of life. PTED has a focus on symptom cluster and types of emotional dysregulation (such as embitterment, rumination and revenge phenomenon), over and above causation (such as type of traumatic experience). Perhaps in this way, objectively discriminating and classifying this construct is possible; whereas MI may be a subjective idea, focused primarily on causation (such as betrayal and breach of one's moral code) and therefore, one's personal experience, opposed to psychopathology and symptoms. This may explain why there have been at least eighteen variations on the concept of MI and researchers have been unable to agree on a single construct.

PTED criteria requires causation to be an exceptional, yet common negative life event. However, this may be insufficient grounds for discriminating PTED from PTSD. PTED and PTSD share many symptoms, such as, thinking about the event over and over again, distorted cognitions, feelings of negative self-concept, guilt, blame and shame, hyperarousal, suicidal thoughts and feelings, disproportionate anger, withdrawal from others and challenging ones' ideas about the world and others. This research has identified a significant prevalence of chronic embitterment reactions linked to extraordinary traumatic incidents that have led to post-traumatic symptoms or a diagnosis of PTSD. Therefore, this research suggests consideration is given to the inclusion of 'chronic embitterment' or 'embitterment reactions' as a specific example of emotional dysregulation or distorted cognition, classified in DSM-5 and ICD-11 for PTSD and/or Complex PTSD. However, a classification of PTED may be of importance where the condition is comorbid with Depression or Burnout (for example) and PTSD is not present. It seems the causation and nature of the triggering event(s) is perhaps problematic in distinguishing PTED as a stand-alone disorder. Chronic Embitterment may best serve as a syndrome relating to various disorders. Moral Injury is not a symptom in of itself, so perhaps this model could also be accommodated in the diagnostic criteria for PTSD with the inclusion of the aforementioned. Moral Injury is the causation; yet embitterment reactions are the outcome. Some research has found betrayal to be a significant factor in the onset of PTSD, such as Deprince (2001) who found that betrayal predicted PTSD 'above and beyond' fear. Sense of betrayal is fundamental to the concept of MI and PTED (in the form of injustice). DSM-5 has removed the requirement of fear stating *"intense fear, helplessness or horror, according to DSM-IV— has…….proved to have no utility in predicting the onset of PTSD"*[279] The addition in DSM-5 diagnostic criteria for PTSD, of emotional dysregulation and cognitive distortion (such as guilt, shame and blame) has also brought the construct of PTSD closer to MI and PTED. Though

---

[279] (APA, 2013)

PTED and MI may not be made redundant by the changes to PTSD in DSM-5 or Complex PTSD in ICD-11; it remains to be seen whether further changes to these diagnostic manuals in the future will render the constructs of MI and PTED unnecessary. There still needs to be recognition of the clinical significance of Posttraumatic embitterment, Posttraumatic blame or moral injury and injustice within the experience of (C)PTSD and Chronic Embitterment within the experience of non-clinical populations - including the development of specialist treatment.

(6) Is it beneficial to treat PTED or MI for more effective PTSD recovery?

Treatments being trialled are Adaptive Disclosure Therapy for MI and Wisdom Therapy for PTED. Forgiveness Therapy may also be beneficial for both. Treatment for PTED and MI are said to be different to PTSD interventions. However, Adaptive Disclosure is a repackaged and sequenced mix of therapies which includes those used for PTSD (such as CBT, Exposure therapy and CPT). MI and PTED may maintain symptoms of post-traumatic stress. Researchers have suggested that PTSD treatment is often ineffective and therefore, resolving MI or PTED first may reduce or eradicate PTSD symptoms altogether. If the cause of the PTSD is not fear based and is due to injustice, betrayal or moral injury, then perhaps this sheds light on why treatment for PTSD is often proving to be ineffective.

(7) Should MI be considered a disorder?

MI cannot be considered a disorder unless an agreement has been reached on diagnostic criteria and factors identified, which discriminate MI from other psychosocial constructs and disorders. However, it may be the intention not to do so. Researchers have stated MI should not be a stand-alone construct, nor should it try to replace PTSD.

This research proposes that chronic embitterment reactions in traumatized individuals (such as difficulty with forgiveness, revenge fantasy, negative self-concept, guilt, shame, blame and rumination), are adjusted behaviour, emotions and cognitions adopted to cope with the traumatic event; and not primarily an 'attitude' or personality trait. Therefore, chronic embitterment reactions are likely to be of clinical significance.

Furthermore, the research hypothesizes that chronic embitterment may be a grief reaction to a shocking and unexpected loss, change or event. Therefore, research into whether chronic embitterment is a complicated grief reaction to significant loss and change, requiring specific therapeutic intervention may be beneficial.

Embitterment reactions could fall under the over-arching umbrella of 'affect dysregulation and distorted cognitions which are already criterion for PTSD and CPTSD. However, being characterized as an embittered person who is vengeful and refuses to change, seek help or 'move on'- can have significant implications such as access to treatment, how embittered persons are perceived, employment matters and where responsibility lies. Police officers assessed for early medical retirement may be refused where they present as 'embittered' as official guidance states, 'The SMP's [selected medical practitioner] …..should disregard ….. non-medical factors, such as dissatisfaction…..[and] judgement should be based upon medical criteria alone.'[280] Linden and Maercker (2011), opening notes state, "Embitterment itself can lead to withdrawal from society, including work…..[the] (German Federal Pension Agency), Berlin, …has long realized that many cases of prolonged embitterment ultimately lead to early retirement…..[claiming] pensions due to earning incapacity….[and engagement in] protracted litigation."[281] Case study five, highlights the stance of occupational medical professionals forming the opinion that embitterment is not a medical issue. This is perhaps unsurprising given

---

[280] (PNB, 2004)
[281] (Linden & Maercker, 2011)

the potentially high prevalence of embitterment in the workplace and presentations to occupational health departments. Research into the cost implications (including litigation), of ignoring chronic embitterment in the workplace may be of benefit, for the purpose of reducing risk to employees and employers.

Research largely discusses the cause and correlating symptoms of PTED and MI. However, what is perhaps lesser understood is the motivations and drivers for people to remain embittered. This research has touched on this subject and hypothesized that embitterment may be perceived as helpful to the individual in meeting particular needs; despite the unhelpful consequences produced. Perhaps overcoming embitterment, requires a supported assessment of the advantages, disadvantages and secondary gains involved; one's goals, desired outcomes and behaviour (including how realistic, proportionate and pragmatic these are). What are the hidden motivations which, one may not be consciously aware of as maintaining embitterment.

It is perhaps important to highlight that trauma and moral transgressions will not inevitably lead to PTED, MI or PTSD in everyone. It will depend on the individual and how they perceive the event. Similarly; though embitterment can be experienced by all, few will develop embitterment disorder. This will depend on how the individual assesses and perceives the traumatic experience and whether or not they can assimilate this into their psyche (i.e. come to terms with what has happened and grow from it).[282] Research carried out by Economists at the University of Technology Sydney, explored eighteen significant life events, measured as part of a longitudinal study. They looked at mental wellbeing and life satisfaction pre and post event. They discovered it takes on average, four years for people to recover post shock from the bereavement of a romantic partner or child, separation or experiencing a health scare.[283]

---

[282] (Linden & Maercker, 2011)
[283] (Kettlewell, et al., 2020)

A higher proportion of embitterment reactions and moral injury in frontline services is anticipated compared to the general population; due to 1) the hierarchical   structure of these organisations, 2) higher levels of exposure to trauma and immorality, 3) greater risk of harm and 4) cognitive and emotional adaptation needed to undertake these roles. Research which explores levels of PTED and MI in the general population comparatively with frontline services, (across various demographic parameters) may be   important for raising awareness and developing strategies which reduce heightened risks to this workforce.

Based on empirical evidence (case studies), this research posits, (perhaps controversially), that the individuals' perception may often be, that the primary cause of trauma is the distressing, negative or fearful incident(s) and the cause of one's psychological injury may be attributed to a person(s) or organisation who has capacity, control, and obligation to prevent the traumatic experience and injury, or ameliorate their effect. In case study 1, blame for the injury was attributed towards those who failed (and were obligated) to safeguard the officer (single crewing on scene at a domestic violence incident with no back-up), humiliation suffered at the hands of colleagues and procedural injustice; and not directed towards the violent offender or traumatic incidents. In case study 4, blame for the injury was attributed to the organisation for failing to provide timely support, welfare and treatment which led to protracted ill health and inhibited recovery; not towards the extremist terrorist who detonated a device that killed civilians. In case study 5, blame for the injury was attributed to the supervisor who was obligated to safeguard the officer and failed to provide full protective equipment, and not directed towards the offender who targeted the officer with a bottle during the riot. In case study 8, the senior ranks, those with power and authority and colleagues with knowledge who could have likely prevented the traumatic incident were perceived as the cause of the psychological injury and not the offender who threatened the soldiers life with a loaded weapon. "*In some workplaces dangerous situations can arise....[such as]...police officers, soldiers, fire-fighters [and] nurses....Such events can cause posttraumatic stress disorders...Depending on the context, e.g. insufficient preventive measures or reparation, such events can also lead to a perception of injustice and embitterment reactions"* (Linden and Maercker, 2011:56).

Problem-solving skills are needed for preventing or overcoming embitterment disorder, yet the injury to the brain caused by PTSD affects the cognitive function of 'problem-solving.' Furthermore, neuroscientists have identified areas of the brain responsible for socialization, cooperation with others, reasoning and understanding the mental states of others and therefore; openness to various perceptions and empathy for people, which relates to PTED, MI and PTSD.

This research has identified comorbidity between PTSD and PTED. This may account (in part) for the difficulty in treating embitterment. Covert retaliation may be a type of revenge for humiliation or injustice which affords a sense of power and control to the individual, thereby protecting against the development of PTED, MI, revenge fantasy or escalated forms of violent revenge. Subsequent to the findings of this research, a new theory of Posttraumatic Blame (PTB) is offered. A morally injurious, unfair and unjust incident(s) occurs. Three potential cognitive pathways are likely – 1) reflection, acceptance, positive problem-solving and posttraumatic growth, 2) rumination, unacceptance, a focus on anger and action directed to others (which may include revenge fantasy), resistance to change one's position or adapt to circumstances 3) rumination, unacceptance, a focus on grief, sadness or victimization and a resistance to change or adapt (which may correlate with depression). The proposed psychopathology of PTB is A) Perception of injustice or wrongdoing B) Future Disorientation C) Disorganized Cognition and Emotional Dysregulation D) Organized Cognition, Emotional Regulation and Future Orientation –(no longer pathological). Symptoms of PTB may include: i) embitterment ii) anhedonia iii) guilt or shame iv) grief v) resistance to change vi) victimization vii) anger viii) revenge fantasy ix) future disorientation x) rigid perceptions xi) persistent negative rumination xii) difficulty problem-solving.

Conclusions

Analysis of results conclude, that **the construct of PTSD and CPTSD now accommodate symptoms shared with PTED and Moral Injury**, such as *"Persistent, distorted cognitions about the cause or consequences of the traumatic event(s) that lead the individual to blame himself/herself or others," "persistent and exaggerated negative beliefs or expectations about oneself, others or the world,"*[284] guilt, shame, negative self-concept and emotional dysregulation. **There is significant overlap between the construct of PTED and Moral Injury, which suggests they are fundamentally the same**, even if presented somewhat differently. **This research could not sufficiently discriminate between PTED and MI. Chronic embitterment is pathological, of clinical significance and often a symptom of PTSD which is inextricably linked to the trauma.** Chronic embitterment can maintain PTSD symptoms. Therefore, **chronic embitterment or 'Posttraumatic Blame' are medical issues**, which may require treatment and before PTSD treatment can be effective. The research suggests the DSM-5 or subsequent versions, are amended to 'Persistent cognitions about the cause or consequences of the traumatic event(s) that lead the individual to blame himself/herself or others.' In order to define Posttraumatic Blame (PTB) or blame as 'distorted,' a medical professional would need to make a judgement that there is no foundation, justification, rationale or evidence to support the patients' blame attribution(s). This would neither be a realistic expectation or an ethical one; and certainly not within the remit of a clinical practitioner. The only achievable measure, is the patients' perception and belief that the attribution of blame is appropriate. PTED

---

[284] (APA, Exhibit 1.3-4DSM-5 Diagnostic Criteria for PTSD, 2020)

and Moral Injury may be comorbid with PTSD or the cause of PTSD. For example, **PTSD may be caused by a perception of betrayal or injustice and not 'fear-based, such as resulting from a life-threatening incident(s).'**

Furthermore, PTED may be attributed to traumatic exposure which meets diagnostic criteria for PTSD and/or Complex PTSD; as well as common, yet exceptional negative life events (such as divorce and redundancy). Therefore, **this research could not sufficiently discriminate PTED from PTSD. This research suggests the DSM-5 diagnostic criteria for PTSD is amended, to include the potential symptom and presentation of persistent embitterment.**

Further questions

1) Are Burnout and chronic embitterment significantly related and if so, how?
2) What are the motivations for persistent embitterment (not the cause)? For example, secondary gain, desire to avoid change.
3) Is bereavement or grief counselling beneficial for PTED, Moral Injury and Posttraumatic Blame?
4) What is the financial cost of chronic embitterment to organisations in relation to litigation, sickness absence and medical retirement?
5) Are desired outcomes in embittered and morally injured persons disproportionate and unrealistic, in relation to the perceived injustice? (for example, type of workplace adjustments, compensation, revenge).
6) Are cases of PTED and Chronic Embitterment significantly higher within frontline services, compared with the general population?
7) Does covert retaliation for humiliation or injustice protect against the development of embitterment, revenge fantasy or escalated violent forms of revenge?

Authors' comments

One feels PTSD in the mind and body; and feels Moral Injury in the soul. Trust is a most valued psychosocial resource. It is vital to our survival. Without trust there can be no love, no cooperation and no growth.

Forgiveness is not the act of forgetting or condoning. Forgiveness is the acceptance of inherent fallibility in systems, self and others. Attributing accountability can be productive. There is a chance of positive outcomes. Attributing blame is disparaging and lessens us all.

Hindsight informs our collective foresight. Sometimes we have to look back reflectively to look forwards. Remain open to other perspectives and ideas. Sometimes one needs to receive the same information in multiple formats before reaching one's own understanding.

The desire to regain control drives revenge. To reinstate control, one must reject vengeance. Flourishing in life, despite the abuser is how you reclaim your whole self. Meet change with fear, resistance, ambivalence, sadness, optimism, excitement or flexibility; you will meet change nonetheless. Harness the energy produced by traumatic experience to power personal development and growth; or waste this energy on self-destruction and harm to loved ones.

Never break rank with your values — Sacrifice your own comfort or security if you must.

(Claire Carter © 2020)

Claire Carter

About the Author

About the author, Claire Carter; has been written by retired British Army Major, Dr Brian W. Seggie. His background is as follows:

Major Seggie enlisted into the Regular Army in 1974 as an apprentice marine engineer. He served in 20 Maritime Regt RCT and 17 Port & Maritime Regt RCT/RLC for the majority of his career. This included tours in Belize, Falkland Island, Sierre Leone, Iraq, Bosnia, Kosovo, Angola and Borneo to name a few. He undertook deployments supporting 3 Commando Brigade and various units on amphibious exercises or operations. He is a qualified Army Diving Supervisor and has been an active commercial, military and sports diving instructor since 1985. Major Seggie was recognised in the Queens New Year's Honours list (2015) for Outstanding Service.

He is currently an active Doctor of Education and a Fellow/Member of various developmental organisations: FCIPD, FInstLM, FIfL, FSRA, FCMI, MCGI, MIET, CMgr, IEng. He also supports Adventure Training exercises for the Officer Training Corps and Regular/Reserve Army as an Expedition Sub-Aqua Diving Supervisor. Dr Brian W Seggie, was Learning and Development Manager with Hampshire Constabulary for 11 years and he was medically retired in 2016 due to military related injuries. He is a former director of Team Endeavour Racing for wounded, injured and sick serving personnel and medically discharged veterans, and Mentor for 'Care After Combat' which supports ex-service personnel who have been in the criminal justice system.

He completed 42 years military service when he retired from the Army in 2016. Of Claire Carter, he states:

The researcher and author of this detailed piece, of real-world research is Claire Carter. Claire is an experienced case worker and manager in domestic abuse. During her roles as an advocate in high risk cases she developed a voluntary male perpetrator programme, utilising a strengths-based model. Claire moved to a frontline management position, supporting ex-offenders and domestic abuse victims.

Claire has been employed in frontline services in the care sector for over 30 years. Due to her former husbands' conditions of CPTSD, Anxiety, Depression and experiences as a serving British police officer; she further developed her skills and knowledge as an advocate. Claire identified a lack of support in the police service system, which she selflessly filled. She became the CEO and founder of Safe Horizon UK, (a registered charity) in an unpaid voluntary role for the next five years. The charity was formed in order to help and support police officers and their families. One of the many outcomes was the self-publishing of a book focusing on supporting others in the police family. This book, published in 2014, 'DUTY OF CARE' has been warmly welcomed by many worldwide.

The impact of her former husbands' psychological injury, resulted in Claire experiencing homelessness and leaving her home with her three children in crisis, which is testament to all those who have to do the right thing during a very difficult period in their lives.

The content of this current book; is the accumulative experiences of those who have kindly shared their life stories. This research was conducted over a relatively short time (four months), during the Covid-19 lockdown period in 2020. This research is both reliable and valid, in fact, it is extremely robust. There are significant observations and findings, which are very likely to assist those who are currently serving and retired frontline practitioners worldwide. Employers and families will also potentially benefit from this research, as well as the academic sector.

Claire is a selfless and caring individual, who has taken the time and made the effort to explore, develop and challenge this evolving area of mental health. I applaud her valiant efforts. It is welcome that Claire has been able to engage with so many frontline individuals to complete this research in challenging conditions. This book is refreshing, honest and adds real value to the body of knowledge in this field. This research is testimony to those human beings who wish to make a difference in the real world in which we live and hope to flourish in. Claire Carter is inspiration to us all.

Other publications by Claire Carter

Duty of Care – Psychological Injury in Policing

- **Paperback:** 240 pages **Language:** English

- **Publisher:** CreateSpace Independent Publishing Platform; 1 edition (15 Aug. 2014)

- **ISBN-10:** 1497372968, **ISBN-13:** 978-1497372962

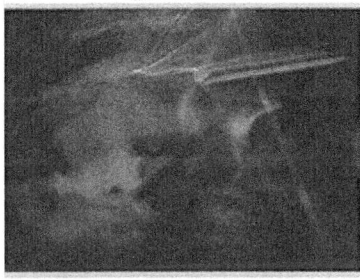

Written by the Ex-wife of a long serving Officer, the author witnessed first-hand the effects of PTSD on her husband and the impact on the family as a whole. This book is the second edition and tells some of that story, of the daily life and struggles of PTSD sufferers and experiences as told by Cops and their partners. Inside the reader will be offered real world advice on how to potentially spot the onset of PTSD, how to seek help and most importantly how to advocate for oneself when dealing with the Constabulary who is responsible for duty of care. The book offers a positive perception of PTSD and through the authors' personal experience and research seeks to offer useful help and guidance to other sufferers and their families. Police Culture and organizational factors which impact on psychological health are explored. The author offers guidance to the Police Service on strategies to reduce levels of sickness absence, improve commitment to the organisation and increase effectiveness whilst safeguarding their greatest asset (the men and women serving our communities). The author was Founder and CEO of Safe Horizon UK, a Registered Charity providing a peer support and advocacy service for (ex) Officers and their families (2014-2020).

Book Reviews

5.0 out of 5 stars This is a must read for every police officer and their families.

Reviewed in the United Kingdom on 20 April 2018

Excellent and informative read. Every person working in the police force, regardless of rank should read this book, also their families. I saw all the signs but had no idea that my son was suffering with PTSD until it was almost too late. No one should underestimate the effect that trauma incidences and lack of follow up support has on a police officer's mental health and well being. This is a must read and highly recommended.

5.0 out of 5 stars A great resource

Reviewed in the United Kingdom on 10 December 2017

This is a must read for anyone affected by PTSD in policing (sufferers, family members, partners and managers/HR). Claire has first-hand experience and provides an accurate picture of this horrible condition and useful ways to manage it.

5.0 out of 5 stars Buy this book

Reviewed in the United Kingdom on 1 October 2015

Having read most self-help type books on mental illness, mainly PTSD I can honestly say that this book is a must buy. Within reading the first few pages I was astounded by how much I could relate to the book and it is written in an easy to read style and provides plenty of helpful advice. If you're a police officer suffering from PTSD or the family of one; buy this book.

5.0 out of 5 stars Five Stars

Reviewed in the United Kingdom on 20 October 2017

Frighteningly accurate!

5.0 out of 5 stars Read this and you will realise You are NOT alone and it's good to talk.

Reviewed in the United Kingdom on 6 August 2018

Makes you aware that there are lots of people out there going through the same awful illness and you are definitely not alone. Great read both comforting and tearful all kinds of emotions.

Testimonials

(SHUK - Safe Horizon UK, 2014-2020)

"Your devotion to each one of us is done with intricacy. You see our unique difficulties and help us in every way you can; and that's what makes us keep moving forward."

"It's great to have your insight and that I can trust, always trust that you speak from a perspective of care and support"

"you're an angel in disguise, a modern-day Florence Nightingale. The help you give to PTSD sufferers is above and beyond"

"you offer lots of hope where people are drowning in despair"

"I'm overwhelmed by how supportive and understanding you are, this world is surely a better place by having someone like you in it."

'The support and understanding you gave stopped me from taking steps to end my life'

"I can't thank you enough... you're a modern-day Florence Nightingale for us Officers... it's 100% true"

"Claire, you are such an inspiration and have helped me do much. I could not have been where I was today without your help and intervention. I would have been a lamb to the slaughter and probably worse. I will always be in your debt"

"As usual, Claire saves the day. You are like a rainbow at the end of a very big storm. Thank you for being there xx"

"You are the absolute polar-opposite of selfish, your help and guidance cannot be compared, your motives are the purist, the modern-day Florence Nightingale"

"Have to say the support and understanding from Claire is a breath of fresh air. Years of mistrust for the establishment are hard to move away from"

"I feel I have to say you are the most positive, efficient and genuine person I have ever encountered!!! Thank you, you have given me confidence"

"A huge thank you for what you have done and what you continue to do, at huge personal cost to yourself. I know that for me you were a flicker of light in my very dark world. And from the start someone 'who got it' without even knowing the circumstances. Thank you, thank you, thank you. X"

"I feel incredibly fortunate to have had someone like Claire in my corner from the start because advocating for my husband has been the toughest fight of all. Very quickly, Claire became my rock, my source of support that helped me to keep going when I felt like giving up."

"As the wife of a Police Officer with PTSD, I cannot explain how Safe Horizon and Claire have helped me. Not only have I gained more understanding of my husbands' condition, I also have gained an inner strength to help him fight a flawed and broken system."

"You've helped save many souls and shown us the way forward."

"An angel to us nowhere men"

Appendices

Version 2 Statements, questionnaire 2, before amendments

41 statements	C PTS D	PTED	MI	Keywords
Memories of it come back to me like it's happening all over again (flashback, intrusive memory)	CP1	TED11		K26
I keep replaying it over and over in my mind (Rumination, intrusive memory)	CP1	TED11		K26
When I am reminded of it I get sensations in my body (hyper-arousal, physical sensation)	CP1			K36
I often feel unable to control my emotions (emotional dysregulation)	CP1, CP7			K23,K24
I struggle to sleep because of recurring bad	CP1			K26,K27

dreams (nightmares)				
I prefer to keep busy so I have less time to think (Avoidance, normal affect when distracted)	CP2	TED8,TED14		K29
there are places or people I avoid because it hurts to be reminded of what happened (Avoidance)	CP2	TED14		K29
I feel on edge for no reason, I can be jumpy (hyper-arousal, (persistent sense of threat)	CP3			K18,K28
I resent people who betrayed my trust		TED19	M1,M5, M10	K3,K7
I was afraid for my life (life-threatening, fear)	CP1, CP4			K1 ,K18
my way of life was under attack (threat to security)	CP4	TED1		K18
I felt threatened that I would lose everything important to me	CP4	TED1		K18

(threat to security, loss)				
I couldn't see a way out, I felt powerless (inescapable, powerless, helpless, hopeless, victim)	CP6	TED1,TED7, TED9, TED19	M9	K5,K8,K9
I had no control over my situation (victim, helpless, powerless)		TED7		K5,K9,K23
I feel useless, a failure and not worth love (negative self-concept, low self-esteem, self-condemnation)	CP8, CP9		M3,M12	K20,K25
I easily lose control of myself, I get angry over little things (emotional dysregulation)	CP7	TED8	M14	K23,K24
I'm not the person I used to be, I used to be happy, confident and fun before the incident (defeated, diminished,	CP8	TED2	M12	K30,

negative self-concept)				
I have no fight left in me, I can't see the point in trying anymore (loss of meaning and purpose, loss of drive)		TED15	M11	K10,K17
I feel ashamed when I think about what happened (shame, self-blame, self-condemnation)	CP9	TED10	M3,M6	K19,K22
I feel guilty about what happened	CP9	TED10	M6	K21
I worry I was to blame (guilt, shame, self-blame, self-condemnation)	CP9	TED10	M3,M6	K19,K20,K21,K22
experiences have taught me that it is only a matter of time before people will betray my trust		TED19	M1,M5, M10	K3,K7
I feel I can't get close to anyone, even though I really want to (difficulty with relationships)	CP10			K31

I find it difficult to keep a job for long, I struggle to work with others (significant impact on occupation, loss of resources)	CP10, CP11	TED5	M2	K10,K33
I struggle to attend family occasions or celebrations (significant impact on personal, family and social areas of life)	CP11	TED5	M2	K31,K33
I feel disgusted by things that other people did. The incident went against my values, morals, beliefs		TED6	M1,M7	K12
I would not be like this now, if this hadn't happened (directly attributes the event to changes in wellness, no pre-existing mental or		TED2,TED4		K6,K32

emotional conditions)				
what happened was unfair, it was an injustice (unfair, unjust, immoral)		TED3	M1,M7	K4,K12,K14,K17
when I think about getting revenge I enjoy it (revenge)		TED17	M13	K16
I struggle to do normal every-day tasks (significant impact on important areas of life)	CP11	TED5	M2	K33
I feel weak for not being able to cope with what happened (self-blame, self-condemnation, negative self-concept)	CP8	TED9,TED10	M3,M12	K19,K20
I find it difficult to forgive those responsible for what happened (embitterment, difficulty with forgiveness)		TED3,TED20	M4	K2,K6
At times I think about ending my life (suicidal		TED12		K34

ideation)			
I have had these thoughts and feelings for over 3 months (PTED criteria)		TED16		K33
I feel punished by God because of what happened (impact on religious/spiritual area of life)			M8	K35
my faith in God has been shaken (impact on religious/spiritual area of life)			M8	K35
Life feels pointless (loss of meaning and purpose, dysphoria, dissatisfaction with life)		TED13	M11	K10,K17
I experienced a threatening incident which lasted a very long time	CP4			K18
I often experienced incidents that made me feel threatened	CP5			K18
I'm not sure if I		TED21	M15	K37

want the wounds to heal			
I sabotage good things that come my way	TED21	MI5	K37

Clusters	CPTSD	PTED	MI
Re-experiencing in the present (such as flashbacks, nightmares, fear, horror, physical sensations, hypervigilance, hyperarousal, persistent sense of threat, avoidance	X		
Threatening event, Prolonged or repetitive	X		
areas of life are significantly affected: personal, family, social, educational, occupational, physical, spiritual or religious (significant impairment on functioning)	X	X	X
Intrusive memories, overwhelming emotions (affect dysregulation), Avoidance	X	X	
horror (fear, shock, disgust)	X	X	X
difficult or impossible to escape (powerlessness, helplessness, victimization, loss of control)	X	X	
diminished, defeated (resignation), worthless, failure (negative self-concept)	X	X	X
guilt, shame, self-blame, (self-condemnation)	X	X	X
Difficulty with relationships, withdrawal from others	X	X	X
Difficulty with forgiveness (embitterment)		X	X
injustice, unfairness		X	
betrayal, violation or breach of values, beliefs or morals		X	X
suicidal ideation		X	X
Loss of meaning and purpose, reduced drive (self-efficacy (R), dissatisfaction with life , loss of hope, (dysphoria) loss of trust		X	X

desire for revenge		X	X
Loss of religious faith			X

Version 1 statements before amendment

Memories of it come back to me like it's happening all over again (flashback, intrusive memory)
I keep replaying it over and over in my mind (Rumination, intrusive memory)
When I am reminded of it I get sensations in my body (hyper-arousal, physical sensation)
my moods are often extreme (emotional dysregulation)
I feel unable to control my emotions (emotional dysregulation)
I struggle to sleep because of recurring bad dreams (nightmares)
Someone close to me was seriously injured or died
I prefer to keep busy so I have less time to think (Avoidance, normal affect when distracted)
there are places or people I avoid because it hurts to be reminded of what happened (Avoidance)
I feel on edge for no reason, I can be jumpy (hyper-arousal)
I'm always looking out for possible threats (hypervigilance)
I feel people can't be trusted (distrust, cynicism, suspicious)
I feel betrayed by those responsible for what happened, I trusted them (distrust, betrayal)
I was afraid for my life (life-threatening, fear)
I thought someone was going to get seriously injured or die
I was in danger (life-threatening, minus fear)
my way of life was under attack (threat to security)
I felt threatened that I would lose everything important to me (threat to security, loss)
I thought it would never end (inescapable, powerless)
It kept on happening (multiple trauma, repeated trauma)
I couldn't see a way out, I felt powerless (powerless, helpless, hopeless, victim, inability to problem solve)
I had no control over my situation (victim, helpless, powerless)

I lost hope that things would be okay (hopelessness)
I feel useless, I feel like a burden to everyone (negative self-concept, low self-esteem, self-condemnation)
I easily lose control of myself, I get angry over little things (emotional dysregulation)
I feel okay when I'm busy, It's when I have quiet time that the thoughts and feelings come back (normal affect when distracted, avoidance)
I panic and feel I have no control over the situation, I can over-react and regret it later (emotional dysregulation)
I feel like a failure, I can't do anything right (negative self-concept, low self-esteem, self-condemnation)
I'm not the person I used to be, I used to be happy, confident and fun and hard-working (defeated, diminished, negative self-concept)
I have no fight left in me, I can't see the point in trying anymore (loss of meaning and purpose, loss of drive)
I feel useless, I feel like a burden to everyone (negative self-concept, low self-esteem, self-condemnation)
I feel ashamed when I think about what happened (shame, self-blame, self-condemnation)
I feel guilty even though I know it wasn't my fault (guilt)
I ask myself why did this happen and I worry I was to blame (guilt, shame, self-blame, self-condemnation)
I feel responsible for what happened, I feel guilty for causing harm to someone else (perpetration of immoral act)
I feel guilty for failing to protect someone else from harm (failure to prevent immoral act)
I find it hard to trust people, I'm always waiting for others to let me down (distrust, cynicism, difficulty with relationships)
I feel I can't get close to anyone, even though I really want to (difficulty with relationships)
I find it difficult to stay in a relationship for long (difficulty with relationships)
I find it difficult to keep a job for long, I struggle to work with others (significant impact on occupation, loss of resources)

I have no motivation to study or work (significant impact on education or occupation, loss of drive)
I struggle to attend family occasions or celebrations (significant impact on personal, family and social areas of life)
I have no energy or drive to take care of myself (significant impact on personal life, loss of drive)
I no longer know what's right or wrong, what happened went against common decency (shattered beliefs, disorientation, violated morals and values)
I was sexually violated (sexual violation, abuse, assault, trauma)
I saw what happened and it was distressing (witnessed immoral act or trauma)
I heard about what happened in great detail (learnt about immoral act or trauma)
I had to go over and over the details of what happened to someone (repeated exposure to details of trauma)
the rules were broken and there is a code of conduct that was breached (violation of values, morals, beliefs)
I would not be like this now, if this hadn't happened (directly attributes the event to changes in wellness, no pre-existing mental or emotional conditions)
I feel really bitter towards the people responsible for what happened (bitterness, embitterment, grudge)
what happened was unfair, it was an injustice (unfair, unjust, immoral)
I feel sad and down (downhearted, dysphoric)
I want those responsible to have a taste of their own medicine (revenge)
when I think about getting revenge I enjoy it (revenge)
I want to publicly shame those responsible for what happened (embitterment, revenge, justice, regain control)
My mental and emotional health was good before this happened
I struggle to do normal every-day tasks (significant impact on important areas of life)
I have lost faith in those with power, those responsible didn't do what's right (injustice, violation of morals and values)

I feel weak for not being able to cope with what happened (self-blame, self-condemnation, negative self-concept)
If I forget what happened it will lose its meaning and purpose
remembering what happened stops me making the same mistake of trusting people again
If I allow myself to forget what happened it means I have forgiven those responsible (difficulty with forgiveness)
It's important I remember what happened in honour of others
I find it difficult to forgive myself (difficulty with forgiveness)
I will never forgive those responsible for what happened (embitterment, difficulty with forgiveness)
I'm not sure I want this pain to go because I am not ready to forgive what happened (embitterment, difficulty with forgiveness)
At times I feel people would be better off without me here (negative self-concept, suicidal ideation)
At times I think about ending my life (suicidal ideation)
I have had these thoughts and feelings for over 3 months (PTED criteria)
I feel punished by God because of what happened (impact on religious/spiritual area of life)
my faith in God has been shaken (impact on religious/spiritual area of life)
I no longer believe in God because of what happened (impact on religious/spiritual area of life)
I've lost interest in my future (loss of meaning and purpose, dysphoria, dissatisfaction with life)
I find it hard to look forward to anything (loss of meaning and purpose, dysphoria, dissatisfaction with life)
Life feels pointless (loss of meaning and purpose, dysphoria, dissatisfaction with life)

Claire Carter

A

abuse, 17, 18, 33, 50, 67, 78, 80, 104, 105, 168, 172, 199, 203, 204, 255

accountability, 82, 195, 197, 214, 236

Accountability, 195

addictive, 37, 104

Adjustment Disorder, 72, 73, 111, 189

affect dysregulation, 65, 182, 183, 185, 186, 187, 188, 228, 252

agoraphobia, 46, 140

anger, 13, 17, 20, 39, 41, 47, 50, 64, 65, 75, 76, 79, 84, 86, 87, 89, 90, 94, 99, 105, 109, 117, 121, 128, 134, 135, 142, 145, 203, 204, 212, 214, 215, 216, 217, 224, 226, 231

Anger. See HSE - Health & Safety Executive

anhedonia, 165, 215, 216, 231

Anxiety, 14, 18, 46, 93, 114, 189

anxious attachment, 113

attachment, 113

attitude, 55, 60, 84, 85, 87, 130, 220, 228

avoidance, 33, 41, 65, 90, 109, 110, 113, 121, 129, 165, 175, 181, 184, 202, 203, 215, 252, 254

avoidant, 113, 131, 143

B

Barnes, 39, 64, 202

beliefs, 15, 18, 32, 34, 38, 39, 40, 41, 50, 66, 67, 75, 86, 92, 98, 101, 102, 103, 105, 108, 115, 117, 132, 143, 144, 167, 175, 176, 177, 178, 179, 182, 185, 187, 190, 199, 202, 203, 204, 213, 215, 216, 217, 219, 232, 249, 252, 255

betrayal, 14, 17, 26, 33, 39, 50, 64, 67, 79, 81, 86, 87, 98, 99, 102, 105, 132, 166, 178, 179, 183, 191, 198, 200, 203, 204, 212, 224, 226, 227, 252, 253

Betrayal, 20, 78, 79, 80, 178, 179, 183

betrayal., 17, 33, 50, 79, 98

bitterness, 13, 27, 36, 37, 61, 79, 99, 109, 110, 135, 145, 192, 255

blame, 14, 15, 49, 65, 66, 86, 87, 92, 98, 99, 101, 109, 160, 167, 178, 179, 186, 192, 193, 194, 195, 196, 198, 199, 200, 212, 217, 221, 224, 226, 227, 230, 232, 236, 248, 254

Bryan, 38, 132, 204

bullying, 42, 43, 49, 170, 172, 173, 206

Burnout, 73, 74, 75, 123, 226, 233

C

capacity, 54, 91, 100, 194, 196, 213, 216, 218, 220, 221, 230

causation, 19, 190, 224, 225

CBT, 57, 59, 60, 61, 95

clinical significance, 15, 33, 72, 165, 227, 228, 232

Combat, 169, 171

comorbid, 17, 18, 19, 20, 34, 35, 64, 98, 99, 115, 155, 174, 175, 198, 199, 202, 217, 224, 226

Cubela, 81

Currier, 39, 40, 41, 175, 201

cynicism, 34, 74, 200, 203, 253, 254

D

Dean, 17, 39, 132, 203

depression, 34, 39, 42, 44, 45, 48, 49, 55, 59, 75, 81, 89, 93, 95, 109, 110, 117, 126, 128, 136, 140, 142, 174, 214, 231

diagnostic criteria, 19, 36, 64, 66, 72, 94, 98, 99, 174, 175, 177, 212, 226, 227

disciplinary, 42, 43, 56, 57, 107, 124, 207

Disorganized Cognition, 215, 216, 231

dissociation, 78, 202

DSM-5, 64, 66, 93, 110

DSM-IV, 64, 65, 72, 93, 174, 226

U

V

W

Claire Carter

Bibliography

Alicke, M. (2000). *Culpable Control and the Psychology of Blame*. Retrieved from Researchgate:
https://www.researchgate.net/profile/Mark_Alicke/publication/12
418323_Culpable_Control_and_the_Psychology_of_Blame/links
/542407440cf26120b7a71256/Culpable-Control-and-the-
Psychology-of-Blame.pdf

APA. (2013). *DSM-5 Criteria for PTSD*. Retrieved 2014, from U.S
Department Of Veterans Affairs: National Center for PTSD:
www.ptsd.va.gov

APA. (2020). *DSM-5 Factsheets, Changes in PTSD Criteria*. Retrieved from
American Psychiatric Association:
https://www.psychiatry.org/psychiatrists/practice/dsm/educationa
l-resources/dsm-5-fact-sheets

APA. (2020). *Exhibit 1.3-4DSM-5 Diagnostic Criteria for PTSD*. Retrieved
from NCBI:
https://www.ncbi.nlm.nih.gov/books/NBK207191/box/part1_ch3.
box16/

Bakker, A., & Heuven, E. (2006). Emotional Dissonance, Burnout and In-
Role Performance Among Nurses and Police Officers. (A. P.
Association, Ed.) *International Journal of Stress Management, 13*(4),
423-440. doi:10.1037/1072-5245.13.4.423

Barnes, H., Hurley, R., & Taber, K. (2019, April). *Moral Injury and PTSD:
Often Co-Occurring Yet Mechanistically Different*. Retrieved from
The Journal of NeuroPsychiatry and Clinical Neurosciences:
https://neuro.psychiatryonline.org/doi/10.1176/appi.neuropsych.1
9020036

BBC. (2019, August 16). *Strength of British Military Falls for Ninth Year*.
Retrieved from BBC News: https://www.bbc.co.uk/news/uk-
49365599

Blom, D., van Middendorp, H., & Greenen, R. (2012, December). *Anxious attachment may be a vulnerability factor for developing embitterment.* Retrieved from ResearchGate: https://www.researchgate.net/publication/232320941_Anxious_a ttachment_may_be_a_vulnerability_factor_for_developing_emb itterment

Bollmann, G., Krings, F., Maggiori, C., & Rossier, J. (2015). *Differential Associations of Personal and General Just-World Beliefs with the FiveFactor and the HEXACO Models of Personality.* Retrieved from https://core.ac.uk/download/pdf/77145492.pdf

Bowcott, O. (2017, February 2). *Phil Shiner: Iraq human rights lawyer struck off over misconduct.* Retrieved from The Guardian: https://www.theguardian.com/law/2017/feb/02/iraq-human-rights-lawyer-phil-shiner-disqualified-for-professional-misconduct

Bryan, C., Anestis, M., Bryan, A., & Anestis, J. (2015). *Measuring Moral Injury.* Retrieved from Research Gate: https://www.researchgate.net/publication/278787735_Measuring _Moral_Injury

Caddick, N., & Smith, B. (2014). *Psychology of Sport and Exercise.* Retrieved from Elsevier: https://www.journals.elsevier.com/psychology-of-sport-and-exercise

Carey, L., & Hodgson, T. (2018, December 5). *Chaplaincy, Spiritual Care and Moral Injury: Considerations Regarding Screening and Treatment.* Retrieved from Frontiers in Psychiatry: https://www.ncbi.nlm.nih.gov/pmc/articles/PMC6290645/

Carlier, I., Lamberts, R., & Gersons, B. (1997). *Risk Factors for Posttraumatic Stress Symptomatology in Police Officers: A Prospective Analysis (Abstract).* Retrieved 2014, from The Journal of Nervous and Mental Disease: http://journals.lww.com

Carter, C. (2014). *Duty of Care - Psychological Injury in Policing.* Kindle Direct Publishing.

Carter, C. (2021, September). *Organisational Injustice in UK Frontline Services and Onset of Moral Injury, Post Traumatic Embitterment Disorder (PTED) and PTSD.* Retrieved from International Journal of Law, Crime and Justice: http://doi.org/10.1016/j.ijlcj.2021.100483

Cloitre, M. (2013, May 15). *Evidence for proposed ICD-11 PTSD and complex PTSD: a latent profile analysis.* Retrieved from NCBI: https://www.ncbi.nlm.nih.gov/pmc/articles/PMC3656217/

Cloitre, M., Gavert, D., Brewin, C., Bryant, R., & Maercker, A. (2013). *Evidence for proposed ICD-11 PTSD and complex PTSD: a latent profile analysis.* Retrieved from Taylor and Francis Online: https://www.tandfonline.com/doi/full/10.3402/ejpt.v4i0.20706

(2014). *Code of Ethics.* Coventry: College of Policing. Retrieved July 15, 2014, from www.college.police.uk

Collier, L. (2016, November). *Growth after Trauma.* Retrieved from American Psychological Association: https://www.apa.org/monitor/2016/11/growth-trauma

Corbishley, S. (2019, September 28). *Thousands protest prosecution of 'Soldier F' over Bloody Sunday massacre.* Retrieved from Metro: https://metro.co.uk/2019/09/28/hundreds-protest-prosecution-soldier-f-bloody-sunday-massacre-10825215/

Currier, J. (2017). Development and evaluation of the Expressions of Moral Injury Scale—Military Version. *Clinical Psychology and Psychotherapy,* 474-488.

Dalbert, C., & Donat, M. (2015, March). *Belief in a Just World.* Retrieved from ResearchGate:

https://www.researchgate.net/publication/276090224_Belief_in_
a_Just_World

Dean, W., Talbot, S., & Dean, A. (2019). *Reframing Clinician Distress:
Moral Injury Not Burnout.* Retrieved from NCBI:
https://www.ncbi.nlm.nih.gov/pmc/articles/PMC6752815/

Deprince. (2001). *Trauma and posttraumatic responses: An examination of
fear and betrayal.* Retrieved from APA PsychNet:
https://psycnet.apa.org/record/2001-95024-199

Deprince, A. (2001). *Trauma and Posttraumatic Responses: An Examination
of Fear and Betrayal.* Retrieved from ResearchGate:
https://www.researchgate.net/publication/34280779_Trauma_an
d_posttraumatic_responses_An_examination_of_fear_and_betr
ayal

Dobby, J., Anscombe, J., & Tuffin, R. (2004). *Police leadership: expectations
and impact.* Retrieved 2014, from Internet Memory Foundation:
http://collection.europarchive.org

Dobricki, M. (2010, February). *(Post-traumatic) embitterment disorder:
Critical evaluation of its stressor criterion and a proposed revised
classification.* Retrieved from Research Gate:
https://www.researchgate.net/publication/41423161_Post-
traumatic_embitterment_disorder_Critical_evaluation_of_its_st
ressor_criterion_and_a_proposed_revised_classification

Dunn, J. (2016, June). *Chronic Embitterment in the NHS.* Retrieved from
https://pure.royalholloway.ac.uk/portal/files/26903332/2016Joann
eDunnDClinPsy.pdf

Dunn, J., & Sensky, T. (2018, January). *Psychological processes in chronic
embitterment: The potential contribution of rumination.* Retrieved
from NCBI PubMed:
https://www.ncbi.nlm.nih.gov/pubmed/29323521

Durvasula, R. (2020, June 30). *The narcissist and the shame-rage spiral.* Retrieved from YouTube: https://www.youtube.com/watch?v=xYWPuJNuvMc

(2011). *Employment Statutory Code of Practice.* Equality and Human Rights Commission. Retrieved 2014, from www.equalityhumanrights.com

Equality Act 2010 Guidance; The Definition Of Disability. (2011, May). Retrieved 2013, from GOV.UK: www.gov.uk

Ethics Checklist. (2020). Retrieved from University of Leicester: https://www2.le.ac.uk/institution/ethics/resources/checklist

Franco, F. (2020). *What Is Affect or Emotion Dysregulation?* Retrieved from PsychCentral: https://psychcentral.com/blog/what-is-affect-or-emotion-dysregulation/

Freedman, S., & Enright, R. (2017, May). *The Use of Forgiveness Therapy with Female Survivors of Abuse.* Retrieved from ResearchGate: https://www.researchgate.net/publication/317350212_The_Use_of_Forgiveness_Therapy_with_Female_Survivors_of_Abuse

Freyd, J. (2019). *What is Betrayal Trauma Theory?* Retrieved from https://dynamic.uoregon.edu/jjf/defineBT.html

Freyd, J., & Smith, C. (2013). *Institutional Betrayal.* Retrieved from University of Oregon: https://dynamic.uoregon.edu/jjf/articles/sfinpress.pdf

Fujisawa, T., Jung, M., Kojima, M., Saito, D., Kosata, H., & Tomoda, A. (2015, August 20). *Neural Basis of Psychological Growth following Adverse Experiences: A Resting-State Functional MRI Study.* Retrieved from NCBI: https://www.ncbi.nlm.nih.gov/pmc/articles/PMC4546237/

Galatzer-Levy, I., Brown, A., Henne-Haase, C., Metzler, T., Neylan, T., &

Marmar, C. (2013, Jan 21). *Positive and Negative Emotion Prospectively Predict Trajectories of Resilience and Distress Among High-Exposure Police Officers.* Retrieved from NCBI: https://www.ncbi.nlm.nih.gov/pmc/articles/PMC3974969/

Gerevich, J., & Ungvari, G. (2014, October 29). *The Description of the Litigious Querulant: Heinrich von Kleist's Novella Michael Kohlhaas.* Retrieved from ResearchGate: https://www.researchgate.net/publication/267746920_The_Desc ription_of_the_Litigious_Querulant_Heinrich_von_Kleist's_No vella_Michael_Kohlhaas

Giordano, C. (2019, May 9). *Police officers suffering PTSD on 'alarming' scale, study finds.* Retrieved from Independent: https://www.independent.co.uk/news/uk/home-news/ptsd-police-survey-mental-health-cambridge-university-a8906051.html

Golis, C. (2020). *Practical Emotional Intelligence.* Retrieved from https://www.emotionalintelligencecourse.com/increase-your-eq/

Government. (2020, April 4). *Coronavirus (COVID-19): what you need to do.* Retrieved from Gov.UK: https://www.gov.uk/coronavirus

Graef, R. (1990). *Talking Blues: The Police In Their Own Words.* London: Fontana Paperbacks.

Greene, T. (2018). *Blame, PTSD and DSM-5: an urgent need for clarification.* Retrieved from Taylor and Francis Online: https://www.tandfonline.com/doi/full/10.1080/20008198.2018.14 68709

Grierson, J. (2020, March 31). *Calls for Funds to House Domestic Violence Victims During Covid-19 Outbreak.* Retrieved from Guardian: https://www.theguardian.com/society/2020/mar/31/call-for-uk-domestic-violence-refuges-to-get-coronavirus-funding

Guardian. (2020, March 28). *Lockdowns Around the World Bring Rise in Domestic Violence*. Retrieved from The Guardian: https://www.theguardian.com/society/2020/mar/28/lockdowns-world-rise-domestic-violence

Hayes, J., VanElzakker, M., & Shin, L. (2012, October 9). *Emotion and cognition interactions in PTSD: a review of neurocognitive and neuroimaging studies*. Retrieved from NCBI: https://www.ncbi.nlm.nih.gov/pmc/articles/PMC3466464/

Herman, J. (1997). *Trauma And Recovery: The Aftermath Of Violence - From Domestic Abuse To Political Terror*. New York: Basic Books.

Heshmat, S. (2015, November). *What is Attachment Anxiety?* Retrieved from Psychology today: https://www.psychologytoday.com/gb/blog/science-choice/201511/what-is-attachment-anxiety

Holland, K. (2018, September 25). *What You Should Know About the Stages of Grief*. Retrieved from Healthline: https://www.healthline.com/health/stages-of-grief#order

Informal care-giving and mental health. (2018, October 27). Retrieved from Understanding Society - The UK Household Longitudinal Study: https://www.understandingsociety.ac.uk/2018/10/27/informal-care-giving-and-mental-health

ITV. (2020, April 1st). *Coronavirus: 13-year-old with Covid-19 'died alone' without his family around him, friend says*. Retrieved from ITV News: https://www.itv.com/news/2020-04-01/coronavirus-13-year-old-victim-died-alone-friend-says-ismail-mohamed-abdulwahab-kings-college-hospital/

Jinkerson, J. (2016). *Defining and assessing moral injury: A syndrome perspective*. Retrieved from APA Psychnet:

https://psycnet.apa.org/doiLanding?doi=10.1037%2Ftrm0000069

Jordan, A., & Litz, B. (2014). *Prolonged Grief Disorder: Diagnostic, Assessment, and Treatment*. Retrieved from American Psychological Association: https://www.apa.org/pubs/journals/features/pro-a0036836.pdf

KCL. (2018, October 8). *Increase in probable PTSD among British military*. Retrieved from Kings College London News Centre: https://www.kcl.ac.uk/news/increase-in-probable-ptsd-among-british-military

Kettlewell, N., Morris, R., Ho, N., Cobb-Clark, D., Cripps, S., & Glozier, N. (2020, April). *The differential impact of major life events on cognitive and affective wellbeing*. Retrieved from ScienceDirect: https://www.sciencedirect.com/science/article/pii/S235282731903 02204?via%3Dihub

Koenig, H. (2018, March). *Measuring Symptoms of Moral Injury in Veterans and Active Duty Military with PTSD*. Retrieved from MDPI: https://www.mdpi.com/2077-1444/9/3/86

Koenig, H. (2018). *Military Medicine: Screening for Moral Injury: The Moral Injury Symptom Scale – Military Version Short Form*. Retrieved from AMSUS: https://academic.oup.com/milmed/article/183/11-12/e659/4934229

Koenig, H. (2019). *Assessment of Moral Injury in Veterans and Active Duty Military Personnel With PTSD: A Review*. Retrieved from Frontiers in Psychology: https://www.frontiersin.org/articles/10.3389/fpsyt.2019.00443/full

Koenig, H., Ames, D., & Bussing, A. (2019). *Editorial: Screening for and Treatment of Moral Injury in Veterans/Active Duty Military With PTSD*. Retrieved from Frontiers in Psychology:

https://www.ncbi.nlm.nih.gov/pmc/articles/PMC6712088/

Koenig, H., Youssef, N., Ames, D., & Oliver, J. (2017). *The Moral Injury Symptom Scale-Military Version.* Retrieved from Research Gate: https://www.researchgate.net/publication/321442165_The_Moral_Injury_Symptom_Scale-Military_Version

Krizan, Z., & Johar, O. (2014, December). *Narcissistic Rage Revisited .* Retrieved from ResearchGate: https://www.researchgate.net/publication/270291891_Narcissistic_Rage_Revisited

Kubany, E. (2003). *Guilt: An Elaboration of a Multidimensional Model.* Retrieved from Southern Illionis University: https://opensiuc.lib.siu.edu/tpr/vol53/iss1/4/

Lamiani, G., Borghi, L., & Piergiorgio, A. (2015). *When Healthcare Professionals Cannot Do The Right Thing: A Systematic Review of Moral Distress and its Correlates.* Retrieved from Researchgate: https://www.researchgate.net/publication/280587981_When_healthcare_professionals_cannot_do_the_right_thing_A_systematic_review_of_moral_distress_and_its_correlates

Lansing, K. (2012). *The Rite Of Return: Coming Back From Duty-Induced PTSD.* U.S.A: High Ground Press.

Lees, A. (2019). *Post Traumatic Growth.* Retrieved from Psychology today: https://www.psychologytoday.com/us/blog/surviving-thriving/201904/posttraumatic-growth

Lehrner, A., & Yehuda, R. (2018, January). *Trauma across generations and paths to adaptation and resilience.* Retrieved from ResearchGate: https://www.researchgate.net/publication/322407819_Trauma_across_generations_and_paths_to_adaptation_and_resilience

Lester, G. (2020). *The Unreasonable, Querulent and Vexatious as Litigants in Person*. Retrieved from https://www.aija.org.au/wp-content/uploads/2017/08/Lester.pdf

Lester, G., Wilson, B., Griffin, L., & Mullen, P. (2004). Unusually persistent complainants. *British Journal of Psychiatry*, 352-356.

Linden, M. (2003). *Post Traumatic Embitterment Disorder*. Retrieved from NCBI PubMed: https://www.ncbi.nlm.nih.gov/pubmed/12792124

Linden, M. (2007). *Posttraumatic embitterment disorder in comparison to other mental disorders*. Retrieved from NCBI PubMed: https://www.ncbi.nlm.nih.gov/pubmed/18087208

Linden, M. (2020, May 19). *Querulant delusion and post-traumatic embitterment disorder*. Retrieved from Taylor and Francis Online: https://www.tandfonline.com/doi/full/10.1080/09540261.2020.17 47410?scroll=top&needAccess=true

Linden, M., & Maercker, A. (2011). *Embitterment - societal, psychological, and clinical perspectives*. New York: Springer Wien.

Linden, M., & Rotter, M. (2018, January). *Spectrum of embitterment manifestations*. Retrieved from NCBI PubMed: https://www.ncbi.nlm.nih.gov/pubmed/29323520

Linden, M., Baumann, K., Lieberei, B., & Lorenz, C. (2011, April). *Treatment of Posttraumatic Embitterment Disorder with Cognitive Behaviour Therapy Based on Wisdom Psychology and Hedonia Strategies*. Retrieved from ResearchGate: https://www.researchgate.net/publication/51052199_Treatment _of_Posttraumatic_Embitterment_Disorder_with_Cognitive_B ehaviour_Therapy_Based_on_Wisdom_Psychology_and_Hedo nia_Strategies

Linden, M., Baumann, K., Lieberei, B., & Rotter, M. (2009, March-April). *The Post-Traumatic Embitterment Disorder Self-Rating Scale (PTED*

Scale). Retrieved from NCBI PubMed:
https://www.ncbi.nlm.nih.gov/pubmed/19229838

Linden, M., Baumann, K., Rotter, M., & Schippan, B. (2007, February).
The psychopathology of posttraumatic embitterment disorders.
Retrieved from NCBI PubMed:
https://www.ncbi.nlm.nih.gov/pubmed/17318008

Litz, B., Lebowitz, L., Gray, M., & Nash, W. (2016). *Adpative Disclosure: A*
New Treatment for Military Trauma, Loss and Moral Injury. New
York: Guilford Press.

Maercker, A. (2018, October). *Andreas Maercker: Introduction to*
Prolonged Grief Disorder (PGD, ICD-11). Retrieved from You Tube:
https://www.youtube.com/watch?v=lnPb5nh1u4c

Maguen, S., & Litz, B. (2020). *Moral Injury in the Context of War.*
Retrieved from US Department of Veterans Affairs:
https://www.ptsd.va.gov/professional/treat/cooccurring/moral_in
jury.asp

Maguen, S., Metzier, T. M., Inslicht, S., Henn-Haase, C., Neylan, T., &
Marmar, C. (2009). Routine Work Environment Stress and
PTSD Symptoms in Police Officers. *Journal of Nervous and Mental*
Disease, 197(10), 754-760. doi:10.1097/NMD.0b013e3181b975f8

Malik, N. (2020, March 30). *In This Crisis, The Tory Cuts Can No Longer Be*
Hidden by Empty Gestures. Retrieved from Guardian:
https://www.theguardian.com/commentisfree/2020/mar/30/coro
navirus-crisis-tories-cuts

Malle, B., & Monroe, A. (2014, April). *Theory of Blame.* Retrieved from
ResearchGate:
https://www.researchgate.net/publication/266394032_A_Theory
_of_Blame

Marmar, C., & McCaslin. (2006). Predictors Of Post-Traumatic Stress In Police And Other First Responders. *Annals New York Academy of Sciences,* 1-18. doi:10.1196/annals.1364.001

Mattingly, V., & Kraiger, K. (2019, June). *Can emotional intelligence be trained? A meta-analytical investigation.* Retrieved from Science Direct: https://www.sciencedirect.com/science/article/abs/pii/S10534822 18301840

McMenemy, R. (2018, October 15). *38 years off sick in just 12 months - Merseyside Police mental health epidemic revealed by striking figures.* Retrieved from Liverpool Echo: https://www.liverpoolecho.co.uk/news/liverpool-news/38-years-sick-just-12-15273620?utm_source=facebook.com&utm_medium=social&utm_campaign=sharebar&fbclid=IwAR2sAs0vpoNo1M1HZIsfRmc HmBOXC0XELPwkE1Yf8aCmF3tz2ukEMFlo2sQ

MentalHealth.net. (2020). *Gestalt Therapy: The Empty Chair Technique.* Retrieved from MentalHealth.net: https://www.mentalhelp.net/blogs/gestalt-therapy-the-empty-chair-technique/

Michailidis, E., & Cropley, M. (2018, September 3). *Investigating the predictors of workplace embitterment using a longitudinal design.* Retrieved from https://academic.oup.com/occmed/article/68/8/523/5090107

Mikolajczak, M., Petrides, V., & Hurry, H. (2009). Adolescents choosing self-harm as an emotion regulation strategy: The protective role of trait emotional intelligence. *British Journal of Clinical Psychological,* 48, 181–193.

Miller, J. (2020). *Police Workforce: Almost One in Five Suffer With A Form of PTSD.* Retrieved from https://www.cam.ac.uk/policeptsd

Mitchell, G. (2019, April 29). *Figures spark call for inquiry into 'alarming' levels of nurse suicide*. Retrieved from Nursing Times: https://www.nursingtimes.net/news/workforce/figures-spark-call-for-inquiry-into-alarming-levels-of-nurse-suicide-29-04-2019/

Mitchell, M., Stevenson, K., & Poole, D. (2001). *Managing Post Incident Reactions In The Police Service*. Sudbury, Suffolk: HSE Books. Retrieved 2014

Molendijk, T., Kramer, E., & Verweij. (2018). *Moral Aspects of "Moral Injury": Analyzing Conceptualizations on the Role of Morality in Military Trauma*. Retrieved from Taylor and Francis Online: https://www.tandfonline.com/doi/full/10.1080/15027570.2018.1483173

Morgan, B., & Randhawa, K. (2015, September 1). *Notting Hill Carnival: More than 400 arrested and eight police officers injured as street party hit by rise in violence*. Retrieved from Evening Standard: https://www.standard.co.uk/news/crime/notting-hill-carnival-more-than-300-arrested-and-eight-police-officers-injured-as-street-party-hit-a2924371.html

Mullen, P., & Lester, G. (2006, May). *Vexatious Litigants and Unusually Persistent Complainants and Petitioners: From Querulous Paranoia to Querulous Behaviour*. Retrieved from ResearchGate: https://www.researchgate.net/publication/7075290_Vexatious_Litigants_and_Unusually_Persistent_Complainants_and_Petitioners_From_Querulous_Paranoia_to_Querulous_Behaviour

NAFD. (2020, April 3). *Covid-19 Updates*. Retrieved from National Association of Funeral Directors: https://nafd.org.uk/wp-content/uploads/2020/04/Public-FAQ-3-April-2020-Final.pdf

Nakagawa, S., Sugiura, M., Sekiguchi, A., Kotozaki, Y., Miyauchi, C., Hanawa, S., . . . Kawashima, R. (2016, September 27). *Effects of post-traumatic growth on the dorsolateral prefrontal cortex after a*

disaster. Retrieved from NCBI:
https://www.ncbi.nlm.nih.gov/pmc/articles/PMC5037468/

Nash, W. (2013, June). *Military Medicine: Psychometric Evaluation of the Moral Injury Events Scale*. Retrieved from AMSUS:
https://academic.oup.com/milmed/article/178/6/646/4320207

Nickerson, A. (2016). *The factor structure of complex posttraumatic stress disorder in traumatized refugees*. Retrieved from Taylor and Francis Online:
https://www.tandfonline.com/doi/full/10.3402/ejpt.v7.33253

Nickerson, A. (2018, December). *A Longitudinal Investigation of Moral Injury Appraisals Amongst Treatment-Seeking Refugees*. Retrieved from Frontiers in Psychiatry:
https://www.frontiersin.org/articles/10.3389/fpsyt.2018.00667/full

Norman, S., Elbogen, E., & Schnurr, P. (2014). *Research Findings on PtSD and Violence*. Retrieved 2014, from U.S Department of Veterans Affairs, National Center for PTSD: www.ptsd.va.gov

O'Grady, S. (2020, March 19). *The NHS is getting us through this crisis. Once it's over, the people will remember exactly who tried to destroy it*. Retrieved from Independent:
https://www.independent.co.uk/voices/coronavirus-nhs-austerity-welfare-cuts-bbc-licence-fee-a9411226.html

Pai, A., Suris, A., & North, C. (2017). *Posttraumatic Stress Disorder in the DSM-5: Controversy, Change, and Conceptual Considerations*. Retrieved from NCBI:
https://www.ncbi.nlm.nih.gov/pmc/articles/PMC5371751/

Park, C., Smith, P., Lee, S., Mazure, C., S, M., & Hoff, R. (2018, January 1). *Positive and Negative Religious/Spiritual Coping and Combat Exposure as Predictors of Posttraumatic Stress and Perceived Growth*

in Iraq and Afghanistan Veterans. Retrieved from NCBI:
https://www.ncbi.nlm.nih.gov/pmc/articles/PMC5310632/

Parliament. (2017). *Defence committee report on IHAT*. Retrieved from
parliament.uk:
https://www.parliament.uk/business/committees/committees-a-
z/commons-select/defence-
committee/defencesubcommittee/news/mod-support-report-
published-16-17/

PFEW. (2018). *Single Crewing Policy Document Version 3*. Retrieved from
polfed: https://www.polfed.org/media/13785/pfew_policy_-
_single_crewing_-_may_2017_v3.pdf

PNB. (2004). *IMPROVING THE MANAGEMENT OF ILL HEALTH*.
Retrieved from College of Policing:
https://www.college.police.uk/What-we-do/Support/Health-
safety/Documents/03-19.pdf2010.pdf

Porter, C. (2021, December). *Book review, Overwhelming Injustice and
Posttraumatic Blame Theory: Psychological Wellbeing in Frontline
Services*. Retrieved from International Journal of Law, Crime and
Justice: http://doi.org/10.1016/j.ijlcj.2021.100492

Price, J. (2014). *When a child's parent has PTSD*. Retrieved 2014, from
U.S Department of Veterans Affairs, National Center for PTSD:
www.ptsd.va.gov

PsychologyToday. (2020). *Gestalt Therapy*. Retrieved from Psychology
Today: https://www.psychologytoday.com/us/therapy-
types/gestalt-therapy

Regel, S., & Joseph, S. (2010). *Post-traumatic Stress: the facts*. New York:
Oxford University Press. Retrieved 2014

Sabic, D., Sabic, A., & Batic-Mujanovic, O. (2018, April). *Embitterment in*

War Veterans with Posttraumatic Stress Disorder. Retrieved from NCBI: https://www.ncbi.nlm.nih.gov/pmc/articles/PMC5911170/

Salston, M., & Figley, C. (2003). *Secondary Traumatic Stress Effects of Working With Survivors of Criminal Victimization.* Journal of Traumatic Stress. Retrieved July 2014

SAMHSA. (2020). *Exhibit 1.3-4 DSM 5 Diagnostic Criteria for PTSD.* Retrieved from NCBI: https://www.ncbi.nlm.nih.gov/books/NBK207191/box/part1_ch3.box16/

SAMHSA. (2020). *Table 3.11DSM-IV to DSM-5 Specific Phobia Comparison.* Retrieved from NCBI: https://www.ncbi.nlm.nih.gov/books/NBK519704/table/ch3.t11/

SAMHSA. (2020). *Table 3.19DSM-IV to DSM-5 Adjustment Disorders Comparison.* Retrieved from NCBI: https://www.ncbi.nlm.nih.gov/books/NBK519704/table/ch3.t19/

Saurel, S. (2019, April 29). *Going out of your comfort zone for reaching the growth zone.* Retrieved from Medium.com: https://medium.com/@ssaurel/going-out-of-your-comfort-zone-for-reaching-the-growth-zone-1e069f4932e5

Sensky, T., Salimu, R., Ballard, J., & Pereira, D. (2015, July 1). *Associations of Chronic Embitterment among NHS Staff.* Retrieved from Occupational Medicine: https://academic.oup.com/occmed/article/65/6/431/1422113

Shay, J. (2002). *Odysseus In America: Combat Trauma And The Trials Of Homecoming.* New York, U.S.A: Scribner.

Shay, J. (2003). *Achilles in Vietnam:Combat trauma and the undoing of character.* New York: Scribner.

Shay, J. (2014, March). The hidden wounds of war, Keynote address.

Retrieved 2014

Shevlin, M. (2018). *A psychometric assessment of Disturbances in Self-Organization symptom indicators for ICD-11 Complex PTSD using the International Trauma Questionnaire.* Retrieved from NCBI: https://www.ncbi.nlm.nih.gov/pmc/articles/PMC5774393/

Sinek, S. (2014). *Leaders eat last.* Penguin Books.

Skilling, G., Øfstegaard, M., Brodie, S., & Thomson, L. (2012, April). *Unusually Persistent Complainants against the Police in.* Retrieved from sipr.ac.uk: http://www.sipr.ac.uk/Plugin/Publications/assets/files/PCCS_querulous_complainers.pdf

SoHeeLee. (2017, November). *Social Support as a Mediator of Posttraumatic Embitterment and Perceptions of Meaning in Life Among Danwon Survivors of The Sewol Ferry Disaster.* Retrieved from Yonsei Medical Journal: https://pdfs.semanticscholar.org/2ebd/ca72cc15b195175e3491951546ee46e1e7b6.pdf?_ga=2.53983912.1894980223.1574588558-2044627457.1570114414

Sommers, J. (2013). *Quarter Of Officers At High PTSD Risk.* Retrieved 2014, from Police Oracle: www.policeoracle.com

Stroebe, K. (2015, March). *Belief in a Just What? Demystifying Just World Beliefs by Distinguishing Sources of Justice.* Retrieved from NCBI PubMed: https://www.ncbi.nlm.nih.gov/pmc/articles/PMC4372594/

Stubley, P. (2020, April 4). *Coronavirus: Boris Johnson urged to reconsider lockdown strategy by virus adviser.* Retrieved from Yahoo News: https://uk.news.yahoo.com/coronavirus-boris-johnson-urged-reconsider-230814319.html

Szczygiel, D., & Mikolajczak, M. (2018, December 21). *Emotional Intelligence Buffers the Effects of Negative Emotions on Job Burnout in Nursing*. Retrieved from NCBI: https://www.ncbi.nlm.nih.gov/pmc/articles/PMC6309155/

Tedeschi, R., & Calhoun, L. (2004). *Posttraumatic Growth: Conceptual Foundations and Empirical Evidence*. Retrieved from Semantic Scholar: https://sites.uncc.edu/ptgi/wp-content/uploads/sites/9/2013/01/PTG-Conceptual-Foundtns.pdf

Telles-Correai, D. (2018). *Mental Disorder - The Need for an Accurate Definition*. Retrieved from NCBI: https://www.ncbi.nlm.nih.gov/pmc/articles/PMC5857571/

Travis, A. (2017, November 22). *Public services face real-terms spending cuts of up to 40% in decade to 2020*. Retrieved from Guardian: https://www.theguardian.com/uk-news/2017/nov/22/public-services-face-real-terms-spending-cuts-of-up-to-40-in-decade-to-2020

Trochim, W. (2006). *Statistical Terms in Sampling*. Retrieved 2014, from Research Methods Knowledge Base: www.socialresearchmethods.net

Wenzel, K. (2017, October). *General Belief in a Just World Is Positively Associated with Dishonest Behavior*. Retrieved from Frontiers in Psychology: https://www.frontiersin.org/articles/10.3389/fpsyg.2017.01770/full#B4

WHO. (2016). *Phobic Anxiety*. Retrieved from ICD-10: https://icd.who.int/browse10/2016/en#/F40

WHO. (2019). *6B40 Post traumatic stress disorder*. Retrieved from ICD-11 for Mortality and Morbidity Statistics (Version : 04 / 2019): https://icd.who.int/browse11/l-m/en#http%3a%2f%2fid.who.int%2ficd%2fentity%2f2070699808

WHO. (2019). *6B41 Complex post traumatic stress disorder.* Retrieved from ICD-11 for Mortality and Morbidity Statistics (Version : 04 / 2019): https://icd.who.int/browse11/l-m/en#http%3a%2f%2fid.who.int%2ficd%2fentity%2f585833559

WHO. (2019). *6B43 Adjustment Disorder.* Retrieved from ICD-11: https://icd.who.int/browse11/l-m/en#/http://id.who.int/icd/entity/264310751

WHO. (2019). *QD85 Burn-Out.* Retrieved from ICD-11: https://icd.who.int/browse11/l-m/en#http%3a%2f%2fid.who.int%2ficd%2fentity%2f129180281

Wier, K. (2017). *Forgiveness Can Improve Mental and Physical Health.* Retrieved from APA: https://www.apa.org/monitor/2017/01/ce-corner

Wikipedia. (2020). *Coronavirus Act 2020.* Retrieved from Wikipedia: https://en.wikipedia.org/wiki/Coronavirus_Act_2020

Wikipedia. (2020). *Health Protection (Coronavirus) Regulations 2020.* Retrieved from Wikipedia: https://en.wikipedia.org/wiki/Health_Protection_(Coronavirus)_Regulations_2020

Wikipedia. (2020). *Iraq Inquiry.* Retrieved from Wikipedia: https://en.wikipedia.org/wiki/Iraq_Inquiry

Wikiwand. (2020). Retrieved from https://www.wikiwand.com/en/Moral_injury

Williamson, V., Greenberg, N., & Murphy, D. (2019, June 21). *Impact of moral injury on the lives of UK military veterans: a pilot study.* Retrieved from BMJ Military Health: https://militaryhealth.bmj.com/content/early/2019/06/21/jramc-

2019-001243

Wood, B. (2020). *Double Crossed: A Code of Honour, A Complete Betrayal.* Virgin Books.

Woojin, K. (2019, October 24). *Effect of Burnout on Post-traumatic Stress Disorder Symptoms Among Firefighters in Korea: Data From the Firefighter Research on Enhancement of Safety & Health (FRESH).* Retrieved from NCBI: https://www.ncbi.nlm.nih.gov/pmc/articles/PMC6893225/

Worthington, E. (2004, September 1). *The New Science of Forgiveness.* Retrieved from Greater Good Magazine: https://greatergood.berkeley.edu/article/item/the_new_science_of_forgiveness

Yaghini, F. (2020). Retrieved from Camp Aftermath: https://campaftermath.org/camp-aftermath/

Zisook, S., & Shear, K. (2009). *Grief and Bereavement: What Psychiatrists Need to Know.* Retrieved from NCBI: https://www.ncbi.nlm.nih.gov/pmc/articles/PMC2691160/

Printed in Great Britain
by Amazon

27397074R00156